Collins
Advanced Spanish Grammar

WITH PRACTICE EXERCISES

HarperCollins Publishers
Westerhill Road
Bishopbriggs
Glasgow
G64 2QT

First Edition 2013

Reprint 10 9 8 7 6 5 4 3 2 1 0

© HarperCollins Publishers 2013

ISBN 978-0-00-749032-5

Collins® is a registered trademark of
HarperCollins Publishers Limited

www.collinslanguage.com

A catalogue record for this book is
available from the British Library

Typeset by Aptara in India

Printed in India by Gopsons Papers Ltd

Acknowledgements
We would like to thank those authors and publishers
who kindly gave permission for copyright material to be
used in the Collins Corpus. We would also like to thank
Times Newspapers Ltd for providing valuable data.

All rights reserved. No part of this book may be
reproduced, stored in a retrieval system, or transmitted
in any form or by any means, electronic, mechanical,
photocopying, recording or otherwise, without the
prior permission in writing of the Publisher. This book is
sold subject to the conditions that it shall not, by way of
trade or otherwise, be lent, re-sold, hired out or
otherwise circulated without the Publisher's prior
consent in any form of binding or cover other than that
in which it is published and without a similar condition
including this condition being imposed on the
subsequent purchaser.

Entered words that we have reason to believe constitute
trademarks have been designated as such. However,
neither the presence nor absence of such designation
should be regarded as affecting the legal status of any
trademark.

HarperCollins does not warrant that www.
collinsdictionary.com, www.collinslanguage.com or
any other website mentioned in this title will be
provided uninterrupted, that any website will be error
free, that defects will be corrected, or that the website
or the server that makes it available are free of viruses or
bugs. For full terms and conditions please refer to the
site terms provided on the website.

WRITTEN BY
Ronan Fitzsimons

EDITOR
Teresa Alvarez

COMPUTING SUPPORT
Dave Wark

FOR THE PUBLISHER
Gerry Breslin
Lucy Cooper
Kerry Ferguson
Elaine Higgleton

CONTENTS

Introduction v

1 - Nouns 1
Gender and inflection of nouns 1
Forming plurals 8
Practice 10

2 - Definite and indefinite articles 13
Use of the definite article 13
Use of the neuter article *lo* 17
Use of the indefinite article 18
Practice 20

3 - Adjectives and comparison strategies 23
Agreement of adjectives 23
Comparison strategies 30
Practice 34

4 - Indefinite adjectives and pronouns 37
Indefinite adjectives 37
Indefinite pronouns 42
Practice 46

5 - Demonstratives and possessives 48
Demonstratives 48
Possessives 50
Practice 54

6 - Personal pronouns 56
Subject pronouns 56
Direct object pronouns 57
Word order with direct object pronouns 58
Indirect object pronouns 59
Loísmo, laísmo, leísmo 60
Combining direct and indirect object pronouns 60
Pronouns after prepositions 62
Practice 63

7 - Relative pronouns and linking devices 66
Relative pronouns 66
Nominalisers 69
Cleft sentences 70
Practice 71

8 - Prepositions and conjunctions 74
Prepositions 74
Conjunctions 87
Practice 91

9 - *Por / para* and the personal *a* 95
Por versus *para* 95
Por 95
Para 99
The personal *a* 100
Practice 102

10 - Numerals 104
Ordinal numbers 104
Cardinal numbers 106
Practical uses of numerals 110
Practice 111

11 - Indicative verb tenses 113
The present tense 113
Ways of expressing the future 116
The perfect tense 119
The preterite 121
Combinations of past tenses 124
The pluperfect tense 125
The conditional tense 125
The future perfect tense 127
The conditional perfect tense 127
Practice 128

12 - Other types of verb: continuous forms, the gerund, the infinitive, the past participle, reflexive verbs and *se* 131
Continuous forms 131
The infinitive 135
The past participle 137
Reflexive verbs and *se* 138
Practice 140

13 - The subjunctive – 1 143
Notes on the subjunctive 143
Formation of the present subjunctive 145
Formation of the imperfect subjunctive 147
Formation of compound tenses 149
Practice 151

14 - The subjunctive – 2 153
Using the subjunctive 153
Practice 165

15 - The imperative and how to express commands and invitations 168
Giving commands in Spanish 168
Forms of the imperative 168
Reflexive forms of the imperative 171
Using object pronouns with the imperative 172
The impersonal 'passive *se*' imperative 173
Other ways of expressing commands and invitations 174
Practice 176

CONTENTS

16 - Conditional sentences — 178
- Fulfilled conditions — 178
- Open conditions — 178
- Remote conditions — 179
- Unfulfilled conditions — 180
- Expressing conditions without using *si* — 181
- Practice — 182

17 - Indirect speech — 184
- Reporting a statement — 184
- Reporting a question that is not a request — 186
- Reporting a command — 186
- Reporting a request — 187
- Practice — 189

18 - Expressing English modal auxiliary verbs in Spanish — 191
- Difference between *poder* and *saber* — 191
- Use of *poder* — 192
- Use of *deber* — 193
- Use of *deber de* — 195
- Use of *tener que* — 195
- Use of *haber que* — 197
- Use of *haber de* — 197
- Use of *querer* — 198
- Use of *soler* — 198
- Practice — 199

19 - The passive and its alternatives — 201
- The passive in Spanish — 201
- *Estar* and the past participle — 202
- Other verbs used with the past participle in passive situations — 202
- Other ways of expressing an English passive in Spanish – avoidance techniques — 203
- Misleading English 'passives' — 205
- Practice — 206

20 - *Ser*, *estar* and *haber* — 209
- Uses of *ser* — 209
- Uses of *estar* — 210
- Areas of overlap between *ser* and *estar* — 212
- Words whose meaning changes when used with *ser* or *estar* — 213
- Uses of *haber* — 214
- Potential confusion between *haber* and *estar* — 215
- Practice — 216

21 - More on syntax — 218
- Word order in Spanish — 218
- Concession — 221
- Conditions — 223
- Purpose — 224
- Practice — 225

22 - Adverbs and time expressions — 228
- Adverbs in Spanish — 228
- Time expressions — 232
- Practice — 237

23 - Spelling and the written accent — 239
- Spelling — 239
- The written accent — 241
- Practice — 247

Solutions — 250

Index — 262

INTRODUCTION

Whether you are working towards Spanish A Level, are studying Spanish as part of a degree or other high-level course, or have reached the point in your independent learning at which you want to focus on more complex areas of how the language works, *Collins Advanced Spanish Grammar* will be an invaluable tool.

The book focuses mainly on European Spanish, but offers full coverage of the main features of the verb system in Latin American Spanish, especially the *vos* form used in Argentina and elsewhere.

After re-capping on basic and intermediate elements of grammar, the book aims to guide you carefully through higher-level concepts, with clear, user-friendly explanations and illustrations, including warnings about how Spanish works differently from other languages in the Romance family.

The units work systematically through the grammar areas to be discussed, to offer comprehensive coverage of how each concept works, what its quirks are, and how its difficulties may best be overcome. Frequently, it is useful for the learner to cross-check an element of grammar which may be discussed, or feature prominently, at more than one point in a unit, or across several units. To assist in this, our 'Cross-reference' system takes you to areas of importance elsewhere in the book, which will consolidate your knowledge of the point being covered, and how it works in Spanish. For example:

> ⇨ *For full coverage of comparisons involving* **tanto** *see Unit 3.*

Equally important is the development of a range of tricks to help you remember how areas of grammar work, as well as information to help you put the grammatical point into its cultural context. As aids to this, the book features a series of tips in shaded boxes, which will draw your attention to snippets designed to complement the main grammatical focus. For example:

> Be careful to distinguish between *a* and *en* when translating 'to', 'at' and 'in' into Spanish. A repetitive but useful sentence to remember is: *Vamos a la estación – cuando lleguemos a la estación, estaremos en la estación*. 'We're going to the station – when we get to the station, we'll be at the station.'

Each unit ends with a Practice section, where you can put the nuts and bolts into action. The exercises are designed to develop your confidence and enable you to write correct, useful Spanish. At each stage, the exercises seek to include a range of irregular forms and structures discussed in the unit. There is a Solutions section towards the back of the book for you to check your answers.

The final unit serves as a useful check-list for how to spell correctly in Spanish, and add accents in the right places and for the right reasons. It can stand alone as a resource to dip into, and can also be used in conjunction with points of the main text of the book, where spelling is affected by a range of grammatical factors.

We hope that you will find *Collins Advanced Spanish Grammar* a clear, enjoyable and useful resource in your high-level Spanish studies, and that it will solve many of the conundrums to which you had always sought an answer.

SPANISH GRAMMAR

UNIT 1

Nouns

Gender and inflection of nouns

Nouns in Spanish are considered to be either masculine or feminine, and this **gender** affects the ways in which articles, adjectives and pronouns are used with them. To say that masculine nouns tend to end in -o, and feminine nouns in -a, is a useful starting-point, but doesn't tell the whole story. A noun also has one or more **inflections**, which are the endings it uses to indicate its number (singular / plural) and gender. In this unit, we will look closely at the genders of a wide range of groups and types of Spanish nouns, and the importance of inflections in each case.

Nouns referring to people

Most nouns referring to male humans are masculine:

el padre	the father
el duque	the duke

Most nouns referring to female humans are feminine:

la madre	the mother
la princesa	the princess

If a noun is used to refer to either a male or a female, and has just one ending or inflection, its gender is made clear by the article working with it:

el intérprete	the (male) interpreter
la intérprete	the (female) interpreter
el idiota	the (male) idiot
la idiota	the (female) idiot

Some nouns have only one possible gender, regardless of whether they are being used to refer to a male or a female:

la estrella	the star (of TV show, etc.)
el ligue	the date; short-term boyfriend or girlfriend
el bebé	the baby
la persona	the person

Most masculine nouns referring to a male person and ending in -o have an equivalent feminine form ending in -a. Here are some examples of how both gender and inflection can change:

el amigo / la amiga	the friend
el compañero / la compañera	the companion, classmate, workmate, etc.

1

UNIT 1 NOUNS

> Note a few common exceptions to the above:
>
> | | |
> |---|---|
> | el / la piloto | the pilot |
> | el / la modelo | the fashion model |
> | el / la soldado | the soldier |
> | el / la soprano | the soprano |

Other 'person' nouns ending in -o and not sharing a stem work in pairs to express the masculine and feminine:

el marido	the husband
la mujer / la esposa	the wife
el yerno	the son-in-law
la nuera	the daughter-in-law

Masculine nouns ending in -a do not change in their feminine form:

el / la tenista	the tennis-player (all nouns ending in -ista behave in this way)
el / la atleta	the athlete
el / la internauta	the internet user, web surfer
el / la belga	the Belgian man / woman
el / la policía	the male / female police officer (la policía is also 'the police force')
el / la guía	the male / female guide (la guía also means 'the guidebook')

Most masculine 'person' nouns ending in a consonant make their feminine form by adding -a. Any accent on the final vowel of the masculine disappears in the feminine form:

el traductor / la traductora	the translator
el bailarín / la bailarina	the dancer
el español / la española	the Spaniard
el campeón / la campeona	the champion
el capitán / la capitana	the captain
el francés / la francesa	the Frenchman / Frenchwoman

In recent years there has been some uncertainty in the Spanish-speaking world regarding the feminine forms of jobs traditionally undertaken by men. The terms 'male nurse' and 'male model' are examples of similar issues from the English-speaking world. Here are some notes on current usage:

Masculine form		Recommended feminine form(s)
el abogado	(lawyer)	la abogado / la abogada
el jefe	(boss)	la jefe / la jefa
el juez	(judge)	la juez / la jueza

el médico	(doctor)	la médico / la médica
el miembro	(member of club, etc.)	la miembro
el ministro	(minister)	la ministra

Masculine nouns ending in -nte generally do not change in the feminine:

    el / la cantante   the singer
    el / la amante   the lover
    el / la estudiante   the student

> Note the following exceptions, however, where the masculine -nte changes to the feminine -nta:
>
> el dependiente / la dependienta   (shop assistant)
> el sirviente / la sirvienta   (servant)
> el presidente / la presidenta   (president)

Plural nouns referring to a mixture of male and female people are quite common, and take the masculine plural form. This can be quite confusing:

e.g. *los hermanos* can mean both 'the brothers' and 'the brothers and sisters', and *los alumnos* can mean 'the pupils', implying boys only or a mixture of boys and girls.

The meaning of an expression like *tengo cuatro hijos* ('I have four children / four sons') can be unclear until something further is added to specify the children's genders:

Tengo cuatro hijos: tres hijas y un hijo.

Nouns referring to animals

Some animals have straightforward masculine / feminine inflections in -o / -a:

    el perro / la perra   the dog / bitch
    el gato / la gata   the male cat / female cat
    el mono / la mona   the male monkey / female monkey
    el cerdo / la cerda   the pig / sow

A second category consists of animals that have different inflections for the feminine, which must be learned individually:

    el elefante / la elefanta   the male / female elephant
    el tigre / la tigre, la tigresa   the male / female tiger
    el león / la leona   the lion / lioness
    el gallo / la gallina   the cockerel / hen

UNIT 1 NOUNS

Others exist as pairings of words that do not share a stem:

el caballo / la yegua	the stallion / mare
el macho / la cabra	the billy-goat / female goat
el carnero / la oveja	the ram / ewe
el toro / la vaca	the bull / cow

A final category – made up mainly of wild animals – shows genders that are fixed and cover both the male and the female of the species:

el castor	the beaver
el sapo	the toad
la rana	the frog
la araña	the spider
la ballena	the whale

If it is desirable to clarify whether the animal being referred to is male or female, the best way is to use add-on terms for 'male' and 'female':

la rana macho	the male frog
el sapo hembra	the female toad

Nouns referring to things

Without the guideline of a person's (or an animal's) sex, it is harder to pin down a gender for inanimate objects and concepts in Spanish. Nevertheless, there are various helpful rules we can follow:

Nouns ending in -o tend to be masculine:

el libro	the book
el suelo	the floor
el comunismo	communism

> Some common exceptions to the above:
>
> | | |
> |---|---|
> | la mano | (the hand) |
> | la moto | (the motorbike) |
> | la disco | (the disco / nightclub) |
> | la foto | (the photo) |

Despite the tendency for nouns ending in -a to be feminine, many common ones are masculine:

el día	the day
el bocata	the sandwich
el mapa	the map
el planeta	the planet
el tranvía	the tram

Similarly, many (but by no means all) nouns ending in *-ma* are masculine:

el drama	the drama
el problema	the problem
el clima	the climate
el panorama	the panorama
el programa	the program(me)
el sistema	the system
el tema	the topic

There are various categories of noun that are masculine, usually because of an underlying noun embedded in their meaning:

Category	Example	English
Rivers	*el (Río) Tajo*	the (River) Tagus
Mountains	*el Everest*	Mount Everest
Oceans	*el (Océano) Pacífico*	the Pacific (Ocean)
Seas	*el (Mar) Mediterráneo*	the Mediterranean (Sea)
Lakes	*el (Lago) Como*	Lake Como
Cars	*el Ford*	the Ford
Days	*el martes*	Tuesday
Months	*un noviembre soleado*	a sunny November
Wines	*un buen Rioja*	a good Rioja
Infinitives	*el beber*	drinking
Colours	*el azul*	blue
Sports teams	*el Real Madrid*	Real Madrid

> Note, however, that the gender of some teams is influenced by a clear feminine noun: *La Real Sociedad* (Real Sociedad from San Sebastián).

Compound nouns of one word tend to be masculine:

el rascacielos	the skyscraper
el sacacorchos	the corkscrew

Compound nouns made up of two words usually take the gender of the first word:

la hora punta	the rush hour
el hombre rana	the frogman

Nouns ending in *-a* tend to be feminine:

la casa	the house
la mesa	the table
la filosofía	philosophy

UNIT 1 NOUNS

⇨ *See pages 4 and 5 for lists of common masculine nouns ending in -a.*

Despite the existence of many masculine nouns ending in *-ma*, a large number of common nouns with this ending are feminine:

la alarma	the alarm
el alma	the soul
la crema	the cream
la fama	fame
el arma	the weapon
la broma	the joke
la firma	the signature
la forma	the form, shape
la lágrima	the tear (of crying)
la llama	the flame, llama
la norma	the rule
la cama	the bed

Nouns with the following endings are usually feminine:

Ending	Example	English
-ez	*la niñez*	childhood
-eza	*la pobreza*	poverty
-ción	*la acción*	action
-ía	*la biología*	biology
-sión	*la diversión*	fun, entertainment
-dad	*la hermandad*	brotherhood
-tad	*la lealtad*	loyalty
-tud	*la multitud*	multitude, crowd
-umbre	*la muchedumbre*	crowd
-ie	*la calvicie*	baldness
-nza	*la trenza*	plait
-cia	*la farmacia*	pharmacy, chemist's shop
-sis	*la dosis*	dose
-itis	*la apendicitis*	appendicitis

There are some common exceptions to the above:

el análisis	the analysis
el énfasis	the emphasis
el paréntesis	the parenthesis
el pez	the fish – but *la pez* means 'tar'

Words for countries, regions, provinces, cities, towns and villages are usually feminine if they end in an unstressed -*a*; otherwise they tend to be masculine:

Gender	Examples
Feminine	*Francia, Cantabria, Barcelona* (BUT **Nueva York, Bogotá**)
Masculine	*Canadá, Moscú, Estrasburgo*

There are various categories of noun that are feminine, usually because of an underlying noun embedded in their meaning:

Category	Example	English
Companies	*la Ford*	Ford
Letters of the alphabet	*la eme*	the letter 'm'
Islands	*las Baleares*	the Balearic Islands
Roads	*la N7*	the N7
Motorbikes	*una Suzuki*	a Suzuki motorbike (compare *un Suzuki* for a Suzuki car)

Some nouns exist in both masculine and feminine forms, with different meanings for each. Here are some of the most common:

capital	(m) capital (money); (f) capital (city)
coma	(m) coma; (f) comma
cometa	(m) comet; (f) kite
cura	(m) priest; (f) cure
final	(m) end; (f) final (e.g. of cup competition)
frente	(m) military front; (f) forehead
orden	(m) order (tidiness, sequence, peacefulness, etc.); (f) command, religious order
pendiente	(m) earring; (f) slope
radio	(m) radius; (f) radio

Genders differing between Spanish and other romance languages

Quite a few common nouns have a different gender from their equivalent noun in French, Italian, Portuguese etc., so students of a combination of these languages are advised to keep a close eye on genders as they develop their vocabulary. Here are some examples:

Spanish	Other languages
el diente (tooth)	la dent (French)
la sangre (blood)	le sang (French), il sangue (Italian)
la flor (flower)	il fiore (Italian)

Forming plurals

Plurals ending in -s and -es

If a singular noun ends in a vowel, its plural is generally formed by adding -s:

Singular	Plural	English
el patio	los patios	the patio(s), the yard(s)
el chiste	los chistes	the joke(s)
la casa	las casas	the house(s)

If a singular noun ends in a consonant, its plural is generally achieved by adding -es:

Singular	Plural	English
el traductor	los traductores	the translator(s)
el animal	los animales	the animal(s)
el reloj	los relojes	the clock(s), the watch(es)

Some foreign words ending in a consonant and used in Spanish take -s rather than -es:

Singular	Plural	English
el chalet	los chalets	the chalet(s)
el jersey	los jerseys	the jersey(s)

If a singular noun ends in -s and has an unstressed final vowel, the plural is the same word:

Singular	Plural	English
el jueves	los jueves	Thursday(s)
la crisis	las crisis	crisis / crises
el paraguas	los paraguas	the umbrella(s)

However, a singular noun ending in a stressed final vowel plus -s or -n needs -es to form the plural. The accent is dropped in the plural:

Singular	Plural	English
el autobús	los autobuses	the bus(es)
el inglés	los ingleses	the Englishman / the English
el mes	los meses	the month(s)
el país	los países	the country / -ies (note that this word keeps its accent to highlight the separate pronunciation of the 'a' and the 'i')
la opinión	las opiniones	the opinion(s)

Singular nouns ending in an accented vowel need special attention, as some receive -s for the plural, while others require -es:

Singular	Plural	English
el tabú	los tabúes	the taboo(s)
el rubí	los rubíes	the ruby / -ies

el sofá	los sofás	the sofa(s)
el café	los cafés	the coffee(s), café(s)
el menú	los menús	the menu(s)

Compound nouns consisting of one word do not change between singular and plural. This is because they end in an unstressed -s in the singular:

| el rascacielos | los rascacielos | the skyscraper(s) |

In compound nouns consisting of two words, the first one usually pluralises:

Singular	Plural	English
la hora punta	las horas punta	the rush hour(s)
el hombre rana	los hombres rana	the frogman / frogmen

Singular nouns of more than one syllable which end in -en and don't already have an accent need to add one in the plural:

Singular	Plural	English
el joven	los jóvenes	the young person / people
el examen	los exámenes	the exam(s)

For singular nouns ending in -z, change the -z to -c before adding the -es:

Singular	Plural	English
la luz	las luces	the light(s)
el altavoz	los altavoces	the loudspeaker(s)

Some nouns can pluralise in Spanish, while their English equivalents cannot:

Singular	Plural	English
el pan	unos panes	bread / some loaves of bread
el consejo	unos consejos	advice / pieces of advice

Conversely, note the following items of clothing, which are plural in English but can be either singular or plural in Spanish:

el pantalón / los pantalones   trousers
la braga / las bragas   knickers

It's also worth remembering that while English generally uses a plural verb for sports teams, Spanish rigidly uses a singular one. Compare the following:

Liverpool es una ciudad animada.   Liverpool is a lively city.

El Liverpool es un equipo muy bueno.   Liverpool are a very good team.

PRACTICE

1 What are the feminine forms of the following nouns?

  1 el tío..

  2 el gato..

  3 el atleta..

  4 el economista..

  5 el estudiante...

  6 el dependiente..

2 Give the feminine equivalents of the following:

  1 el padre..

  2 el hombre..

  3 el marido...

  4 el rey..

  5 el actor...

  6 el toro..

3 Add the correct definite article (*el / la*) to each of the following nouns:

  1 ....sistema

  2 ....sobredosis

  3 ....dedal

  4 ....carne

  5 ....catástrofe

  6 ....énfasis

  7 ....foto

PRACTICE

8 .... cine

9 .... reloj

10 .... hambre

11 .... perro-guía

4 Give the genders of the following Spanish nouns. Students of two or more Romance languages may find it useful to compare the genders of the equivalent nouns in French, Italian etc.:

1 calor..

2 límite..

3 oasis..

4 período..

5 flor..

6 color..

7 leche..

8 origen..

9 coche..

5 Complete the grid on the basis of the example given:

el inglés   la inglesa   los ingleses   las inglesas

1 el conductor   la............................   los............................   las............................

2 el catalán   la............................   los............................   las............................

3 el belga   la............................   los............................   las............................

4 el bailarín   la............................   los............................   las............................

5 el anfitrión   la............................   los............................   las............................

PRACTICE

6 Give the plural of each of the following nouns:

1. nieto..
2. mesa..
3. coche...
4. taxi..
5. tribu..
6. papá..
7. café...
8. pakistaní..
9. hindú...
10. menú...
11. autobús...
12. imagen..
13. origen...
14. luz...
15. portavoz..

UNIT 2 — Definite and indefinite articles

This unit looks in detail at the usages (particularly in contrast with patterns in English) of the Spanish definite article – *el / la / los / las* – and indefinite article – *un / una / unos / unas*.

Use of the definite article

A good general rule to follow is that if the definite article is used in a particular construction in English, it will be used in the equivalent construction in Spanish, with two notable exceptions:

For the titles of monarchs, popes, etc., Spanish does not use the definite article:

Enrique octavo	Henry the eighth
Juan Pablo segundo	John Paul the second

Certain set expressions have a definite article in English, but not in Spanish, e.g.:

a / en nombre de	in the name of
a corto / largo plazo	in the short / long term

Otherwise, we need to focus carefully on the subtleties of where usage coincides and differs between the two languages. The following notes will help you to determine whether you need to use the definite article in Spanish.

Definite article used in Spanish but not in English

To refer generally to people, animals or things:

Los médicos cobran mucho.	Doctors earn a lot of money.
Me encantan los gatos.	I love cats.
Los platos suelen ser redondos.	Plates tend to be round.

To refer to abstract qualities, concepts or notions:

La salud es importante.	Health is important.
Lo que más odio es la violencia.	What I hate most is violence.

> The above rule is broken in some set expressions involving *tener* + a noun, or following certain prepositions:
>
> | | |
> |---|---|
> | ***Tengo sed.*** | I'm thirsty. |
> | ***con cautela*** | with care |

UNIT 2 — DEFINITE AND INDEFINITE ARTICLES

Liquids and substances in general are another category requiring the definite article in Spanish:

El vino / El carbón es bastante caro.	Wine / Coal is quite expensive.
El agua es esencial.	Water is essential.

> *Agua* here remains feminine, but falls into a category of feminine singular nouns (those beginning with a stressed *a-* or *ha-*) which take *el* instead of *la* as their definite article. The same thing happens with the indefinite article, where *un agua* would replace *una agua*). This is a device to aid pronounciation, a bit like saying 'thee apple' for 'the apple', or writing and saying 'an apple' instead of 'a apple', in English. This rule does not apply when there is an adjective between the article and the noun, and in all cases the plurals *las* and *unas* are unaffected:
>
> | | |
> |---|---|
> | *el alma / las almas* | the soul(s) |
> | *la bendita alma* | the blessed soul |
> | *el águila / las águilas* | the eagle(s) |
> | *la majestuosa águila* | the majestic eagle |
> | *el haba / las habas* | the bean(s) |
> | *la humilde haba* | the humble bean |

The definite article is used in Spanish in referring to colours:

El azul es un color atractivo.	Blue is an attractive colour.

If you are talking about body parts, these usually take a definite article in Spanish, but not in English. Notice also the use of a possessive adjective in English, and a personal pronoun in Spanish, in some of the examples:

Tengo los ojos verdes.	I have green eyes.
Me duele la garganta.	I've got a sore throat.
Veo que te has roto la pierna.	I see you've broken your leg.

When referring to someone (but, importantly, not addressing them directly) by their title, Spanish uses the definite article (but not with *don*, *doña*, *san* or *santa*):

He quedado con la señora Muñoz.	I've arranged to meet Ms. Muñoz.
Buenos días, señora Muñoz.	Good morning, Ms. Muñoz.
Vamos a rezar a san Antonio	Let's pray to Saint Anthony.
San Antonio, ora por nosotros.	Saint Anthony, pray for us.

When using structures that refer to institutions such as church, university, school, prison, etc. with prepositions, it's important to remember to include the definite article in Spanish:

Voy a la iglesia.	I'm going to church.
Vamos al colegio / a la universidad cinco días por semana.	We go to school / to university five days a week.
Mi hermano está en la cárcel.	My brother is in prison.

DEFINITE AND INDEFINITE ARTICLES — UNIT 2

Meals, games and sports usually take the definite article in Spanish:

después del desayuno	after breakfast
Prefiero el golf.	I prefer golf.

> When using *jugar* to say that you 'play' a particular sport or game, remember to use both the preposition *a* and the definite article:
>
> | | |
> |---|---|
> | *Me gusta jugar al fútbol.* | I like playing football. |
> | *Juguemos a las cartas.* | Let's have a game of cards. |
>
> The verb *practicar* (to 'play' or 'do' an activity), on the other hand, takes the definite article but not the preposition *a*:
>
> | | |
> |---|---|
> | *Practico el footing / el yoga los fines de semana.* | I go jogging / do yoga at the weekends. |

Prices and rates usually take the definite article (often in cases where English would use 'a' or 'per'. The Spanish *por* would also be possible here):

Vale tres euros el litro.	It costs three euros a litre.
Cobramos diez euros la hora.	We charge ten euros an hour.

Numbered nouns (including percentages) take the definite article:

Vivimos en el número 29.	We live in / at number 29.
El 40% de los jóvenes...	40% of young people...

The time of the day uses the definite article to equate to the English 'o'clock':

Es la una. / Son las dos y media.	It's one o'clock. / It's half past two.

Spanish uses the definite article to equate to the English 'on' in many structures involving days of the week. Look carefully at the inclusion / omission of definite articles in the second example:

Tengo mucho que hacer el martes / los martes.	I have a lot to do on Tuesday / on Tuesdays.
La conocí el viernes, doce de junio.	I met her on Friday the twelfth of June.

Notice the following usages with the verb *ser*:

Hoy es domingo.	Today is Sunday.
Fue el domingo por la tarde.	It was (i.e. happened, took place) on Sunday afternoon.

UNIT 2 — DEFINITE AND INDEFINITE ARTICLES

The definite article with names of languages

There are some important subtleties to be noted when dealing with Spanish names for languages:

➤ The definite article is not used after *en*, and is generally omitted after the verbs *aprender*, *hablar* and *saber* (unless the verb is qualified by an adverb):

Prefiero leer revistas en italiano.	I prefer to read magazines in Italian.
Estamos aprendiendo portugués.	We're learning Portuguese.
Hablas estupendamente (el) alemán.	You speak German marvellously.

➤ The definite article is used with other prepositions:

Tenemos que traducir este texto del español al inglés. — We have to translate this text from Spanish into English.

➤ After *entender*, *escribir* or *estudiar*, the use of the definite article is optional:

Llevo muchos años estudiando (el) inglés. — I've been studying English for many years.

➤ If a language is the subject of a verb, the definite article must be used:

El francés es muy difícil. — French is very difficult.

The definite article with names of countries

A small (and diminishing) number of countries are named using the definite article in English (e.g. the United Kingdom, the Lebanon). In Spanish, the definite article is used sparingly in this context, but is generally seen in *el Reino Unido* (though not in *Gran Bretaña*), *la India*, *los Países Bajos*, *la República Checa* and *la República Dominicana*. *(Los) Estados Unidos* carries an optional definite article. Note also that any country can carry the definite article when it is qualified:

la España de nuestros abuelos — the Spain of our grandparents

Names of streets, avenues, etc.

Note the contrast between 'I live in / on London Street' and *Vivo en la calle (de) Londres*.

The definite article in names of sports teams, etc.

Sports teams require the definite article, whereas they don't in English (e.g. Spanish says *el Manchester United*). A separate issue – though worth pointing out here – is that teams are generally taken to be masculine, unless there is a clear or underlying feminine noun forming their basis. Notice also the singular verb:

El Real Madrid juega contra la Real Sociedad. — Real Madrid (masculine, because *el club* is assumed) are playing against Real Sociedad (*sociedad* is feminine).

DEFINITE AND INDEFINITE ARTICLES — UNIT 2

Some subtleties of inclusion / omission of the definite article

Notice the difference between the modified and unmodified statements below:

Estamos estudiando filosofía.	We're studying philosophy (generally).
Estamos estudiando la filisofía de Platón.	We're studying the philosophy of Plato (specifically).

⇨ For another example of the definite article being required for a modified (qualified) use, see the section 'The definite article with names of countries'.

Note also the following sentences, which express generality and specificity – the third example can be understood in both ways:

Suelo salir con italianos.	I usually go out with Italians (people of that nationality generally).
Suelo salir con los italianos.	I usually go out with the Italians (the specific handful of my friends who are Italian).
Los italianos son simpáticos.	Italians are nice (as a nationality) / The Italians are nice (referring to specific ones).

Use of the neuter article *lo*

The neuter article *lo* is used to express concepts, repetitions, etc., that are neither masculine nor feminine. It is never used with a noun, but can be used in the following combinations:

With a masculine singular adjective, or with a past participle:

Lo importante es terminar.	The important thing is to get finished.
Vamos a enfocarnos en lo escrito.	Let's focus on what's written down.

As part of some common set expressions:

por lo menos	at least
por lo general	generally
a lo mejor	perhaps, maybe

Lo que + a verb construction means 'what' in the sense of 'that which':

Sabemos muy bien lo que pasa.	We know full well what's happening.
¿Viste lo que hizo?	Did you see what s/he did?

Lo + adjective + *que* can be used to state how important / big / red, etc. something is or was:

No sabe lo guapa que es.	She doesn't know how beautiful she is.
Es difícil comprender lo trabajadores que son.	It's difficult to understand how hard-working they are.

UNIT 2 — DEFINITE AND INDEFINITE ARTICLES

The *lo* + adjective + *que* construction also works with an adverb in the place of the adjective:

No sabe lo mucho que la quiero. She doesn't know how much I love her.

Lo de + a noun or noun phrase can be used to convey the idea of 'that thing that happened (to)...', 'that business of...', etc.:

Lo de la profesora de historia fue terrible. That business with the history teacher was terrible.

Cuéntanos lo de la reunión. Tell us what happened at the meeting.

Use of the indefinite article

Generally, usage in Spanish matches usage in English, with a few categories in which the two languages work differently:

Indefinite article used in English but not in Spanish

Job titles and 'occupations' in structures involving the verb *ser* — equating to the English 'to be + a + profession' (unless the noun is qualified by an adjective):

Soy estudiante. I'm a student.
Laura es profesora. Laura is a teacher.
Laura es una profesora maravillosa. Laura is a great teacher.

After certain verbs — especially *tener*, *buscar*, *haber* and *llevar (puesto)* — when it is normal for only one of the following nouns to be the case, the indefinite article is generally omitted:

¿Tienes novio? Have you got a boyfriend?
Suele llevar chaqueta. S/he usually wears a jacket.
Creo que hay mercado hoy. I think there's a market today.

The indefinite article is not used with the words *otro*, *cien*, *mil* and *qué*:

¿Quieres otra cerveza? Do you want another beer?
Tengo casi cien primos. I've got almost a hundred cousins.
Me costó mil euros. It cost me a thousand euros.
¡Qué pena! What a pity!

Similarly, *cierto* and *sin* usually work without the indefinite article, but *un cierto...* is sometimes heard, and you can use *sin un...* to emphasise that there really is not a single example of what is being talked about:

Detecté (una) cierta ironía en tus palabras. I detected a certain irony in your words.
¿Viajaste sin maleta? Did you travel without a suitcase?
Acabamos sin un céntimo. We ended up without a cent to our names.

DEFINITE AND INDEFINITE ARTICLES — UNIT 2

Indefinite article used in Spanish but not in English

This occurs when an abstract noun is qualified by an adjective:

Tienen una gran paciencia. They have great patience.

Spanish can use the plural *unos / unas* in the following way:

Son unos cobardes. They're (a bunch of) cowards.

Other usages of the indefinite article with *ser*

Look carefully at the following examples of usage. The brackets indicate that a usage is optional:

Hoy es fiesta.	Today is a holiday / bank holiday.
Es (una) parte de la exposición.	It's part of the exhibition.
Es (una) cuestión de tacto.	It's a question of tact.
Es un problema.	It's a problem.
Fue una lástima.	It was a shame.
Va a ser un éxito.	It's going to be a success.
No es (un) problema.	It's not a problem.

PRACTICE

1 Translate the following sentences into Spanish:

1. Patience is important.

   ....

2. I love dogs.

   ....

3. Cars tend to be expensive.

   ....

4. Teachers don't earn much.

   ....

5. I'm hungry.

   ....

6. Lunch is at one o'clock.

   ....

7. Beer is strong.

   ....

8. My favourite colour is red.

   ....

9. You have blue eyes.

   ....

10. My leg hurts.

    ....

2 Insert the correct definite article, and any other pronouns and prepositions, where it is appropriate to do so:

1. Mi hermano...........................ha roto...........................dedo.

2. ....águila volaba encima de...........................arena.

PRACTICE

3 Hoy no voy a .... universidad porque mi padre está en

.... hospital.

4 Vamos a jugar .... fútbol después de .... cena.

5 Tengo una serie de citas con .... doctora Fernández.

6 Buenas tardes, ... señora Ruiz.

7 .... quince por ciento de .... portugueses creen que el plan es bueno.

8 Son .... cinco menos .... cuarto de .... tarde.

9 Hoy es .... lunes.

10 Nací .... martes, ... ocho de .... febrero.

3 **Say whether each of the following sentences is correct or incorrect, making any adjustments you consider necessary:**

1 Italiano es una lengua muy bonita.

....

2 ¿Hablas ruso?

....

3 Prefiero leer este libro en el inglés.

....

4 ¿Te importa traducírmelo a español?

....

5 Vivo actualmente en Reino Unido.

....

6 La Francia es mi país favorito.

....

PRACTICE

7 Vivo en calle Calderón.

....

8 Esta tarde Barcelona juega contra Liverpool.

....

9 Catalanes no beben mucho.

....

10 Me gusta hablar con los irlandeses que viven al lado.

....

4 Add *un*, *una*, *unos* or *unas* where appropriate:

1 ¿Sabes si hay .... fiesta esta noche?

2 Tengo .... coche desde hace dos meses.

3 Es .... actor, y vive con .... científico muy famoso.

4 Esos hombres son .... borrachos.

5 Posee .... gran inteligencia.

6 ¿Quieres .... otro vaso de leche?

7 Es aconsejable ir a la playa sin .... dinero.

8 ¡Qué .... lástima!

5 Match the fragments in the left-hand column with the best continuations in the right-hand column:

1 Lo imprescindible   a lo de la semana pasada.
2 Mi amiga no sabe   b lo que haces.
3 Me impresionó   c lo olvidado.
4 No intentes recordar   d es ganar.
5 Ten cuidado con   e lo bonita que es.

UNIT 3

Adjectives and comparison strategies

Agreement of adjectives

In this unit, we'll revise how to make adjectives feminine and plural, and look at their positioning in relation to the noun they describe, along with how to construct and use comparative and superlative forms.

Masculine and feminine singular

Starting from the masculine singular form, which is what we find when we look up an adjective in a dictionary, we need to know how to make the adjective feminine (and, in a separate process, plural). The simplest format, applicable to adjectives ending in -o, looks like this:

Masc. sing.	Fem. sing.	Masc. pl.	Fem. pl.
blanco	blanca	blancos	blancas

Unfortunately, by no means all adjectives work as straightforwardly as *blanco*, so we need a series of rules – based on the nature of the masculine singular form – to determine how to proceed to feminine and hence plural forms.

A   The first cluster of adjectives are those with a separately inflected feminine singular form (as is the case with *blanco*, above). This cluster is made up as follows:

1   Adjectives whose masculine singular form ends in -o, -án, -és, -ín, -ón, -or, -ote, -ete.

In each case, if the word ends in a vowel, change this vowel to -a for the feminine; if it ends in a consonant, add -a to the end and remove any accent that may have been present on the final syllable of the masculine form:

Masc. sing	Fem. sing.	Meaning
blanco	blanca	white
catalán	catalana	Catalan
francés	francesa	French
parlanchín	parlanchina	chatty
burlón	burlona	mocking
trabajador	trabajadora	hard-working
grandote	grandota	huge
regordete	regordeta	chubby

UNIT 3 ADJECTIVES AND COMPARISON STRATEGIES

2. Adjectives of nationality and regional identity which end in a consonant receive -*a* on the end to make the feminine form, and again any final-syllable accent is removed in the feminine. This is the case with *francés / francesa* in the table on the preceding page, but there are other consonants affected:

Masc. sing.	Fem. sing.	Meaning
español	*española*	Spanish
andaluz	*andaluza*	Andalusian

> Remember that names of both languages and nationalities are spelt with a small letter in Spanish. Students of French (where nationalities of people take a capital and languages don't) should pay particular attention here.

B The second cluster contains adjectives with no difference in inflection between the masculine and feminine singular. This cluster is made up as follows:

1. Adjectives ending in an unaccented vowel, other than those set out in the first cluster:

Masc. sing.	Fem. sing.	Meaning
importante	*importante*	important
realista	*realista*	realistic
caqui	*caqui*	khaki

2. Adjectives whose masculine singular form ends in a consonant (other than those noted at point **A**):

Masc. sing.	Fem. sing.	Meaning
joven	*joven*	young
fácil	*fácil*	easy
feliz	*feliz*	happy

3. Adjectives whose masculine singular form ends in an accented vowel:

Masc. sing.	Fem. sing.	Meaning
hindú	*hindú*	Hindu
iraní	*iraní*	Iranian

4. There is a group of 11 adjectives that end in -*or* (and therefore ought to belong to the first cluster), but which have no change between the masculine and feminine singular. These are all comparative forms, so we'll see some of them again later. The one exception is that *superior* can be made feminine in the term *madre superiora* ('mother superior' in a convent):

Masc. / Fem. sing.	Meaning
anterior	earlier, previous
exterior	exterior, outer

inferior	inferior, lower
interior	interior, inner
mayor	older, larger
mejor	better, best
menor	younger, smaller
peor	worse, worst
posterior	rear, subsequent
superior	superior, higher
ulterior	further, later

5   There are five reasonably common exceptions to the rules already listed, three ending in *-és* and two ending in *-ón*:

Masc. sing.	Fem. sing.	Meaning
cortés	*cortés*	polite
descortés	*descortés*	impolite
montés	*montés*	(of animals) wild
marrón	*marrón*	brown
afín	*afín*	similar, related

C   The final cluster is made up of the invariables – a group of adjectives (actually, in many cases, nouns working as adjectives, modifying another noun) whose form doesn't inflect for gender or number. Firstly, here is a collection of fairly common adjectives fitting this description:

Sole form	Meaning
alerta	alert
clave	key (essential)
crack	crack (expert)
estándar	standard
extra	extra (additional)
gratis	free (without cost)
heavy	heavy-going
hembra	female
light	lightweight (concept, etc.)
macho	male
porno	porn(ographic)
sport	sport, sports, sporting
tabú	taboo
ultra	extreme right-wing

UNIT 3 — ADJECTIVES AND COMPARISON STRATEGIES

To these, we can add *hirviendo* ('boiling') and *ardiendo* ('burning'), which are the only two gerunds capable of being used as adjectives, and are also invariable:

agua hirviendo	boiling water
piel ardiendo	burning skin

Adjectives of colour also merit a brief mention. Whilst many are inflected in the conventional ways (e.g. *blanco*, *verde*, *azul*), some are invariable – this is because they are nouns working as adjectives. Here is a list of the most common of these:

Sole form	Meaning
naranja	orange
rosa	pink
malva	mauve
violeta	violet
esmeralda	emerald
café	coffee
cereza	cherry
chocolate	chocolate
grana	dark red
lila	lilac
oro	gold(en)
turquesa	turquoise

If a colour is used in a compound form, e.g. *azul claro* ('light blue'), *verde botella* ('bottle-green'), it is generally invariable in form. Consider the following examples:

Example	English
una chaqueta verde botella	a bottle-green jacket
unas medias azul oscuro	some dark blue tights

Short forms of adjectives ('apocopation')

A small number of adjectives drop their final *-o* before a masculine singular noun, or before a combination of an adjective + a masculine singular noun. Their feminine and plural forms are unaffected, and the masculine singular reverts to its full form if placed <u>after</u> the noun (e.g. *un buen hombre*; *un hombre bueno*). Notice that *algún* and *ningún* receive accents in this usage:

Basic form	Short form	Example	English
alguno	*algún*	*algún amigo; algún íntimo amigo*	some friend or other; some intimate friend or other
bueno	*buen*	*un buen partido de fútbol*	a good football match

ADJECTIVES AND COMPARISON STRATEGIES — UNIT 3

malo	mal	Hace mal tiempo.	The weather is bad.
ninguno	ningún	Ningún profesor me lo dijo.	No teacher told me.
primero	primer	Vivo en el primer piso.	I live on the first floor.
santo	san	San Juan	Saint John
tercero	tercer	Es su tercer marido.	He's her third husband.
uno	un	un día de estos	one of these days

The adjective *grande* ('big', 'great') forms a category of its own, in that the shortening process to *gran* happens before <u>any</u> singular noun, whether masculine or feminine. The exception is that it doesn't shorten when either *más* or *menos* precedes it. Again, it reverts to its full when placed <u>after</u> the noun. We'll look at changes in meaning triggered by position of adjectives later in the unit:

un gran palacio	a great palace
el más grande escritor de su época	the greatest writer of his era
un palacio grande	a large palace
una gran sala	a great room
una sala grande	a large room

Similarly, *cualquiera* ('any', 'any old') drops its final *-a* before any singular noun, retaining it if placed <u>after</u> the noun:

cualquier libro	any book
un libro cualquiera	any old book

The numeral *ciento* ('a hundred') shortens to *cien* before any plural noun, and before *mil* ('thousand') and *millones* ('millions'). The full form of *ciento* is used before all other numbers. For more detail, see the unit on Numerals.

cien veces	a hundred times
cien mil personas	a hundred thousand people
cien millones de euros	a hundred million euros
ciento tres, ciento cuarenta	a hundred and three, a hundred and forty

Making adjectives plural

This process is considerably easier than dealing with masculine / feminine singulars. Essentially, there are two main groups and two smaller groups to focus on. Before we look at the formations, though, it's important to remember that if an adjective describes a combination of masculine and feminine things or people, it needs to be expressed in the masculine plural form:

El aceite y la gasolina son caros.	Oil and petrol are expensive.
árboles y plantas magníficos	magnificent trees and plants

UNIT 3 — ADJECTIVES AND COMPARISON STRATEGIES

Here are the formation rules:

1. Any singular adjective – masculine or feminine – ending in an unaccented vowel (other than the invariables, naturally), adds **-s** to form its plural:

un regalo precioso	a gorgeous gift
unos regalos preciosos	(some) gorgeous gifts
la puerta roja	the red door
las puertas rojas	the red doors
una oficina grande	a large office
unas oficinas grandes	(some) large offices

2. Any singular adjective – masculine or feminine – ending in a consonant (other than the invariables, naturally), adds **-es** to form its plural. Any accent present on the final syllable in the singular disappears in the plural, but notice the case of *joven*, where an accent is added only in the plural):

catalán	catalanes
francés	franceses
marrón	marrones
fácil	fáciles
espectacular	espectaculares
joven	jóvenes

   In the case of invariables, as the term suggests, there is no change in the adjective ending from singular to plural:

una entrada gratis / varias entradas gratis	a free ticket / several free tickets

   It's interesting to note that adjectives coming from the English are generally used only in the singular in Spanish. This is probably because an attempt at pluralisation could lead to pronunciation difficulties:

las políticas más light	the most lightweight policies

3. If an adjective has a singular form ending in **-í** or **-ú**, the plural is formed by adding **-es**, but this time the accent is retained in the plural:

hindú	hindúes
iraní	iraníes

4. For adjectives ending in **-z** in the singular, change the **-z** to **-c** before adding **-es** for the plural form:

capaz	capaces
feliz	felices
andaluz	andaluces

ADJECTIVES AND COMPARISON STRATEGIES — UNIT 3

Word order of adjectives

Generally speaking, whilst the norm in English is for adjectives to precede the noun ('a happy boy', 'an important event'), in Spanish the default setting is for them to follow the noun (*un chico feliz, un acontecimiento importante*).

If two or more adjectives describe a noun in Spanish, they generally go after the noun, and the last two are separated by *y* ('and'):

una mujer guapa, delgada y rubia   a beautiful, slim, blonde woman

Adjectives that always come before the noun

There are a few categories of adjective that always precede the noun in Spanish. Here's a summary:

Category	Example of category	Example of usage
demonstratives	este, ese, aquel	este libro
short possessives	mi, tu, su	mi madre
numbers	cinco, quinto	cinco veces, la quinta vez
interrogatives	¿cuánto?	¿cuántas veces?
exclamations	¡qué!	¡qué pena!
indefinites	cada, ninguno	cada semana
shortened forms	buen, mal	un buen chico

Here is a list of some of the more common instances of adjectives preceding the noun – some belong to categories in the table above, and others don't, but it should help to highlight typical usages:

Ambos documentos contienen los mismos detalles.   Both documents contain the same details.
El llamado 'sistema' ha vuelto a fallar.   The so-called system has failed again.
La mera mención de la huelga me afectó.   The mere mention of the strike affected me.
Había mucha gente en la plaza.   There were a lot of people in the square.
Vamos a tener que hacerlo otra vez.   We're going to have to do it again (lit: another time).
Se desnudó en pleno mercado.   He stripped off in the middle of the market.
Menudo caos has armado.   What chaos you've caused.
Hay poca tranquilidad en esta casa.   There's very little peace and quiet in this house.
Es el presunto asesino.   He's the alleged murderer.
El supuesto robo fue ayer.   The supposed robbery took place yesterday.
No esperaba tantas dificultades.   I didn't expect so many difficulties.

There is a certain amount of personal judgement available in placing an adjective before a noun: choosing to do so can give a sense of personal opinion, reaction, emotion and so on:

Recuerdo la deliciosa cena que me preparaste.   I remember the delicious dinner you cooked for me.
Su increíble fuerza me impresionó.   His / her incredible strength impressed me.

UNIT 3 — ADJECTIVES AND COMPARISON STRATEGIES

Adjectives that can precede or follow a noun, with differing meanings

It's also worth taking a close look at a number of adjectives whose meaning changes depending on whether they precede or follow a noun:

Before the noun	Meaning	After the noun	Meaning
mi antiguo profesor	my former teacher	la casa antigua	the ancient house
cierto interés	a certain amount of interest	una explicación cierta	a true explanation
en diferentes ocasiones	on various occasions	dos casos diferentes	two different cases
un gran intelectual	a great intellectual	un campo grande	a large field
medio bocadillo	half a sandwich	el porcentaje medio	the average percentage
la misma oportunidad	the same opportunity	el príncipe mismo	the prince himself
un nuevo coche	a new (different) car	un coche nuevo	a brand-new car
el pobre niño	the poor (unfortunate) child	el niño pobre	the poor (penniless) child
en raras ocasiones	on rare occasions	un chico raro	a strange boy
una rica paella	a delicious paella	una mujer rica	a rich woman
un verdadero experto	a real (genuine) expert	una explicación verdadera	a truthful explanation
un viejo amigo	an old (long-standing) friend	una camisa vieja	an old shirt

Comparison strategies

Comparative adjectives

A comparative adjective in English either ends in '-er' ('warmer') or uses 'more' ('more intelligent') or 'less' ('less friendly') to indicate a comparison with another person or thing. In Spanish, the equivalent form involves *más* + adjective to indicate 'more', and *menos* + adjective to indicate 'less'. The equivalent of the English 'than', before the person or thing you are making the comparison with, is *que*:

Esta camisa es más fina.	This shirt is thinner.
Mis diccionarios son más completos que los tuyos.	My dictionaries are more complete than yours.
Soy menos comunicativo hoy día.	I'm less communicative these days.
Laura es menos problemática que Lidia.	Laura is less problematic than Lidia.

There are a few irregular comparative adjectives in Spanish (just as in English, where for the comparative of 'good' we say 'better' instead of 'gooder'). These irregular forms have the same *-or* inflection for both masculine and feminine singular, and add *-es* for both genders in the plural. You will see that *grande* and *pequeño* have two forms: the regular one is generally used to refer to physical size, while the irregular one refers more to age:

Adjective	Meaning	Comparative	Meaning
bueno	good	mejor	better
malo	bad	peor	worse

ADJECTIVES AND COMPARISON STRATEGIES — UNIT 3

grande	big	mayor	bigger, older
		más grande	bigger
pequeño	small	menor	smaller, younger
		más pequeño	smaller

If 'than' needs to be followed by a verb construction (e.g. 'I know more than you think'), the *que* becomes *de lo que*:

Es más inteligente de lo que crees. — S/he's more intelligent than you think.
Me parece peor de lo que me dijeron. — It seems worse than they told me.

This also applies when there is an adverb, rather than an adjective, in the comparison:

Te quiero más de lo que sabes. — I love you more than you know.
Hizo menos de lo que dijo. — S/he did less than s/he said.

Note also the following usages involving a noun, where *del que, de la que, de los que* or *de las que* is used, depending on the number and gender of the noun being compared:

Tienes más tiempo del que necesitas. — You've got more time than you need.
Hay más leche de la que puedo beber. — There's more milk than I can drink.
Me han dado más diarios de los que podría leer en un día. — They've given me more newspapers than I could read in one day.
Nos exigen más horas de las que estamos dispuestos a dedicarles. — They're demanding more hours than we're prepared to give them.

Care must be taken with the use of 'more than' or 'less than' / 'fewer than' + numbers or quantities. The rule is that this must be expressed by *más de / menos de*, except in instances such as the last example below, where the comparison is not strictly with a number, but with a group of people (*carreteros* are 'cartwrights', but are used in Spanish similes of smoking and swearing heavily):

Tengo más de cien amigos. — I have more than a hundred friends.
Hace menos de diez grados. — The temperature's less than ten degrees.
Fuma más que dos carreteros. — S/he smokes more than two chimneys (would).

Comparisons of equality

These are constructions in which, in English, we use 'as... as...' to indicate that two people or things have the same level of whatever the adjective or adverb suggests (e.g. 'I am as tall as my brother'). The Spanish equivalent is to use **tan**+ adjective / adverb + **como**... (e.g. *Soy tan alto como mi hermano*). A common mistake to avoid is to say *tan alto que*...

Mi hermana es tan guapa como mi madre. — My sister is as pretty as my mother.
Mis primos son tan inteligentes como sus padres. — My cousins are as intelligent as their parents.
Este restaurante es tan bueno como me habían comentado. — This restaurant is as good as I'd been told.

If the English adjective requires you to use a noun in Spanish (e.g. 'to be thirsty' = *tener sed* = 'to have thirst'), use *tanto* instead of *tan* to introduce the construction. You can expand this to include ideas such as having 'as much ... as' or 'as many ... as', by using the corresponding inflection of *tanto / tanta / tantos / tantas*:

Tengo tanta sed como vosotros.	I'm as thirsty as you are.
Bebo tanta leche como agua.	I drink as much milk as water.
Hay tantas mujeres como hombres en el consejo.	There are as many women as men on the committee.

Superlative adjectives

In English, superlative adjectives have the suffix '-est' ('biggest', 'fittest') or are formed using 'most' or 'least' ('most intelligent', 'least appetising'). In Spanish, they appear in the following formats:

1 *el / la / los / las* + *más / menos* + adjective: e.g. *Es la más alta de la clase* ('she's the tallest in the class').

2 *el / la / l os / las* + noun + *más / menos* + adjective: e.g. *Es la niña más alta de la clase* ('she's the tallest girl in the class').

Notice that, to express the English 'in' (which introduces the 'field' under discussion), Spanish uses *de* rather than *en*. Here are some more examples involving both types:

Soy el menos ambicioso de todo el grupo.	I'm the least ambitious in the whole group.
Tienes los muebles más caros de la calle.	You've got the most expensive furniture in the street.
Son las películas menos interesantes que he visto.	They are the least interesting films I've seen.
Es la cosa más hortera que te puedes imaginar.	It's the tackiest thing you can imagine.

> Students of French should note that Spanish doesn't insert a second article immediately before the *más* or *menos* in this structure.

The group of four irregular comparative forms (*mejor, peor, mayor, menor*) we met in the section on Comparative adjectives feature again as superlatives, only this time preceded by *el / la / los / las*:

Es la mejor (artista) del colegio	She's the best (artist) in the school.
Son los peores (ejemplos) que he visto.	They're the worst (examples) I've seen.

Finally, another way of expressing a superlative is to give an adjective the *-ísimo* suffix, which lends the base adjective the meaning of 'extremely ...'. It's really an intensifier rather than a superlative (though most Spanish grammars refer to it as a superlative anyway), but is worth mentioning at this point for what it can bring to a base adjective. The formation involves removing any final vowel then adding the *-ísimo* suffix (*altísimo, grandísimo*), or adding it directly to any base adjective ending in a consonant (*facilísimo*):

Adjective	Superlative	Example	Meaning
gracioso	*graciosísimo*	*Esas chicas son graciosísimas.*	Those girls are hilarious.
fácil	*facilísimo*	*La tarea fue facilísima.*	The task was a piece of cake.

Notice that – as is the case for all adjectives bearing an accent – *fácil* loses its base accent when the *-ísimo* suffix is added. There are a few more key rules associated with this suffix:

1 Not all adjectives can take it. There are various obscure categories which, for reasons of word structure, would not lend themselves to the addition of this suffix, but some more useful ones are outlined below:

Example	Meaning	Reason
perfecto, fantástico	perfect, fantastic	Concepts which do not allow for further intensification
anual, tercero	annual, third	Adjectives of time and number (though the exception *primerísimo* – 'very first of all' – is sometimes used)
nacionalista	nationalist	Most adjectives ending in *-ista*

A rule of common sense applies: if you would not use an intensifying structure in English (e.g. 'very infinite', 'extremely tenth') it might be best to avoid the *-ísimo* suffix for the corresponding adjective in Spanish.

2 Notice the spelling changes occurring in the following examples, designed to ensure that the correct pronunciation and spelling conventions are maintained:

Adjective	Superlative	Meaning
blanco	*blanquísimo*	very white
amargo	*amarguísimo*	really bitter
feliz	*felicísimo*	as happy as Larry

3 With adjectives ending in *-ble*, you need to change this ending to *-bil* before adding the *-ísimo* suffix:

Adjective	Superlative	Meaning
amable	*amabilísimo*	very pleasant
factible	*factibilísimo*	very feasible

4 The following irregular intensive forms should be studied closely – some involve the *-ísimo* suffix; others don't, but are usefully learned at the same time:

Adjective	Superlative	Meaning
antiguo	*antiquísimo*	very old
cursi	*cursilísimo*	extremely twee / affected
joven	*jovencísimo*	extremely young
lejos	*lejísimos*	very far, 'miles away'
mayor	*máximo*	greatest, supreme, 'top'
menor	*mínimo*	least, slightest
mejor	*óptimo*	superb, very best
peor	*pésimo*	very worst, dreadful

PRACTICE

1 Write the appropriate form of the adjective given in each case below:

1. Tengo muchísimas amigas (alemán) .... y (belga) ....

2. Mis primos viven en el (tercero) .... piso, no en el (primero) ....

3. No somos (capaz) .... de acabar las secciones (azul) ....

4. ¿Por qué no has hecho (ninguno) .... ejercicio? Podrías haber hecho (alguno) ....

5. Mi mujer es (español) ...., pero concretamente es (andaluz) ....

6. El agua (frío) .... es (bueno) .... para quitar la sed.

2 Make as many changes as necessary to the following fragments to make them fully feminine:

1. El traductor catalán ....
2. Un intérprete canadiense ....
3. Un hombre descortés ....
4. El joven modelo ....
5. El colega andaluz ....
6. Unos chicos felices ....

3 Translate the following noun phrases into Spanish, paying close attention to the position of each adjective:

1. The former teacher (masculine) ....
2. The brand-new cars ....
3. The poor (penniless) girls ....
4. A strange man ....
5. Certain theories ....

PRACTICE

6   A big book..

7   The great princess..

8   The poor (unfortunate) Frenchman...

9   The ancient furniture..

10 A new friend (feminine)..

4 Fill in each of the gaps with *tan*, *tanto*, *tanta*, *tantos* or *tantas*, as appropriate:

1   Mi hermana es .... rápida como mi hermano.

2   Tenemos .... sed como vosotros.

3   Somos .... corteses como ellos.

4   ¿Estabas .... alerta como ella?

5   Tuviste .... problemas como éxitos.

5 Fill each of the gaps below with *mejor*, *mejores*, *el mejor*, *la mejor*, *los mejores* or *las mejores*, as appropriate:

1   Mis hijas son .... del grupo.

2   ¿Crees que estos libros son .... que los otros?

3   El agua que has traído es .... que he probado.

4   Pepe dice que Juan es .... artista de la clase.

5   A María le parece .... la primera.

6 Insert *que*, *de*, *de lo que*, *del que*, *de la que*, *de los que* or *de las que* into each of the gaps below, as appropriate:

1   Han servido más carne .... podremos comer.

2   Estudio con más paciencia .... esos alumnos.

PRACTICE

3 Creo que es menos simpática .... parece.

4 Habíamos completado más .... cincuenta proyectos juntas.

5 Ha habido menos problemas .... esperábamos.

6 Sé más .... tú.

7 Suele ponernos menos queso .... querríamos.

8 Me ha dado más tareas .... estaba dispuesta a hacer.

9 La verdad es que tengo menos oportunidades .... ayer.

10 Este ejercicio es menos complicado .... crees.

7 Use an appropriate variant of the *-ísimo* suffix to make each of the following statements more emphatic, as shown in the example:

Mi hermano es muy alto – es altísimo

1 Esta bebida es muy barata – ....

2 Tus padres son muy majos – ....

3 La directora es muy joven – ....

4 Es una chica muy cursi – ....

5 Pedro y Laura son muy amables – ....

6 Estas reglas son muy antiguas – ....

7 El barco es muy grande – ....

8 Sois muy simpáticas – ....

9 Mi casa está muy lejos – ....

10 Mis tías son muy felices – ....

UNIT 4 Indefinite adjectives and pronouns

Indefinite adjectives

Indefinite adjectives are used to refer to people or things without being specific as to who or what they are, how many of them there are, etc. Examples in English would be 'some', 'few', 'several'. Here is a table featuring the main indefinite adjectives to be learned in Spanish:

Base adj.	Masc. sing.	Fem. sing.	Masc. pl.	Fem. pl.	Meaning
alguno	algún	alguna	algunos	algunas	some, any
ambos			ambos	ambas	both
bastante	bastante	bastante	bastantes	bastantes	enough
cada	cada	cada			each, every
cierto	cierto	cierta	ciertos	ciertas	certain, specific
cualquiera	cualquier	cualquier	cualesquiera	cualesquiera	any
demasiado	demasiado	demasiada	demasiados	demasiadas	too much, too many
medio	medio	media	medios	medias	half
mismo	mismo	misma	mismos	mismas	same
mucho	mucho	mucha	muchos	muchas	a lot of
ninguno	ningún	ninguna	ningunos	ningunas	no
otro	otro	otra	otros	otras	other, another
poco	poco	poca	pocos	pocas	little, few
tanto	tanto	tanta	tantos	tantas	so much, so many
todo	todo	toda	todos	todas	all

Most of the adjectives behave as you would expect them to, but there are a couple of general rules worth bearing in mind. Firstly, as in English, indefinite adjectives go before the noun:

Tengo mucha paciencia.   I have a lot of patience.
Han surgido algunas dificultades.   Some difficulties have arisen.

Secondly, the English 'some' and 'any', when used before uncountable nouns (e.g. milk, bread), do not need to be translated into Spanish by *alguno/a*:

Quiero mantequilla.   I want some butter.
¿Hay agua en la nevera?   Is there any water in the fridge?
No me dieron información / trabajo.   They didn't give me any information / work.

UNIT 4 — INDEFINITE ADJECTIVES AND PRONOUNS

It's a good idea to look more deeply into the specifics of each adjective from the table on the previous page, to clarify issues of meaning and quirks of usage:

Alguno

Whilst generally omitted in translating the English 'some' + a singular noun, *alguno* is very useful for conveying the vague sense of 'some ... or other', and often features in translations of 'some' + a plural noun. Notice its shortened form before a masculine singular noun:

Algún día lo haré.	I'll do it one day / one of these days.
He quedado con algunos amigos.	I've arranged to meet a few friends.

When it comes after a noun, its takes on the emphatic meaning of 'no ... at all':

No había información alguna sobre él.	There was no information whatsoever about him.

Ambos

The plual adjective *ambos / ambas*, meaning 'both', is less common (and less safe to use) than the alternative *los dos / las dos*. A couple of warnings about its usage: don't use an article with it – for 'both men', say *ambos hombres* rather than *ambos los hombres* – and don't try to use it in structures like 'both my mother and my father' (which we'll cover in a later unit). Here are some examples of good usage:

Usage of *ambos / ambas*	Alternative	Meaning
Ambos libros son buenos.	Los dos libros son buenos.	Both (the) books are good.
Soy consciente de ambas consecuencias.	Soy consciente de las dos consecuencias.	I'm aware of both consequences.

Bastante

Aside from its adverbial meaning of 'quite' or 'fairly', *bastante* works as an adjective to express the notions of 'enough', 'sufficient', 'quite a bit of' or 'quite a few'.

Hay bastante leche para todos.	There's enough milk for everyone.
Hubo bastantes quejas después del programa.	There were quite a few complaints after the programme.

Cada

Cada is always followed by a singular noun, always precedes the noun, and is invariable. An alternative that can often be used is *todos los / todas las* + the plural noun (which, naturally, has the additional meaning of 'all... '):

Usage of *cada*	Alternative	Meaning
Hago la compra cada día.	Hago la compra todos los días.	I do the shopping every day.
Cada profesor tiene su clase.	Todos los profesores tienen su clase.	Each / every teacher has his / her class.

It's also worth noting that *cada uno* is a useful way of saying 'everyone' in the sense of 'each person', and that *cada vez más / menos* + adjective / adverb is a neat way of expressing English comparative adjectives and adverbs such as 'bigger and bigger', or 'more and more painstakingly'. We'll come across this usage again in our unit on Adjectives.

Cierto

This adjective differs in its meaning depending on whether it precedes or follows the noun:

Buscamos una explicación cierta.	We're looking for a true, accurate explanation.
Muestra cierta inquietud en su conducta.	S/he shows a certain uneasiness in his / her behaviour.
Ciertos mapas te pueden servir.	Certain maps may be of use to you.

Cualquiera

Cualquiera ('any') shortens to *cualquier* before a singular noun (whether masculine or feminine) or noun phrase. Its plural *cualesquiera* is rarely seen in modern Spanish, as most usages can be conveyed successfully via the singular. It normally precedes the noun, but can also follow it, in which case it retains its final *-a* and its meaning alters to a slightly more random 'any old ... ':

Cualquier sistema será válido.	Any system will be valid.
Dame una bolsa cualquiera.	Give me any old bag (you can lay your hands on).

Demasiado

Similarly to *bastante*, *demasiado* has a separate adverbial usage, but here as an adjective it means 'too much' (of something singular) or 'too many' (of something plural), and always comes before the noun.

He bebido demasiado café.	I've drunk too much coffee.
Has actuado con demasiada arrogancia.	You've acted with too much arrogance.
Tienes demasiados libros en tu oficina.	You've got too many books in your office.
Hemos faltado demasiadas veces.	We've been absent too many times.

Medio

Medio can work as an adjective (with full inflections) or as an adverb (invariable, followed by an adjective). In both instances, it means 'half':

Spanish	English	Function
Estuve media hora bebiendo medio litro.	I spent half an hour drinking half a litre.	Adjectival
Mis amigas están medio dormidas.	My friends are half asleep.	Adverbial

UNIT 4 INDEFINITE ADJECTIVES AND PRONOUNS

Mismo

As an adjective, *mismo* has two main meanings: 'the same ...', in which case it always comes before the noun), and 'the very / selfsame ...', in which case it can precede or follow the noun:

Es la misma chica que nos ayudó ayer.	She's the same girl who helped us yesterday.
El ladrón consiguió entrar en el mismo palacio / en el palacio mismo.	The thief managed to get into the very palace.

There are a few other snippets worth noting:

1. *Mismo* (as a fully inflected adjective) can be used emphatically after a pronoun:

   Yo misma puedo hacerlo si quieres.   I can do it myself if you like.

2. The invariable *mismo* can be used after an adverb or adverbial phrase, to give emphasis:

   aquí mismo   right here
   por eso mismo   for that very reason

3. Take care with *lo mismo*, as it has three slightly different functions: it can mean the same as *la misma cosa* ('the same thing') or can have a more obviously adverbial usage, in a sentence such as:

   Lo mismo bebo ginebra que vodka.   I'm just as likely / happy to drink gin as vodka.

   and can work as another way of saying 'perhaps':

   Lo mismo me paso por tu casa hoy.   I might just pop round to your place today.

4. The emphatic *mismísimo* is available to add strength to *mismo* in the sense of 'very / selfsame': *la mismísima reina* ('the queen herself').

Mucho

Used adjectivally, *mucho* is quite straightforward:

Tengo mucha paciencia.	I have a lot of patience.
Tienes muchos amigos.	You have a lot of friends.

There are two additional comments to make about *mucho*. One relates to its usage before *más*, *menos*, *mayor* or *menor* + a noun. In this case, *mucho* must agree in both number and gender with the noun in question:

Hay muchas menos posibilidades.	There are far fewer possibilities.
Bebes mucha más agua hoy en día.	You drink a lot more water these days.

The other usage is where *mucho* takes on the meaning of 'too much' – this can, for example, occur in moments of gentle complaint:

Me has puesto mucha comida.	You've given (served) me too much food.
No puedo con todo, es mucho trabajo.	I can't manage all this – it's too much work.

Ninguno

Used before a noun, *ninguno* gives the meaning of 'no (example of that noun)'. Notice the shortened form before a masculine singular noun. It can also feature after the noun for emphasis:

Ningún hombre debería comportarse así.	No man should behave like that.
Ninguna ciudad cumple con los criterios.	No city meets the criteria.
No veo problema ninguno en que vayas.	I see no problem with you / your going.

Otro

The first thing to remember is that *otro* means both 'other' and 'another' – the combination *un otro* is bad Spanish:

Quiero otra ración de pulpo.	I want another portion of octopus.
El otro sillón es más cómodo.	The other armchair is more comfortable.
He hablado con ellos en otras ocasiones.	I've spoken to them on other occasions.

It's useful to be aware that 'the others' – in the sense of 'the remainder' or 'the rest' of a group of people or things – is better translated by *los demás / las demás* than by *los otros / las otras*.

Poco

Structurally, *poco* works very similarly to *mucho*, though clearly it has the opposite meaning of 'little' / 'few':

Tengo poca paciencia.	I have little patience.
Tengo pocos amigos.	I have few friends.

Tanto

As an adjective, *tanto* agrees in number and gender with the noun to which it is attached.

⇨ *For full coverage of comparisons involving **tanto** see Unit 3.*

No me eches tanto vino.	Don't pour me so much wine.
Tanta frivolidad no te favorece.	So much frivolity doesn't suit you.
Hay tantos problemas que no sé con cuál empezar.	There are so many problems that I don't know which one to start with.
No quiero tantas patatas fritas.	I don't want so many chips.

UNIT 4 — INDEFINITE ADJECTIVES AND PRONOUNS

Todo

There is no real difficulty with the adjectival use of *todo*, but it's worth pointing out that it can translate back into English in various ways, according to the context. Consider the following examples:

Spanish	English	Notes
Lo sabe toda la clase.	The whole class knows (it).	When followed by a definite article
Ya han llegado todos los invitados.	All the guests have arrived.	
Hay obras por todo el pueblo.	There are roadworks throughout / right across the village.	
Todos los sábados	Every Saturday	With a definite article + period of time
Todo Canadá participó.	All of / the whole of Canada took part.	When followed by a place or place name
Toda infracción será sancionada.	Any infringement will be punished.	When not followed by an article

Indefinite pronouns

Indefinite pronouns refer to people or things generally, without specifying who or what they are. Examples in English include 'somebody', 'anything' and 'nothing'. Here is a table featuring the main indefinite pronouns to be learned in Spanish – *cada uno*, while not strictly a pronoun, is included for its usefulness in the list:

Base pronoun	Masc. sing.	Fem. sing.	Masc. pl.	Fem. pl.	Meaning
algo					something, anything
alguien					somebody, anybody
alguno	alguno	alguna	algunos	algunas	some, a few
cada uno	cada uno	cada una			each (one)
cualquiera	cualquiera	cualquiera	cualesquiera	cualesquiera	any, anybody
mucho	mucho	mucha	muchos	muchas	much, many
nada					nothing, anything
nadie					nobody, anybody
ninguno	ninguno	ninguna	ningunos	ningunas	none
otro	otro	otra	otros	otras	another one, others
poco	poco	poca	pocos	pocas	little, few
tanto	tanto	tanta	tantos	tantas	so much, so many
todo	todo	toda	todos	todas	everything, all

Algo

This pronoun is invariable, and comes to mean 'something' or 'anything', depending on the structure in which it is used:

¿Has encontrado algo?	Have you found anything?
Algo no va bien.	Something's not quite right.

Alguien

Alguien is the human equivalent of *algo*, being used to express 'somebody' or 'anybody', depending on the structure in which it is used:

Alguien ha abierto la puerta.	Somebody has opened the door.
¿Has hablado con alguien?	Have you spoken to anybody?

Alguno

In the singular, the pronoun *alguno / alguna* (never *algún* as a pronoun) means 'one or two', 'the odd one'. In the plural, its meaning is the more straightforward 'some' or 'a few':

—¿Tienes plantas en casa? —Sí, tengo alguna.	'Have you got any plants in your house?' – 'Yes, I've got the odd one.'
Algunos ya han hecho la matrícula.	Some people have already enrolled.

Cada uno

Cada uno, and its feminine *cada una*, are used to mean 'each one' or 'everybody':

Venga, chicas: ¡cada una a su habitación!	Come on, girls: everybody to their room!
Cada uno tiene sus puntos de interés.	Each one has its points of interest.

Cualquiera

As a pronoun, *cualquiera* retains its final *-a* at all times. The plural *cualesquiera* is very rare.

Cualquiera diría que estás loco.	Anyone would think (lit: say) you're mad.
Aceptaría cualquiera de las ofertas.	I would accept any of the offers.

UNIT 4 INDEFINITE ADJECTIVES AND PRONOUNS

Mucho

In its singular forms, *mucho* means 'much' or 'a lot'; the plural forms translate as 'many' or 'a lot'. There are additional shades of meaning that can affect translation into English – see the last two examples, below:

No queda mucho.	There's not much left.
Muchas de las chicas hicieron sugerencias.	A lot of the girls made suggestions.
Esta noche han bebido mucho.	They've had too much to drink this evening.
Nos vemos mucho.	We see each other very often.

Nada

Meaning 'nothing' and being essentially the opposite of *algo*, *nada* is not problematic, but the examples below show how it can work with double negatives. There is an additional meaning of 'not at all' in expressions like *no me gusta nada* ('I don't like it at all') or *no es nada fácil* ('it's not at all easy') – where *nada* is working as an adverb followed by an adjective – and note that *nada* can be used (just like 'nothing' in English) as a single-word reply to a question.

Use of negatives	English	Notes
<u>No</u> sabes <u>nada</u>.	You don't know anything.	As direct object of verb
<u>No</u> juego con <u>nada</u>.	I'm not playing with anything.	After a preposition
<u>Nada</u> es más importante.	Nothing is more important.	As subject of verb

Nadie

Meaning 'nobody' and being essentially the opposite of *alguien*, *nadie* functions very similarly to *nada*. It's worth pointing out that if *nadie* is the object of a verb, the personal *a* must be inserted. Similarly to *nada*, *nadie* can be used (just like 'nobody' in English) as a single-word reply to a question.

Use of negatives	English	Notes
<u>No</u> he visto a <u>nadie</u>.	I haven't seen anybody.	As direct object of verb
<u>No</u> estoy con <u>nadie</u>.	I'm not with anybody.	After a preposition
<u>Nadie</u> querrá hacerlo.	Nobody will want to do it.	As subject of verb

Ninguno

Ninguno/a/os/as (never *ningún* as a pronoun) follows the same double-negative pattern as *nada* and *nadie*. It can also be used as a single-word reply to a question.

Ninguna de las directoras estuvo en la reunión.	None of the female directors was at the meeting.
—¿Cuántos quieres? —Ninguno.	'How many do you want?' – 'None.'

INDEFINITE ADJECTIVES AND PRONOUNS — UNIT 4

Otro

As a singular pronoun, *otro/a* has the meaning of 'another one'; the plural *otros/as* equates to 'others'. There are no special issues to worry about:

Si quieres, te doy otro.	I'll give you another one if you like.
Las he dejado en casa, pero no importa: tengo otras.	I've left them at home, but it doesn't matter: I've got others (some more).

Poco

In its singular forms, *poco/a* means 'little' ('not very much'); the plural forms translate as 'few' or 'not many'. It's also worth noting its adverbial use, when it can be followed by an adjective to mean 'not very' (see the third example, below):

¿Leche? Me queda poca.	Milk? I've not got much left.
Hay pocos pero son tuyos.	There are few of them, but they're yours.
una herramienta poco útil	not a very useful tool

Tanto

Functioning as 'so much' in the singular and 'so many' in the plural, *tanto/a/os/as* works quite straightforwardly as a pronoun:

—¿Has tenido suerte? —No tanta.	'Have you had any luck?' – 'Not so much.'
Me gustan los jerseys, pero no tengo tantos.	I like jerseys, but I haven't got so many.

Todo

Here are some typical usages of this pronoun, meaning 'all', 'everything', 'the whole lot', 'everybody', etc.:

Todo va a acabar mal.	It's all going to end badly.
Vamos a participar todas.	We're all going to take part.

PRACTICE

1 Fill in the gaps in the following sentences, using the words from the grid:

| cada | nada | muchas | bastante | ninguno |
| algún | poco | alguna | cualquier | nadie |

1. Antes tenía muchos libros de ese tipo pero ahora no me queda ....
2. .... ayuda económica me vendría bien.
3. No hay .... que se pueda hacer para mejorarlo.
4. Me dijo que no aceptaría excusa ....
5. ¿Tenemos .... gasolina para llegar al destino?
6. Si buscas una chaqueta elegante, mi hermano tiene ....
7. .... quiso ayudarme.
8. Normalmente la veo .... semana.
9. Lo has hecho en muy .... tiempo.
10. Dice que .... año de estos lo hará.

2 Translate the following sentences into Spanish:

1. We have the same system.

   ....

2. I have so many sisters.

   ....

3. I don't want to do any work whatsoever.

   ....

4. Certain men have arrived at the prison.

   ....

5. No boy should behave like that.

   ....

PRACTICE

6 Both plans are excellent.

....

7 I have three bottles of water. Do you want another one?

....

8 All of Spain wants to celebrate the victory.

....

9 I want some butter but there isn't any.

....

10 Nobody said anything.

....

3 **The following sentences contain examples of single negatives and double negatives. Re-express each one (changing single to double, or vice versa), without altering the meaning:**

1 No ha venido nadie.

....

2 Nada me sorprende en esta ciudad.

....

3 Ninguno de los chicos lo entiende.

....

UNIT 5 | Demonstratives and possessives

> This unit clarifies the difference between demonstrative adjectives ('<u>that</u> book') and demonstrative pronouns ('<u>that</u> was fantastic'), before moving on to look at possessive adjectives ('<u>my</u> book') and possessive pronouns ('the book is <u>mine</u>').

Demonstratives

Demonstrative adjectives and pronouns are used to indicate the closeness or distance of a particular person, thing or experience in relation to the speaker. In English we use the terms 'this' (singular) and 'these' (plural) for proximity, and 'that' (singular) and 'those' (plural) to describe someone or something we consider further away. It is important to establish that this closeness or distance relates not only to physical, spatial distance ('this table', 'that field') but also to matters of time ('this Thursday', 'that year').

Demonstrative adjectives

Spanish works with three levels of distance: *este* ('this' – close by in time or space), *ese* ('that' – further away from the speaker), and *aquel* (a second type of 'that', suggesting a further distance in time or space – the old English 'yonder' is perhaps a rough approximation). Here is a table with the full set of forms:

Meaning	Masc. sing.	Fem. sing.	Masc. pl.	Fem. pl.
this	este	esta	estos	estas
that (not far away)	ese	esa	esos	esas
that (further away)	aquel	aquella	aquellos	aquellas

There are a few useful points to note about these adjectives:

1. They usually go (as in English) before the noun: *este libro*, 'this book'.

2. There is a degree of overlap in the usage of *ese* and *aquel*. The choice is generally personal: if you want to create a real sense of spatial or temporal distance in your statement, use *aquel*; to say 'that' in the everyday sense of 'the further away of two visible or easily imagined items', or to refer to something that is closer to the listener than to the speaker, *ese* is the better option.

3. Students of Italian, note the masculine singular form above. We will look at the neuter form *esto* later in the unit.

4. Don't be tempted to put an accent on any of these adjectival forms. The section on demonstrative pronouns, later in the unit, contains a discussion of when to use an accent.

DEMONSTRATIVES AND POSSESSIVES — UNIT 5

5   If you are planning to follow any of the feminine singular forms (*esta*, *esa*, *aquella*) with a feminine singular noun that begins with a stressed *a-* or *ha-* (*esta arma*, *esa hacha*, *aquella águila*), the best advice is to go ahead and do so, with no alterations required! Rules we learned earlier in the book about forms such as *el agua* are not rigidly enforced in the context of demonstratives, and modern practice is to keep the adjective 'fully feminine'.

Este verano voy a hacer un cursillo.	I'm going to do a short course this summer.
No me parece muy sólida esta silla.	This chair doesn't seem very solid.
Estos planes son mejores que los otros.	These plans are better than the others.
¿Te gustan estas gafas de sol?	Do you like these sunglasses?
Ese collar es el más caro.	That necklace is the most expensive one.
Esa ciudad tiene mucha marcha.	That city's got a buzz about it.
Esos zapatos no te van muy bien.	Those shoes don't really suit you.
Esas vacaciones te vinieron bien.	That holiday did you good.
¿No te acuerdas de aquel chico de Dublín?	Don't you remember that boy from Dublin?
Aquella vez no me dejaron entrar.	That time they didn't let me in.
Se dice que aquellos años fueron maravillosos.	People say those years were magnificent.
Mi casa está detrás de aquellas torres.	My house is behind those towers over there.

Demonstrative pronouns

These are a very similar group of words to those visible in the Demonstrative adjectives table on the previous page, but their role is different. Demonstrative pronouns stand alone – they are not followed by a noun, although in the majority of cases they refer to a noun which is either not present, or located in another part of the sentence. For example, if you and a friend are talking about cars, you can say 'this is my favourite' or 'that one is better', and you are both aware of what items you're talking about, even though 'car' is not specifically mentioned. The same thing happens in Spanish. In each of the examples below, it will be clear whether the person(s) or thing(s) being referred to are masculine or feminine, singular or plural:

Creo que este me gusta más	I think I like this one better / best.
Estas son mis favoritas.	These are my favourites / my favourite (ones).
Llévate esa si quieres.	Take that one away with you if you want.
Aquellos no valían la pena.	Those (ones) weren't worth bothering with.

Aquel and *este* (with appropriate inflections for number and gender) can be used respectively to translate the English 'the former' and 'the latter' in formal contexts, when it is undesirable to repeat the nouns or persons under discussion:

Daniel y Laura quieren hablar contigo: aquel de la presentación y esta del examen.	Daniel and Laura want to talk to you: the former about the presentation and the latter about the exam.
Tengo arañas y ratones en casa. Aquellas no me importan pero estos sí.	I've got spiders and mice in my house. The former don't bother me, but the latter do.

You may have seen some demonstrative pronouns written with an accent: *éste*, *ésas*, *aquéllos*, etc. This was a historical strategy to distinguish them from the corresponding demonstrative adjectives (e.g. <u>este</u> coche es el más rápido / el coche más rápido es <u>éste</u>). Nowadays, however, it is acceptable to drop these accents, and you will only need to use one on the very rare occasions when you feel that your sentence could otherwise be ambiguous (e.g. *esta muestra* = 'this sample'; *ésta muestra* = 'this (one / woman) shows').

A key difference from the adjectival list is that there is an additional layer of demonstrative pronoun provision. It is known as the neuter demonstrative pronoun, and is used when the 'this' or 'that' you're talking about doesn't refer to any noun that is clearly masculine or feminine. The three neuter pronouns all end in *-o* (and must be kept carefully separate from the masculine singular forms) and must never carry an accent:

<u>Esto</u> *es lo que más me gusta de la universidad.*   This is what I like best / most about university.
Ten cuidado con <u>eso</u>.   Be careful with that.
<u>Aquello</u> *fue horrendo.*   That was horrendous.

Possessives

Possessives are used to denote belonging. In Spanish, as in English, there are adjectival forms ('<u>my</u> house', 'the house is <u>mine</u>') and pronominal forms (' <u>Mine</u> is the house at the end of the row').

Possessive adjectives

In Spanish, these divide into two groups, each equating to one of the adjectival usages noted above: 'my house'; 'the house is mine'. They are generally known as the 'short' and 'full' forms respectively.

1   Short form

Meaning	Masc. sing.	Fem. sing.	Masc. pl.	Fem. pl.
my	*mi*	*mi*	*mis*	*mis*
your (*tú* usage)	*tu*	*tu*	*tus*	*tus*
his, her, its, your (*usted* usage)	*su*	*su*	*sus*	*sus*
our	***nuestro***	***nuestra***	***nuestros***	***nuestras***
your (*vosotros/as* usage; NB not used in Latin America or the Canary Islands)	***vuestro***	***vuestra***	***vuestros***	***vuestras***
their, your (*ustedes* usage)	*su*	*su*	*sus*	*sus*

Note the following observations about usage of the short forms:

➤ These short forms always precede a noun or noun phrase.

➤ If you want to state possession of more than one noun, the possessive adjective must be repeated (which isn't necessarily the case in English):

<u>mi</u> *papel y* <u>mi</u> *bolígrafo*   my pen and paper
<u>tu</u> *médico y* <u>tu</u> *dentista*   your doctor and dentist

DEMONSTRATIVES AND POSSESSIVES — UNIT 5

➤ Only the *nuestro* and *vuestro* forms have a visible inflection for gender.

➤ As the *vosotros* form of verbs is not used in Latin America or the Canary Islands, all plural variants of 'your' are expressed via *su/s* in those territories.

➤ *Su/s* is, by its nature, potentially ambiguous: it can mean 'his', 'her', 'its', 'your' (belonging to *usted*), 'their' or 'your' (belonging to *ustedes*). A useful tool for disambiguation is to use *de él, de ella, de usted*, etc., as follows – the pronouns used will be studied in the next unit:

Ambiguous possessive	Possible meaning	Solution
su vida	his life	*la vida de él*
	her life	*la vida de ella*
	its life (animal)	*la vida de él / ella*
	your life (*usted*)	*la vida de usted*
	their life	*la vida de ellos / ellas*
	your life (*ustedes*)	*la vida de ustedes*

➤ It's vital to remember – particularly when you are working with *nuestro* or *vuestro* – that the number and gender inflections are determined by the <u>thing(s) possessed</u>, not the possessor(s):

nuestra madre　　　　　　　　　　　　　　our mother
tus buenos amigos　　　　　　　　　　　　your good friends

➤ One of the main differences between Spanish and English usage of the short possessive adjective is that whereas English generally uses it to refer to parts of the body, items of clothing and possessions that would normally be carried about the body, Spanish tends to use the definite article. Study the following examples, which show the most common, preferred rendering in Spanish. Also worthy of note are the reflexive pronouns included, and the singularity of 'the passport', being something of which each person ordinarily has only one:

Me he quitado <u>la</u> chaqueta.　　　　　　I've taken <u>my</u> jacket off.
¿Te duele <u>la</u> pierna?　　　　　　　　　Does <u>your</u> leg hurt?
Miguel se rascó <u>la</u> cabeza.　　　　　　Miguel scratched <u>his</u> head.
Tuvimos que entregar <u>el</u> pasaporte.　　We had to hand <u>our</u> passports over.

This can be overridden if clarification or emphasis is required:

Tenemos <u>mi</u> pasaporte, pero falta el de mi hermana.　　We've got <u>my</u> passport, but my sister's is missing.

2　Full form

Meaning	Masc. sing.	Fem. sing.	Masc. pl.	Fem. pl.
(of) mine	*mío*	*mía*	*míos*	*mías*
(of) yours [*tú* usage]	*tuyo*	*tuya*	*tuyos*	*tuyas*
(of) his, (of) hers, (of) its, (of) yours [*usted* usage]	*suyo*	*suya*	*suyos*	*suyas*

UNIT 5 — DEMONSTRATIVES AND POSSESSIVES

(of) ours	nuestro	nuestra	nuestros	nuestras
(of) yours [*vosotros / as* usage]; NB: not used in Latin America or the Canary Islands	vuestro	vuestra	vuestros	vuestras
(of) theirs, (of) yours [*ustedes* usage]	suyo	suya	suyos	suyas

Full-form possessive adjectives go after the noun they describe, and must agree with it in both number and gender. They can also go after the verb *ser*:

una amiga nuestra	a friend of ours
unos documentos tuyos	some documents of yours
La culpa es tuya.	It's your fault (the fault is yours).
¿Es vuestro ese coche?	Is that car yours?

The *mío / mía* pair also appear in a range of exclamations and forms of addressing people, where the English equivalent would perhaps be a short-form adjective:

hija mía	my dear daughter
¡Dios mío!	My God!
amor mío	my love
muy señor mío	Dear Sir

Possessive pronouns

Possessive pronouns are used to denote possession, and are used in place of the noun to which they refer. They are formed identically to full-form possessive adjectives, but usually have a definite article attached (e.g. *el mío, la tuya, las nuestras*). Compare the examples below, which contrast the use of possessive adjectives and pronouns. In the third example, we assume that the concept of 'houses' is already under discussion in the conversation, so we can say 'mine' in the knowledge that 'house' is understood – in both languages, the pronominal form allows us to drop the ungainly repetition of the noun in such circumstances:

Short-form adjective	**Mi casa está al final de la calle.**	My house is at the end of the street.
Full-form adjective	**La casa al final de la calle es mía.**	The house at the end of the street is mine.
Pronoun	**La mía está al final de la calle.**	Mine is at the end of the street.

There are a few subtleties to be observed in the inclusion or omission of the definite article:

1 After *ser* ('to be') the definite article is usually omitted to denote ownership:

Las sillas rotas son nuestras.	The broken chairs are ours.

To include the article in a sentence like this changes the focus from ownership to clarification / distinguishing one example from another:

Las sillas rotas son las nuestras.	Ours are the broken chairs (i.e. identifying or distinguishing them – ownership is not the issue).

2   Otherwise, if the pronoun is the subject or the object of the verb, the definite article is used:

La mía brilla más.   Mine [something feminine singular] shines
                                                more brightly.
Veo que prefieres **los nuestros**.   I see you prefer ours [masculine plural things]

3   If an ambiguity arises over who is being referred to in *el suyo, la suya*, etc., the option of saying *el de usted, la de ellos*, etc., is open to you:

mi oficina y **la suya**   mi oficina y **la de ella**   my office and hers
los nuestros y **los suyos**   los nuestros y **los de ustedes**   ours and yours

Equally, *el de, la de, los de, las de* can be used before a person's name or a noun referring to them, to denote possession:

El de mi hermano es el más interesante.   My brother's is the most interesting one.
Prefiero **las de** Pablo.   I prefer Pablo's (ones).

4   There is a neuter form of the possessive (*lo* + the masculine singular pronoun: *lo mío, lo nuestro*, etc.) where no specific masculine or feminine noun is visible or implied. *Lo de* can also be used in the manner described in point 3, but can be used with nouns denoting 'things', not just 'people'. The neuter form works like this:

Lo nuestro es algo muy especial.   What we have is something very special.
Acabo de enterarme de **lo tuyo**.   I've just heard about what's happened to you.
¿Sabes **lo de Juan**?   Have you heard that business about Juan?
Lo de la fiesta fue genial.   What happened at the party was brilliant. /
                                                What they said about the party was
                                                brilliant. / The idea of having a party was
                                                brilliant.

PRACTICE

1 Translate the following sentences into Spanish:

1. This book is better than that one.

   ....

2. Those women are more interesting than these ones.

   ....

3. That was impossible.

   ....

4. This water is purer than that one.

   ....

5. This is useful.

   ....

2 Make the following masculine, as in the example:

esas mujeres → esos hombres

1. aquella chica ....
2. esa traductora ....
3. estas niñas ....
4. aquellas canadienses ....
5. esta francesa ....

3 Insert the appropriate possessive adjective or pronoun in each of the sentences below. Assume any 'you' / 'your' usages to take the *tú* form:

1. [My] .... padres son mayores que [yours] ....

2. [Ours] .... es una condición muy interesante.

3. El reloj es [mine] ...., lo compré en Roma.

PRACTICE

4 Creo que [your]..........................jardín es más bonito que [theirs]..........................

5 [Their]..........................condiciones son más rígidas que [mine]..........................

4 Translate the following sentences into English:

1 My feet hurt.

....

2 Give me your hand.

....

3 I'm going to put my shirt on.

....

4 I've broken my arm.

....

5 We had to hand in our wallets.

....

UNIT 6

Personal pronouns

> This unit will look at the different types of personal pronouns, and their usages. Particular attention will be paid to the difference between direct and indirect object pronouns, and when each should be used.

Subject pronouns

Subject pronouns (such as 'I', 'he' or 'they') are essential in English to express the person or thing performing a verb, in the absence of a noun. In Spanish, they are not generally needed as the verb ending (*escribo* – 'I write'; *escribes* – 'you write'; *escribimos* – 'we write') tends to make it clear who or what is the subject of the action. Before we look at usage, here is a table of Spanish subject pronouns:

yo	I
tú	you (singular, informal)
vos	you (singular, informal – some Latin American countries)
él	he
ella	she
usted (Vd.)	you (singular, polite)
nosotros, nosotras	we (masc. & fem.)
vosotros, vosotras	you (plural, informal, masc. & fem.). NB: only used in Spain
ellos	they (masc.)
ellas	they (fem.)
ustedes (Vds.)	you (plural, polite)

Use of subject pronouns

As mentioned above, subject pronouns are generally not needed in Spanish, but there are several circumstances in which their inclusion is needed:

1 To avoid ambiguity:

***Ella** estudia italiano pero **él** no.*	She studies Italian but he doesn't.
*¿**Usted** no me ha oído?*	Did you (formal) not hear me?

In the second example in the table, above, the omission of *usted* could have left 'you,' 'he,' 'she' or 'it' (e.g. a dog) as possible subjects.

2   For contrast, even if the verb endings make the subjects clear:

Tú tienes que hacerlo hoy pero nosotros vamos a hacerlo mañana.	You have to do it today but <u>we're</u> going to do it tomorrow.
—Tengo varias novelas suyas. —Yo las he leído todas.	'I've got several of his / her novels.' – '<u>I've</u> read them all.'
Voy a pedirme un café, pero usted prefiere té, ¿verdad?	I'm going to order a coffee, but you prefer tea, don't you?

3   For emphasis, even if the verb ending is such that a subject pronoun is not strictly required:

Y vosotras, ¿qué opináis?	And what's your opinion?
—Nadie quiere ir. —Yo sí quiero.	'Nobody wants to go.' – 'I do.'
Quiero una cerveza. ¿Tú también quieres una?	I want a beer. Do you want one too?

4   In phrases such as 'It's him', where the pronoun follows a part of the verb *ser* ('to be'):

Es ella.	It's her.
Soy yo.	It's me.

5   In comparisons, after *que* and *como*:

Eres mejor que yo.	You're better than I am / better than me.
No soy tan delgada como ella.	I'm not as slim as she is.

6   In short answers, without a verb:

—¿Quién lo hizo? —Yo.	'Who did it?' – 'I did.'

7   After a small number of prepositions, of which the most common are:

entre tú y yo	between you and me
según tú	according to you
excepto / menos ella	except her
hasta / incluso ellos	even them

Direct object pronouns

Direct object pronouns stand in place of a noun in the object position of the verb, when the identity of the person or thing directly 'suffering' the action has already been established (e.g. 'I like my brother – I like <u>him</u>'). Here is a list of the Spanish forms:

me	me
te	you (for the *tú* form)
lo	him (see note below), it (masc.), you (masc. usage of the *usted* form)
le	him (see note below)
la	her, it (fem.), you (fem. usage of the *usted* form)
nos	us

UNIT 6 PERSONAL PRONOUNS

os	you (for the *vosotros* form – NB in Spain only)
los	them (masc. – both people and things), you (masc. usage of the *ustedes* form)
las	them (fem. – both people and things), you (fem. usage of the *ustedes* form)

> For the Spanish means of expressing 'him' as a direct object pronoun, there has been much debate over the centuries. Current practice suggests that *le* is preferred in Spain, whereas *lo* is safer in Latin American usage. In both cases, *los* is the preferred plural for 'them' (i.e. 'those men / boys').
>
> ⇨ See section on 'Loísmo, laísmo, leísmo'.

Word order with direct object pronouns

Direct object pronouns usually come before the verb with which they are linked:

Os quiero a todos.	I love you all.
No las comas.	Don't eat them.

There are three circumstances in which a direct object pronoun must not (or, in some cases, need not) come before the verb:

1 If it is the object of a <u>positive command</u> (e.g. 'eat this!', as opposed to the negative 'don't eat that!'), it must be tacked onto the end of the command form. Note that you may need to add an accent to maintain the spoken stress on the correct syllable:

¡Termínalo!	Finish it!
¡Mírennos!	Look at us!

2 If it is the object of an <u>infinitive</u>, there are two scenarios: if the infinitive does not depend on a preceding verb, the direct object pronoun must be added to the end of the infinitive:

Es facilísimo hacerlo.	It's a doddle to do.
Ten cuidado al abrirlo.	Take care when you open it.

However, if the infinite does depend on a preceding verb, the direct object pronoun may be added to the end of the infinitive, as above, or placed before the earlier verb. There is very little, if any, difference between the two variants, but some people find the first one safer:

Voy a empezarlo esta tarde. / Lo voy a empezar esta tarde.	I'm going to start it this evening.
¿Puedes ayudarnos? / ¿Nos puedes ayudar?	Can you help us?

The preceding verbs *poder* ('to be able') and *ir a* ('to be going to') have been used in the examples above. Other common verbs affecting this construction are *querer* ('to want'), *deber* ('to have to', plus variants of 'should', 'ought to', etc.), *tener que* (as *deber*), *acabar de* ('to have just'), *llegar a* ('to get to', 'to manage to'), *haber de* (as *deber*), *dejar de* ('to give up', 'to stop'), *volver a* ('to do again') and *hacer* ('to make' in the sense of 'to oblige').

3   If it is the object of a gerund, a pair of rules similar to those in point 2 must be followed. Note the following usages, focusing additionally on the addition of an accent to the gerund form:

Leyéndolo, aprenderás.   You'll learn by reading it.
Lo estoy leyendo. / Estoy leyéndolo.   I'm reading it.

Estar has been used in the example as a preceding verb. Other verbs working with this construction (though less commonly than *estar*) are *venir*, *andar*, *ir*, *quedarse* and *seguir*.

Special use of direct object pronoun *lo*

Lo can be used to refer to a piece of information that is already understood by the speaker and the listener. It equates to the English 'it', which is often omitted in the equivalent English construction:

—He aprobado el examen. —Ya lo sé.   'I've passed the exam.' – 'I know.'
Habían acabado el proyecto pero nadie me   They had finished the project but nobody told
lo dijo.   me.

Indirect object pronouns

Indirect object pronouns differ from their direct cousins in that they refer not to the object of an action, but to the person or thing the action is intended to affect, benefit or harm. As an example, in English the differing role of 'me' can be seen in the following sentences: 'You hate me' (direct object) and 'You gave me a present' (indirect object). In the latter usage, the direct object is 'a present', and 'me' represents the person to whom the present was given. The structure features commonly in English – imagine snippets like 'she told me (= 'to me') a joke', 'pass him (= 'to him') the salt', 'they bought her (= 'for her') a jacket', and so on. It's vital to distinguish which type of pronoun is in play in each usage, so that the correct choice of Spanish equivalent can be made smoothly. Here is a list of Spanish indirect object pronouns:

me	me, to me, for me
te	you, to you, for you (with *tú* form)
le	him, to him, for him; her, to her, for her; it, to it, for it; you, to you, for you (with *usted* form)
nos	us, to us, for us
os	you, to you, for you (with *vosotros* form – in Spain only)
les	them, to them, for them; you, to you, for you (with *ustedes* form)

Clearly *le* and *les* can be problematic, as they have so many potential meanings. A good idea is to clarify with *a ella* ('to her'), *a ustedes* ('to you'), etc., so that it is absolutely clear who the indirect object is. To get a flavour of how indirect pronouns work in Spanish, here are some examples. In studying them, pay close attention to the rules given in the 'Word order with direct object pronouns' section, which also apply here:

Ofrecí ayuda a mi hermana. → Le ofrecí ayuda.   I offered my sister help. → I offered her help.
¿Me pasas la sal? ¡Pásame la sal!   Will you pass me the salt? Pass me the salt!

UNIT 6   PERSONAL PRONOUNS

Es imprescindible decirles la verdad.	It's vital to tell them the truth.
¿Te puedo dar un consejo? / ¿Puedo darte un consejo?	Can I give you a bit of advice?
Prestándome atención, aprenderás.	You'll learn by paying attention to me.
Van a decirme su opinión. / Me van a decir su opinión.	They're going to tell me their opinion.

Loísmo, laísmo, leísmo

These phenomena occur when a speaker uses a direct object pronoun where an indirect object pronoun would have been correct, or vice versa. *Loísmo* is the use of an incorrect *lo* for *le*, *laísmo* an incorrect *la* for *le*, and *leísmo* an incorrect *le* for *lo* or *la*. A person habitually falling into such traps is said to be *loísta*, *laísta* or *leísta*, respectively. Such mistakes do not generally impair understanding, but are frowned upon, as they produce an effect similar to that of an English-speaker saying something like 'Me and my brother can help you'.

When a sentence contains both a direct and an indirect object, there is less of a problem. If there is only one object (referring to a person), and the speaker is unclear as to whether it is direct or indirect, then the confusion between *lo / le* or between *la / le* can be stronger. Usage can often boil down to what is normal in the region the speaker comes from. In different parts of Spain, you might hear the variations outlined in the table below:

Situation	Variants	English
Referring to a man	*Salúdalo de mi parte / Salúdale de mi parte.*	Say hello to him for me.
Talking to a woman (as *usted*)	*¿La molesto? / ¿Le molesto?*	Am I bothering you?

As in so many areas of Spanish and other languages, it's important to be open-minded, listening and reading for variations stemming from geography, class, age, etc. That said, in your own speech and writing, the safest way is to stick to the recommended rules and tendencies.

Combining direct and indirect object pronouns

Often it will be necessary to use a direct and an indirect object pronoun in the same structure, as in the example 'Give me it', where 'it' is the direct object (the thing given) and 'me' is the indirect object (the person to whom the thing is given). Sometimes English assists us by providing a helpful 'to' or 'for' to help us determine which is the indirect pronoun ('give it to them'); other times we have to look more closely ('I'll give you them'). At all times, we should be clear as to what the direct object is, and who or what is the indirect 'beneficiary', 'recipient' or 'sufferer'.

Word order in a combination of direct and indirect object pronouns

In combining two object pronouns in Spanish, it's essential to put the indirect one first, then the direct one. The following examples illustrate correct usage – notice how the indirect pronoun always precedes the direct one, and keep an eye on the application of rules we saw earlier in the unit about where these pronouns are located in relation to positive commands, infinitives and gerunds:

Te lo he mandado.	I've sent it to you / I've sent you it.
Tráemelas.	Bring them to me. / Bring me them.
después de decírnoslo	after telling us (it)
Me lo deberías dar. / Deberías dármelo.	You should give me it. / You should give it to me.
Entregándomelo, aceptas las condiciones.	By handing it in to me, you accept the conditions.
Os los están preparando. / Están preparándooslos.	They're preparing them for you.

Use of *se* instead of *le / les*

One of the stranger rules of object pronoun use is the requirement – when combining either *le* or *les* with *lo / la / los / las* – to replace the *le / les* with *se*. Hence the sentence 'I give it to him' which, when we put the two pronouns together in Spanish would come out as *le lo doy*, is correctly rendered as *se lo doy*.

Se lo he dicho esta tarde.	I've told him / her / them / you (it) this afternoon.
Voy a ofrecérselos hoy. / Se los voy a ofrecer hoy.	I'm going to offer them to him / her / them / you today.

'Redundant' usage of object pronouns

Spanish often includes an indirect object pronoun even if the noun to which it refers is also present in the sentence. However superfluous the 'extra' pronoun might look, its purpose is to reinforce the noun in the indirect object role, and its inclusion is perfectly natural – and good practice well worth imitating – in Spanish:

Les he pasado la información a los directores.	I've passed the information on to the directors.
¿Se lo has dicho a tu madre?	Have you told your mother?

Another usage to note is where a direct object precedes the verb. Here, Spanish again 'doubles up', adding what appears to be an unnecessary direct object pronoun to reinforce or give emphasis to the structure:

Este libro lo estuve leyendo ayer.	I was reading this book yesterday.
La paella la prepararemos nosotros.	We'll make the paella.

Pronouns after prepositions

With the exception of the small number of prepositions noted in 'Use of subject pronouns', when Spanish prepositions have to be followed by a personal pronoun (to produce structures like 'for me', 'behind them', etc.), a separate list of pronouns must be used:

mí	me
ti	you (*tú* form)
él	him
ella	her
usted (Vd.)	you (*usted* form)
sí	himself, herself, yourself (*usted* form)
nosotros, nosotras	us
vosotros, vosotras	you (*vosotros* form – in Spain only)
ellos, ellas	them (masc. / fem.)
ustedes (Vds.)	you (*ustedes* form)
sí	themselves, yourselves (*ustedes* form)

Here are some examples of usage:

detrás de ella	behind her
para nosotros	for us
sin ti	without you

There are special forms for use in combination with the preposition con ('with'):

¿Quieres ir conmigo?	Do you want to go with me?
Esperan pasar el día contigo.	They hope to spend the day with you.
Han traído mucho equipaje consigo.	They've brought a lot of luggage with them.

PRACTICE

1 Respond to each of the following questions with a one-word answer in Spanish, based on the information given in English in brackets:

1 ¿Quién es? [Her] ....
2 ¿Quién lo hizo? [He did] ....
3 ¿Quién quiere más café? [I do] ....
4 ¿Quién va al cine? [We are] ....
5 ¿Quién ha preparado esta comida? [Them] ....

2 Insert the appropriate subject pronouns into the following sentences, for emphasis:

1 .... no tenemos coche, pero .... sí tienen.
2 El encargado soy ...., pero como es tu hermana, ... también puede desempeñar un papel en el proyecto.
3 ¿Lo has visto ....? ¿No? Me parece que .... tampoco lo han visto.
4 Y ...., ¿qué vais a hacer? Pepe dice que .... va a hacer lo mismo.
5 .... haz lo que quieras; .... no estoy tan seguro.

3 In the sentences below, replace each bracketed fragment with an appropriate pronoun, rewriting the sentence to alter the word order:

1 He escrito la carta y he enviado [la carta] [a mi hermano]
    ....
2 ¿Habéis escuchado las canciones? Sí, hemos escuchado [las canciones]
    ....
3 Mi marido y yo queremos leer esos libros. ¿Te importaría dejar [a nosotros] [los libros]?
    ....
4 Mi hermana pasará todo el verano viendo esas películas. [A mi hermana] gusta mucho ver [esas películas]
    ....
5 ¿Han entregado los documentos a tu madre? Sí, han entregado [los documentos] [a mi madre] esta mañana.
    ....

PRACTICE

4 **Translate the following into Spanish:**

1. opposite him ....
2. for me ....
3. according to her ....
4. in front of us ....
5. with me ....
6. between you and me ....
7. without them ....
8. thanks to you, my friend ....
9. behind me ....
10. except her ....

5 **Re-order the following elements to create a meaningful sentence. You may need to attach pronouns to other words and / or add accents:**

1. hacer voy a lo
   ....

2. lo he se dado
   ....

3. ¡nos cuando lo da lo tengas!
   ....

4. ¿de lo después enseñas lo pintar me?
   ....

5. las entregar se deberías
   ....

PRACTICE

6 Reinforce the following sentences by including a 'redundant' pronoun, as in the example:

He dado el dinero a mi hermano → <u>Le</u> he dado el dinero a mi hermano

1 Lo dieron a nosotros.

   ....

2 Los hemos pasado al abogado.

   ....

3 Toca a vosotras hacerlo.

   ....

4 Corresponderá a ellos realizarlo.

   ....

5 Quiere a ti.

   ....

7 Correct the form and / or location of the pronouns in the following sentences:

1 La he comprado un reloj para su cumpleaños.

   ....

2 Si quieres puedes lo decir a tus padres.

   ....

3 ¿Pueden ir con ti mañana?

   ....

4 A mi primo se encantan las matemáticas.

   ....

5 Lo voy a decirte después de la reunión.

   ....

UNIT 7 | Relative pronouns and linking devices

Relative pronouns

Relative pronouns are a small group of words (in English: 'which', 'who', 'whom', 'whose' and 'that'), used to link one piece of information with a subsequent, related piece, which is known as a relative clause.

Que

Que is the commonest relative pronoun in Spanish, and can link clauses about things or people:

El hombre que vive en esta casa	The man who / that lives in this house
El libro que compraste ayer	The book you bought yesterday

Note that in the latter example, English has the option of removing the relative ('the book you bought', which could also be expressed as 'the book <u>which</u> you bought' or 'the book <u>that</u> you bought'). Spanish does not allow *que* to be omitted.

Relative pronouns with a preposition

If you want to precede a relative pronoun with a preposition (for examples such as 'to whom', 'next to which', etc.), you have a choice of devices:

1. *el que / la que / los que / las que*

   These pronouns can be used to refer to people or things, and must agree in number and gender with the noun they are replacing:

el chico con el que vivo	the boy I live with / with whom I live
la fundación a la que dediqué el libro	the foundation I dedicated the book to / to which I dedicated the book
los asuntos sobre los que escribes	the issues you write about / about which you write
las mujeres entre las que figuras	the women you feature among / among whom you feature

   Note that, in English, it's possible (though sometimes frowned upon) to end a sentence with a preposition. This must never happen in Spanish, so we need to get into the habit of thinking in 'the Spanish way' when approaching such structures. The English 'the friend with whom I study' (rather than 'the friend I study with') sounds very formal in English, but is the ideal format for a smooth transition into Spanish.

RELATIVE PRONOUNS AND LINKING DEVICES — UNIT 7

If you're using this structure with either *a* or *de* + *el*, note that the resultant form is contracted:

el estadio <u>al que</u> vamos	the stadium we're going to / to which we're going
el tema <u>del que</u> hablas	the topic you're talking about / about which you're talking

2 quien / quienes

This pair of relative pronouns can be used as alternatives to those in section 1, but only for persons, never for things. There is no separate inflection for masculine / feminine, but the plural form must be used when a plural noun is being replaced:

el estudiante con quien suelo estudiar	the student I usually study with / with whom I usually study
la chica a quien debo este dinero	the girl I owe this money (to) / to whom I owe this money
los hombres de quienes te hablé	the men I told you about / about whom I told you
las mujeres sin quienes esto no funcionaría	the women without whom this wouldn't work

Note that *quien* cannot ordinarily replace *que* when *que* functions as the subject of a relative clause and is therefore not preceded by a preposition:

El presentador que leyó las noticias (NOT *el presentador quien leyó las noticias*)	The presenter who / that read the news

However, *quien* is possible if it is preceded by a comma or a pause, indicating that it is introducing a non-defining relative clause (i.e. one that does not limit the meaning of the noun in the main clause):

El presentador, quien leyó las noticias sin alterarse, no se dio cuenta de la gravedad de la situación.	The presenter, who read the news unperturbed, did not realise the severity of the situation.

3 el cual / la cual / los cuales / las cuales

This group of relative pronouns are a more formal means of expressing *el que* (etc.), in section 1:

la situación en la cual me encontraba	the situation I found myself in / in which I found myself
los artistas con los cuales propongo trabajar	the artists I propose to work with / with whom I propose to work

> Notice that, when the noun preceding the relative is a person and this noun functions as the direct object of the relative clause, you could use three options (the choice depending on register and context): *la niña a la que cuidaba mi hermana / la niña a quien cuidaba mi hermana / la niña a la cual cuidaba mi hermana*.
>
> A fourth option – *la niña que cuidaba mi hermana* – is also possible here, but would be impossible if the noun the relative refers to were working as an indirect object in the relative clause: *la niña a la que enseñaba inglés mi hermana / la niña a quien enseñaba inglés mi hermana / la niña a la cual enseñaba inglés mi hermana*, but NOT *la niña que enseñaba inglés mi hermana*.

Lo que and lo cual

These neuter forms are very useful to express the English relative pronoun 'which', when it refers not to an identifiably masculine or feminine noun, but to a whole idea or sentence (e.g. 'I was tired, which made me irritable').

Lo cual is more formal, and is also the one to use after a preposition:

Estaba deprimida, lo que empezó a afectar a mi familia.	I was depressed, which began to affect my family.
Las cortinas estaban corridas, por lo cual deduje que no estabas en casa.	The curtains were drawn, from which I deduced that you weren't at home.

Cuyo

This pronoun, expressing possession like the English 'whose', works adjectivally, and must agree with the noun to which it refers in both number and gender. It can function with or without prepositions, and the resultant constructions can feel very complex, even though they are always logical:

El señor cuya hija trabaja conmigo	The gentleman whose daughter works with me
El chico cuyos padres viven en Madrid	The boy whose parents live in Madrid
La mujer delante de cuyo edificio ocurrió el accidente	The woman in front of whose building the accident happened
El estudiante a consecuencia de cuyas acciones todo empezó a ir mal	The student as a result of whose actions everything started to go wrong

As is the case with the English 'whose', the use of *cuyo* implies an element of formality, and in colloquial speech, users of both languages often avoid this pronoun:

El señor que tiene una hija que [cuya hija] trabaja conmigo	The man who has a daughter who [whose daughter] works with me

Donde, adonde, por donde, etc.

Donde can be readily combined with prepositions such as *a* or *hacia* ('to', 'towards'), *de* or *desde* ('from'), *en* ('in'), *por* ('through', 'along'), etc., to function as a relative. Similarly, the English 'where' can fulfil such a role in examples like 'the street where I live', 'the place where I'm heading for' and 'the shop where I got it'. It's worth noting that *adonde* carries the notion of 'where ... to' (working a bit like the old English 'whither').

Here are some examples of good usage:

el sitio donde nos conocimos	the place (where) we met
la caja de donde sacaste los documentos	the box from which you took the documents
el campo adonde / hacia donde vamos	the field we're heading for / for which we're heading
la carretera por donde íbamos	the road we were driving along / along which we were driving

RELATIVE PRONOUNS AND LINKING DEVICES — UNIT 7

In all of these sentences, you could equally use *el / la / los / las + que*: *el sitio <u>en el que</u> nos conocimos / la caja <u>de la que</u> sacaste / el campo <u>al que</u> / <u>hacia el que</u> / la carretera <u>por la que</u>*.

Nominalisers

Nominalisers generally occur in English in the form of 'the one who…', 'the ones which…', 'those that…', etc. In Spanish, we can immediately identify a new, separate usage for some of the structures we've covered earlier in this unit:

<u>El que</u> me gusta es el rojo.	The one (that) I like is the red one.
Voy a cambiar <u>la que</u> me diste.	I've going to change the one you gave me.
Los mejores son <u>los que</u> ves en el rincón.	The best ones are the ones you can see in the corner.
Saludamos a <u>las que</u> asistieron.	We greeted those (girls / women) who attended.

El que / la que can be replaced by *quien*, and *los que / las que* by *quienes*, when the noun they refer to is a person, although the effect is rather more formal:

<u>Quien</u> dirige el proceso es el señor Ruiz.	The person leading the process is Mr. Ruiz.
Entrevistaba a <u>quienes</u> pasaban.	S/he was interviewing those who were passing by.

The neuter *lo que*, equating to the English 'what' in the sense of 'the thing that' or 'that which', is very commonly used in Spanish:

Me interesó <u>lo que</u> me dijiste.	I was interested by what you told me.
<u>Lo que</u> solemos hacer es tomar el sol.	What we usually do is sunbathe.
Mira <u>lo que</u> ha pasado.	Look what's happened.

A separate set of nominalisers serves to express the English 'the one(s) from …', 'the one(s) belonging to …', 'the one(s) wearing / in …', 'that / those of …', etc. Notice that, as the examples show, the only preposition that can work in this structure is *de*:

Mi primo es <u>el de</u> la gorra.	My cousin is the one in the cap.
Coge <u>la de</u> la izquierda.	Take the one on the left.
He quedado con <u>los de</u> Madrid.	I've arranged to meet the ones (people) from Madrid.
Prefiero <u>las de</u> mis abuelos.	I prefer the ones belonging to my grandparents.

The neuter *lo de* (like its cousin *lo que*, above) has a useful role to play when no gender is apparent and we want to refer to a general idea or episode. It often conveys English fragments like 'that business / affair of …':

⇨ See also Unit 2: Definite and indefinite articles

<u>Lo del</u> accidente fue horrendo.	That business about the accident was awful.
Quiero que me cuentes <u>lo de</u> las vacaciones.	I want you to tell me all about your holiday.

Cleft sentences

Cleft sentences are used in both English and Spanish to alter the focus of basic elements of information. For example, the English sentence 'My brother committed that crime' can have its focus changed, and emphasis added, by a different rendering such as 'It was my brother who committed that crime' or 'It was that crime that my brother committed'. In each of these new versions, we can see that the verb 'to be' has been brought in to provide the emphasis. A similar thing happens in Spanish, with *ser* providing the emphasis, but the tricky thing is to remember that the 'who' / 'that' is provided not just by *que*, but by a full nominaliser (*el que, quien,* etc.). Study the following examples carefully:

Basic sentence	English	Cleft sentence	English
Pepe escribió la carta.	Pepe wrote the letter.	*Fue Pepe el que / quien escribió la carta.*	It was Pepe who / that wrote the letter.
Mis tías llevan el negocio.	My aunts run the business.	*Son mis tías las que / quienes llevan el negocio.*	It's my aunts who / that run the business.
Eso me importaba mucho.	That was very important to me.	*Era eso lo que me importaba mucho.*	It was that which / that was very important to me.

If the first half of a cleft sentence in Spanish contains a preposition, the usual thing is for this to be repeated in the second half. This can look and sound very ungainly to English-speakers, but it is worth perfecting so that the correct meaning is conveyed:

Basic sentence	English	Cleft sentence	English
Voy a esa iglesia.	I go to that church.	*Es a esa iglesia a la que voy.*	It's to that church that I go.
Suelo hablar con esos señores.	I usually speak to those gentlemen.	*Es con esos señores con los que / con quienes suelo hablar.*	It's with those men that I usually speak.
Jugué contra ese equipo.	I played against that team.	*Fue contra ese equipo contra el que jugué.*	It was against that team that I played.
Iban siempre por esa carretera.	They always went by that road.	*Era por esa carretera por la que iban siempre.*	It was by that road that they always went.

PRACTICE

1 Express each of the following phrases in one or (where possible) two ways in Spanish, using *que* or *quien*:

1. The boy with whom I study

    ....

2. The woman close to whom I live

    ....

3. The man to whom you gave the document

    ....

4. The streets in which we play

    ....

5. The actresses without whom

    ....

6. The Frenchmen among whom

    ....

7. The building behind which

    ....

8. The house opposite which

    ....

9. The exams during which

    ....

10. The person against whom

    ....

2 Complete the following sentences by translating the English snippets into Spanish:

1. Esa es la mujer [with whose sons] .... vivía.

2. Muchas gracias a todos los estudiantes [without whose help] .... no habría sido posible.

PRACTICE

3 Te voy a presentar al hombre [in whose car] .... vamos al estadio.

4 Esta es la planta [from whose leaves] .... hicimos la infusión.

5 Fuimos a la casa [underneath whose garden] .... se habían encontrado las monedas romanas.

3 Insert an appropriate nominaliser to complete each of these sentences. More than one may be possible in some sentences:

1 Mi prima es .... organiza estas actividades.

2 .... suelen ganar son los alemanes.

3 .... quiosco es uno de mis mejores amigos.

4 Me impresionó oír .... tu aventura.

5 Mis favoritas son .... esta tienda.

6 Esto es .... más me gusta.

7 Éstos son mejores que .... ayer.

8 De los dos jerseys, me pondré .... tú prefieras.

9 Mi camisa favorita es .... diseño azteca.

10 Tus cartas son .... más ilusión me han hecho.

4 The following cleft sentences are each missing a crucial element. Can you correct them?

1 Fuimos nosotros que construimos la chabola.

   ....

2 Es mi madre que me lleva a la universidad.

   ....

3 Fui yo, Miguel, que te llamé.

   ....

4 Sois vosotras que deberíais tener cuidado.

   ....

PRACTICE

5 Es por este puente que solemos ir.

....

6 Era con mi hermana que ese chico salía.

....

7 Fue entre estas flores que descubrimos el anillo.

....

8 Es por eso que no puedo ir.

....

9 Es a la fiesta de Juan que vamos.

....

10 Fue para estos hombres que hicimos el favor.

....

5 In each instance below, join the two shorter sentences into one complex sentence featuring a relative clause, as in the example:

e.g. Ese vestido es horrible / Ese vestido lo llevaba tu amiga ayer → Ese vestido <u>que</u> llevaba tu amiga ayer es horrible.

1 La chica está embarazada / Hablaste con ella ayer

....

2 Ese hombre ha muerto / Hicimos una barbacoa en su jardín

....

3 La carta es preciosa / Me escribiste un poema en la carta

....

4 Me comentaste algo / Me interesó

....

5 Voy a llamar a mis primas / Estaría perdido sin ellas

....

UNIT 8 — Prepositions and conjunctions

Prepositions

Prepositions are words – or clusters of words – whose purpose is to relate a following noun phrase to the rest of the sentence. Many prepositions have a 'positional' function ('<u>under</u> the table', '<u>opposite</u> the church'), others relate to time ('<u>after</u> the war', '<u>during</u> lunch'), and various other common ones (' <u>with</u> pleasure', ' <u>without</u> anxiety', ' <u>because of</u> my illness', etc.) fall into neither category. This unit looks – in alphabetical order – at the most important Spanish prepositions, but leaves treatment of *por*, *para* and the personal *a* until Unit 9.

Position of prepositions in Spanish

Spanish prepositions can come immediately before the following types of words:

Type of word to follow preposition	Example	English
noun	*con amigos*	with friends
article + noun	*entre las mesas*	between / among the tables
article + adjective + noun	*durante el largo discurso*	during the long speech
adjective + noun	*sin mucha suerte*	without much luck
pronoun	*para ella*	for her
infinitive	*antes de empezar*	before starting

> In the last example above, notice that English is happy to follow a preposition with a gerund ('starting'). This cannot happen in Spanish – the equivalent structure requires the infinitive (*empezar*)

Other notes about Spanish prepositions

In addition to the above, there are a few vital points to bear in mind when using Spanish prepositions:

1   Unlike in English, Spanish prepositions must never end a sentence or clause:

   la persona <u>con la que</u> / <u>con quien</u> vivo   the person I live <u>with</u>

PREPOSITIONS AND CONJUNCTIONS — UNIT 8

2. Prepositions in both languages can be made up of more than one word. It's worth noting that Spanish grammars often refer to these clusters of words not as 'prepositions', but as 'prepositional phrases' – i.e. phrases (or *locuciones*) working as prepositions:

al lado de	next to
a causa de	because of

⇨ See note before *a causa de* for further comment

3. We must always beware 'knee-jerk' translation of a preposition by what we think is the obvious equivalent in the other language. As will become apparent later in the unit, this can be fraught with danger:

Estoy en la estación.	I'm at the station.
Lo vimos en la televisión.	We saw it on (the) television.

a

Here is a summary of the main usages of *a* (with the exception of the personal *a*, which is covered in the next unit):

1. Its main use is to denote 'to' a place or destination, in the sense of 'towards', 'in the direction of'. This can include giving / saying / passing (etc.) something 'to' someone:

Se lo di a mi padre.	I gave it to my father.
La semana que viene voy a Londres.	Next week I'm going to London.

2. It means 'at', in the context of age, prices, rates and the time of day:

Me licencié a los treinta años.	I got my degree at the age of thirty.
Lo venden a dos euros el kilo.	They sell it at two euros a kilo.
Iban a cien kilómetros por hora.	They were travelling at a hundred kilometres per hour.
Nos veremos a las ocho.	See you at eight o'clock.

3. It can mean 'at' when followed by a place, but only after a verb of motion:

Vamos a recogerla al aeropuerto.	We're going to pick her up at the airport.
¿A qué hora llegarás a la iglesia?	What time will you arrive at the church?

Otherwise, for English 'at' usages with places, such as 'at the station / library / doctor's surgery', 'at church / university / school', etc., Spanish uses *en* (see further exemplification under *en*, below):

Voy al colegio. / Estoy en el colegio.	I'm going to (the) school. / I'm at (the) school.
Ha ido al hospital. / Está en el hospital.	S/he's gone to (the) hospital. / S/he's at the / in hospital.

> Be careful to distinguish between *a* and *en* when translating 'to', 'at' and 'in' into Spanish. A repetitive but useful sentence to remember is: *Vamos a la estación – cuando lleguemos a la estación, estaremos en la estación.* 'We're going to the station – when we get to the station, we'll be at the station.'

UNIT 8 — PREPOSITIONS AND CONJUNCTIONS

4 A tricky issue for English-speakers to remember is the requirement, in Spanish, to use *a* to state that a place is 'at' a particular distance from another place. Notice the difference between the Spanish and English structures:

El colegio está a cien metros / a dos minutos de la catedral.
The school is a hundred metres / two minutes from the cathedral.

5 Two usages of *a* + verbs are worth noting together. The first is *ir* + *a* + an infinitive, which expresses that one is 'going to do' something.

⇨ *This structure is covered in greater detail in Unit 11: Indicative verb tenses.*

Vamos a terminarlo esta tarde.
We're going to finish it this evening.

The second one is *al* + infinitive, which equates to the English structure 'on doing' something. This is a good example of the many occasions when the English '-ing' is expressed in Spanish by the infinitive:

Al oír tu voz supe que habías llegado.
On hearing your voice I knew you'd arrived.

6 Also in the context of verbs, some Spanish verbs take *a* and produce a structure that would involve the preposition 'from' in English. These verbs tend to have the meaning of 'buying', 'stealing', 'taking away', 'confiscating', etc. The example involving *comprar* is the one requiring closest attention, as it may look at first glance as if the speaker has bought the shoes for, rather than from, the friend. The verb *oír* ('to hear') also joins this list. Here are the most common examples:

Verb	Meaning	Example	English
comprar	to buy	*He comprado unos zapatos a mi amiga.*	I've bought some shoes from my friend.
confiscar	to confiscate	*Han confiscado el dinero a Pepe.*	They've confiscated Pepe's money (from him).
oír	to hear	*Oí ese chiste a un primo mío.*	I heard that joke from a cousin of mine.
quitar	to take away	*Le han quitado todo el dinero a mi hermana.*	They've taken all my sister's money (from her).
robar	to steal	*Le robaron el coche al cura.*	They stole the priest's car (from him).
sacar	to take out	*A Laura le han sacado una muela.*	Laura has had a tooth taken out.

The preposition *para*, when followed by an infinitive in its meaning of 'in order to', is usually replaced by *a* when preceded by a verb of motion. Compare the following:

Trabajo en una tienda para ganar dinero.
I work in a shop to earn some money.

Voy a la tienda a comprar leche.
I'm going to the shop to buy some milk.

A good number of useful verbs take *a* before a subsequent infinitive or noun phrase. Here is a selection of the most common:

Verb + *a*	Example	English
acercarse a	*No te acerques al animal.*	Don't approach the animal.
acostumbrarse a	*Tuve que acostumbrarme a comer pescado.*	I had to get used to eating fish.
aprender a	*Veo que has aprendido a coser.*	I see you've learned to sew.
arriesgarse a	*Nos arriesgamos a perder.*	We risked losing.
aspirar a	*Aspiraba a ganar cinco medallas.*	S/he aspired to win five medals.
atreverse a	*¿Cómo te atreves a hacer esto?*	How dare you do this?
ayudar a	*Quiero ayudar a preparar la cena.*	I want to help (to) prepare dinner.
comenzar a	*¿Has comenzado a leerlo?*	Have you started reading it?
comprometerse a	*Se han comprometido a ayudarnos.*	They've committed to helping us.
conducir a	*Esto les conducirá al desastre total.*	This will lead them to total disaster.
decidirse a	*Mi prima se ha decidido a hacer una carrera.*	My cousin has made up her mind to do a degree.
dedicarse a	*Hoy día me dedico a la música.*	These days I devote my time to music.
disponerse a	*Os disponíais a salir.*	You were getting ready to go out.
echar(se) a	*(Nos) echamos a correr*	We broke into a run.
empezar a		see *comenzar a*
limitarse a	*Voy a limitarme a pintar las paredes.*	I'm going to limit myself to painting the walls.
llegar a	*Llegaste a conocer al rey.*	You went so far as to meet the king.
llevar a		see *conducir a*
oler a	*Esta sala huele a ajo.*	This room smells of garlic.
pasar a	*Han pasado a construir un garaje.*	They've gone on to build a garage.
ponerse a	*No te pongas a llorar.*	Don't start crying.
prepararse a		see *disponerse a*
resistirse a	*Quiero que te resistas a hacerlo.*	I want you to resist doing it.
saber a	*Este queso sabe a fruta.*	This cheese tastes of fruit.
sonar a	*Me suena a mentira.*	It sounds like a lie to me.
tender a	*Tiendo a no preocuparme tanto.*	I tend not to worry so much.
volver a	*Hemos vuelto a quedarnos sin pan.*	We've run out of bread again.

7 Finally, *a* features in a number of important set expressions:

a caballo   on horseback
a pie   on foot

UNIT 8   PREPOSITIONS AND CONJUNCTIONS

a mano	by hand
a tiempo	on time
escribir a máquina	to type
a final / finales / fines de mes	at the end of the month
a veces	at times
a menudo	often
al sol	in the sun
a la sombra	in the shade
pedir algo a gritos	to shout for something
a la puerta	at the door
estar a dieta	to be on a diet
a largo / corto plazo	in the long / short term
a paso lento	slowly
poco a poco	little by little
a la francesa	in the French style

> Spanish grammars do not normally call clusters of more than one word *preposiciones* but *locuciones preposicionales* (phrases functioning like a preposition). Here we include some of them in alphabetical order, as from the point of view of the English language they are all prepositions.

a causa de

'Because of' / 'on account of' can be rendered by *a causa de* + a noun phrase:

> **No hay servicio de autobuses, a causa de la huelga.**
> There are no bus services, because of the strike.

al lado de

This preposition means 'next to', 'beside', and is straightforward:

> **Mi oficina estaba al lado de la de ella.**
> My office was next to hers.

antes de

This has the straightforward meaning of 'before', in a time sequence, but note that if it comes before the '-ing' form of a verb in English, the infinitive is needed in Spanish:

antes de la guerra	before the war
antes de las diez	before ten o'clock
antes de empezar	before starting

PREPOSITIONS AND CONJUNCTIONS — UNIT 8

bajo

Bajo means 'under' in the literal sense of 'located underneath', but *debajo de* is more commonly used in this context. *Bajo* is required for figurative usages such an 'under a regime', 'under the following conditions', etc. It is also the preferred preposition to convey the English 'below' or 'minus' in temperatures:

la alfombra que se veía bajo la mesa	the carpet that could be seen under the table
bajo la dictadura	under the dictatorship
dos (grados) bajo cero	minus two; two (degrees) below zero

cerca de

Cerca de means 'near' or 'close to' when referring to a person, thing or place, but can also be used to express 'nearly' with numbers:

El hotel estaba cerca del centro de la ciudad.	The hotel was close to the city centre.
Entrevistamos a cerca de cien candidatos.	We interviewed close to a hundred candidates.

con

The use of *con* generally coincides with that of the English 'with', but there are various circumstances where the two languages differ slightly. The following examples illustrate the main ones:

Quiero ver a la chica <u>de</u> la moto.	I want to see the girl <u>with</u> the motorbike.
Fuiste muy cruel <u>conmigo</u>.	You were very cruel <u>to</u> me.
<u>Con</u> saludar, basta.	It's enough just to say hello.
Estoy ilusionada <u>con</u> el plan.	I'm excited <u>about</u> the plan.
Mi hermano se escribe <u>con</u> un italiano.	My brother has an Italian pen pal.
pan <u>con</u> mantequilla	bread <u>and</u> butter
café <u>con</u> leche	white coffee, latte

A few useful verbs take *con* before a subsequent noun phrase or infinitive. Here is a selection of the most common:

Verb + *con*	Example	English
amenazar con	*El hombre amenazó con destrozar la casa.*	The man threatened to destroy the house.
contactar con	*Puedes contactar conmigo si quieres.*	You can contact me if you like.
encontrarse con	*Me he encontrado con tu padre esta mañana.*	I bumped into your father this morning.
pasar con	*Espera, te paso con mi hermano.*	Hang on, I'll pass the phone to my brother.
soñar con	*Anoche soñé contigo. / Sueño con ser astronauta.*	Last night I dreamt of you. / I dream of being an astronaut.
tropezar con		see *encontrarse con*

UNIT 8 PREPOSITIONS AND CONJUNCTIONS

contra

Contra covers all the subtleties of the English 'against', but there are a couple of additional points to make:

1. Where English would use 'at' in contexts of firing, shooting, etc. 'at' a target, Spanish can use *contra*:

   Los soldados dispararon contra los manifestantes. — The soldiers shot at the demonstrators.

2. If 'against' means 'in opposition to', the variant *en contra de* is generally preferred, especially with verbs like *estar*:

   Estoy en contra del divorcio. — I'm against divorce.

de

The following are the main uses of *de*:

1. To express possession, in the sense of 'belonging to' or 'of'. Here it often coincides with the English apostrophe + 's' construction:

   la casa de mi primo — my cousin's house
   el símbolo de la paz — the symbol of peace

2. To indicate origin, usually expressed in English by 'from'. Notice the difference in meaning provided by *ser* and *venir* — English-speakers should beware the trap of trying to say 'I come from London' literally in Spanish:

   Soy de Londres. — I'm from London.
   Vengo de Londres. — I've (just) come from London.

3. As a means of expressing what something is made of, what it contains or what its purpose is:

   una mesa de madera — a wooden table
   una botella de agua — a bottle of water
   el cuarto de baño — the bathroom

4. In comparatives, *más de / menos de* (NOT *más que / menos que*) are used before a number to mean 'more than' / 'less than':

   Le he visitado más de veinte veces. — I've visited him more than twenty times.

5. In superlatives, the English 'in' (e.g. 'the highest mountain in the world') is expressed in Spanish by *de*:

   Es el chico más listo de la clase. — He's the cleverest boy in the class.

6. *De* is commonly used after certain adjectives:

   Estamos contentos de verte. — We're happy to see you.
   Estoy encantada de estar con usted. — I'm delighted to be with you.

Somos capaces de hacerlo.   We are capable of doing it.
Son difíciles de seguir.   They're difficult to follow.

> A common query among students of Spanish is when *de* should be included in examples of the last type – most commonly involving the adjectives *fácil* and *difícil*. Compare the following sentences: 1. *Es difícil leer este libro*. 2. *Este libro es difícil de leer*.
>
> In the first example, the subject of the verb *es* is the infinitive *leer*, and the sentence in effect means 'to read this book is difficult'. In this case, *de* is not used. In the second example, the subject of *es* is *el libro*, which changes the syntax and means that *de* is now required.

Finally, a large number of useful verbs take *de* before a subsequent noun phrase or infinitive. Here is a selection of the most common:

Verb + *de*	Example	English
acabar de	*Acabo de verte.*	I've just seen you.
acordarse de	*Acuérdate de sacar la basura.*	Remember to take the rubbish out.
arrepentirse de	*Me arrepiento de salir con ellos.*	I regret going out with them.
cansarse de	*Me he cansado de ello.*	I've grown tired of it. / I'm tired of it.
dejar de	*Creo que ha dejado de beber.*	I think s/he's given up drinking.
depender de	*Todo depende de ti.*	It all depends on you.
deshacerse de	*Me deshice pronto de ese coche.*	I soon got rid of that car.
encargarse de	*¿Por qué no se encarga usted del proceso?*	Why don't you take charge of the process?
pasar de	*Paso de leer tantas novelas.*	I can't be bothered to read so many novels.
reírse de	*¡No te rías de tu hermano!*	Don't laugh at your brother!
terminar de	*¿Has terminado de escribir el informe?*	Have you finished writing the report?
tratar de	*Voy a tratar de convencerte.*	I'm going to try and / try to convince you.

debajo de, por debajo de

Debajo de shares the meaning of '(physically) underneath' with *bajo*, but doesn't carry the latter's additional figurative meaning ('under the dictatorship', etc.). On a note of subtlety, *debajo de* is generally used to describe a 'static' positioning, whereas 'under' involving movement (e.g. passing a note 'under a door') can be rendered as *por debajo de*:

Creo que la revista estaba debajo de la silla. — I think the magazine was under the chair.
Pasa la llave por debajo de la puerta si puedes. — Push the key under the door if you can.

delante de, por delante de

Delante de means 'in front of', and mustn't be confused with *enfrente de* (which looks as if it ought to mean 'in front of', but actually means 'opposite'). *Por delante de* can be used to add the extra meaning of '(passing) in front of':

Tengo los documentos delante de mí. — I've got the documents in front of me.
El buzón está delante del cine. — The postbox is in front of the cinema.
La imagen pasó por delante de mis ojos. — The image passed in front of my eyes.

dentro de

Dentro de serves firstly as an alternative to *en* for 'inside', but is best used when you want to make it crystal clear that the positioning is 'inside', as opposed to 'on', the item.

Le encontraron dentro de un contenedor de basura. — They found him inside a wheelie-bin.

In the context of time, it also has a useful function to express 'in' in the sense of 'after a period of':

Van a empezar las obras dentro de quince días. — They're going to start the roadworks in a fortnight's time.

desde

Desde has two main meanings: 'since' (a point in time), and 'from' (a departure point or vantage point – though *de* is used for origin in sentences such as *Soy de Valencia*.):

desde las dos, desde 1995 — since two o'clock, since 1995
desde la guerra — since the war
Puedes llamar / empezar desde mi casa. — You can phone / start from my house.
Lo vi desde la ventana. — I saw it from the window.

después de

Meaning 'after', *después de* functions in the same way as its antonym *antes de*, and requires the same word of caution about the English '-ing' becoming a Spanish infinitive:

después de la cena — after dinner
después de verte — after seeing you

detrás de, por detrás de

Detrás de means 'behind', in the literal, positioning sense, and also in the context of (for example) an issue lurking 'behind' a situation. Again, the addition of *por* lends a sense of movement to the preposition:

Estaba detrás de la nevera.	It was behind the fridge.
Creo que hay algo siniestro detrás de su calma exterior.	I think there's something sinister behind his / her outward calm.
Vamos a intentar pasarlo por detrás del radiador.	Let's try passing it behind the radiator.

durante

Alongside the obvious meaning of 'during', *durante* covers various usages of the English 'for' + a period of time expressed as a plural noun. If you are ever unsure whether to use *por* or *para* to mean 'for' in this context, *durante* is often a failsafe solution:

durante la fiesta / guerra	during the party / war
durante el siglo diecinueve	during the nineteenth century
Fui estudiante durante cuatro años.	I was a student for (i.e. 'during a period of') four years.

en

As well as its basic meaning of 'in', *en* covers various usages of the English 'at' and 'on', which can be confusing, although the difficulty is far more acute for Spanish-speakers learning English. The real trick is to avoid automatically translating 'at' by *a*, when *en* would be correct. Let's look at a few illustrative sentences:

Spanish usage	English equivalent	Notes
en la ciudad	in the city	'in' / 'inside'
El dinero está en el cajón.	The money is in the drawer.	'inside' – *dentro de* would work here, but is perhaps a little emphatic
Estabas en la cama.	You were in bed.	'in' / 'inside'
Nos sentamos en la cama.	We sat down on the bed.	'on the surface of' – *sobre* or *encima de* would also work here
Ponlo en la mesa.	Put it on the table.	'on the surface of' – *sobre* or *encima de* would also work here
Sentaos a la mesa.	Sit down at the table.	'at' – in close proximity to
Está en misa / en la estación.	S/he's at mass / at the station.	'at' in English, but *en* required in Spanish
Vamos a convertirlo en garaje.	We're going to turn it into a garage.	'into'

UNIT 8 — PREPOSITIONS AND CONJUNCTIONS

en italiano	in Italian	'in' a language
en coche / tren	by car / train	'by' + many modes of transport
en marzo / primavera / 1970	in March / spring / 1970	'in' + month, season or year
Voy a hacerlo en dos semanas.	I'm going to do it in two weeks.	'in' – meaning 'occupying a period of'
Voy a hacerlo dentro de dos semanas.	I'm going to do it in two weeks' time.	'in' – meaning 'after X period has elapsed'
Estamos en París / en Francia.	We're in Paris / in France.	'in' for both towns / cities and countries – see box below

> Students of French should note that Spanish uses *en* to be in both a village / town / city and a country. You would say *a Madrid* or *a España* when you are talking about movement towards those places.

Many verbs take *en* before a subsequent noun phrase or infinitive. Here is a a selection of the most common:

Verb + *en*	Example	English
consistir en	*Consiste en tres secciones.*	It consists of three sections.
dudar en	*Dudamos en aceptarlo.*	We hesitated over accepting it.
entrar en	*No entres en esa sala.*	Don't enter / go into that room.
fijarse en	*Fijaos en aquellas nubes.*	Look at / focus on those clouds.
insistir en	*No deberías insistir en decir eso.*	You shouldn't insist on saying that.
pensar en	*Pienso siempre en ti.*	I'm always thinking of / about you.
quedar en	*Quedamos en abandonar el proyecto.*	We agreed to abandon the project.
ser el primero / último en	*Fui el primero en saludarle.*	I was the first one to greet him.
tardar en	*Tardaron tres semanas en devolverme la moto.*	It took them three weeks to give me my motorbike back.

encima de, por encima de

Meaning 'on' or 'on top of', *encima de* has a good deal of overlap with *en* and *sobre* (in their meaning of 'on top of'). The inclusion of *por* indicates movement 'over' an item:

Lo pusimos encima de la mesa. We put it on the table.
Tienes que pasarlo por encima de la barrera. You have to pass it over the top of the barrier.

en medio de

En medio de is used to express 'in the middle / midst of':

Está en medio de la calle peatonal. It's in the middle of the pedestrianised street.
Me has pillado en medio de un problema. You've caught me in mid-problem.

entre

This preposition covers the notions of 'between' (two things / people) and 'among' (three or more), with the additional sense of 'amid(st)':

entre el ayuntamiento y la catedral	between the town hall and the cathedral
entre tú y yo	between you and me
Me encontré entre un grupo de turistas franceses.	I found myself among a group of French tourists.
entre todo el papeleo y el ruido de los obreros	what with all the paperwork and the noise of the workers

hacia

Hacia means 'towards', both with places and times – in the latter context, it can sometimes convey the English 'around'. Note also its usage as an equivalent to the English '-ward(s)' suffix to indicate direction:

hacia Madrid, hacia el norte	towards Madrid, towards the north / northward(s)
hacia las seis de la tarde	towards / around six o'clock in the evening
hacia arriba / abajo / adelante / atrás	upward(s) / downward(s) / forward(s) / backward(s)

hasta

Hasta translates the English 'until', 'as far as', 'to' and 'up to'. Note also the farewells:

⇨ See Unit 22 for coverage of the non-prepositional use of **hasta**, meaning 'even'

Voy a quedarme en casa hasta las seis / hasta el fin de semana.	I'm going to stay at home until six o'clock / until the weekend.
Si quieres, te sigo hasta el pueblo.	I'll follow you as far as the village if you like.
Entraron en el agua hasta las rodillas.	They went into the water up to their knees.
Hasta luego / ahora / mañana / la semana que viene.	See you later / in a minute / tomorrow / next week.

junto a

Junto a does more or less the same thing as *al lado de*, but is also translated by the English 'by':

Vivimos junto al parque.	We live by / next to the park.

junto con

This differs from *junto a* in the subtlety of meaning 'together with':

Lo construyó junto con sus hermanos.	S/he built it together with his / her brothers.

UNIT 8   PREPOSITIONS AND CONJUNCTIONS

lejos de

Meaning 'far from', *lejos de* is the opposite of *cerca de*:

> **Madrid está lejos de Barcelona.**   Madrid is a long way from Barcelona.

mediante

This preposition translates the English 'by means of', usually with a machine, instrument or technique. The more common *con* is sometimes an alternative:

> **Consiguieron abrirlo mediante una palanqueta.**   They managed to get it open using / with a jemmy.
>
> **Llegaron a un acuerdo mediante un diálogo cordial.**   They reached an agreement through cordial dialogue.

según

Its two prepositional meanings are 'according to' and 'depending on', as illustrated in the first two examples, below. Pay particular attention to the use of the subject pronouns after *según* in the first example. The third example brings in – just for interest – a non-prepositional usage, where *según* is followed by a verb and means 'as', in the sense of 'while' or 'at the same time as':

> **según el profesor / según yo / según tú**   according to the teacher / according to me / according to you
>
> **Escogeremos el destino según el tiempo que haga.**   We'll choose our destination depending on the weather.
>
> **según se acercaban a nosotros**   as they were approaching us

sin

Meaning 'without', *sin* is fairly straightforward, but care must be taken when translating English fragments involving 'without a...', and also with the English 'without + -ing' structure:

> **Sin tu ayuda, no habría podido hacerlo.**   I wouldn't have been able to do it without your help.
>
> **No salgas hoy sin abrigo.**   Don't go out without an overcoat today.
>
> **¿Cómo aprobaste el examen sin estudiar?**   How did you pass the exam without studying?

sobre

The first meaning of *sobre* is 'on (a surface)', where it equates to *en* and *encima de*:

> **El reloj estaba sobre la mesilla de noche.**   The clock was on the bedside table.

It also carries the meaning of 'about' or 'on' (in the sense of 'concerning', 'on the subject of'):

> **Te voy a regalar un libro sobre Barcelona.**   I'm going to give you a book about Barcelona.

The third main usage is for approximation, equating to the English 'about' or 'around':

La reunión terminó sobre las cinco.   The meeting finished at around five o'clock.

tras

This is a more formal variant of *detrás de*, which is used less in the literal, 'positional' sense and more in expressions of time:

año tras año   year after year
tras varias horas de debate   after several hours of debate

Translating certain English prepositions into Spanish

Various English prepositions coming after a verb can cause difficulty when we want to translate them into Spanish. This is particularly the case when the structure implies some form of movement. Often, there is no straight equivalent in Spanish, and a solution can frequently be found simply by using a single verb form. Here is a selection of such prepositions, with suggested translations:

Preposition	Example, with verb	Spanish solution	Spanish example	English
across	to go across the desert	*cruzar*	*Los exploradores cruzaron el desierto.*	The explorers crossed / went across the desert.
down	to come down	*bajar*	*Baja y ayúdanos.*	Come down and help us.
in	to come in	*entrar*	*Les he dicho que entren pero no quieren.*	I told them to come in but they don't want to.
out	to go out	*salir*	*Suelen salir los domingos.*	They usually go out on Sundays.
over	to jump over	*saltar*	*Salté (por encima de) la valla.*	I jumped over the fence.
through	to wade through	*caminar por*	*Caminamos por el barro durante media hora.*	We waded through the mud for half an hour.
up	to get up	*levantarse*	*Laura se levantó y se duchó.*	Laura got up and had a shower.

Conjunctions

A conjunction is a word, or a cluster of words, serving to link two words or phrases of similar type, or two halves of a sentence. The most common ones in English are 'and', 'but', 'or', 'so', 'if' and 'because'. Here is a summary of the main Spanish conjunctions and their correct usage:

UNIT 8 PREPOSITIONS AND CONJUNCTIONS

y, e

The word for 'and' works very similarly to its English equivalent, but note that it changes to *e* before words beginning with *i-* and *hi-* (but not *hie-*):

el sol y la luna	the sun and the moon
padre e hijo	father and son
acero y hierro	steel and iron

o, u, ó

The word for 'or' exists in three variants: *o* is the standard form, *u* is its spoken and written replacement before words beginning with *o-* or *ho-*, and *ó* can often be found written between numerals (though this is no longer a formal requirement):

carne o pescado	meat or fish
siete u ocho	seven or eight
21 ó 22 años	21 or 22 years

pero, sino

Both words mean 'but'. *Pero* is the general word, but *sino* must be used in cases of a negation followed by a correction ('not blue but red'), and also features commonly in the structure 'not only ... but (also) ...':

> A common error is to confuse *sino* ('but') and *si no* ('if not').

Quiero hacerlo pero no sé cómo.	I want to do it but I don't know how.
No tiene cinco años sino seis.	S/he isn't five years old but six.
He escrito no solo novelas sino poesía también.	I've written not only novels but poetry too.

que

As a conjunction, *que* links two clauses in the same way as 'that' in English (e.g. 'They know <u>that</u> we've arrived'). However, it's vital to remember that whereas English can omit the 'that' here, Spanish must always retain the *que*. Notice also that the Spanish *que* is far more common than its English equivalent, because of its role in introducing subjunctives – such structures are covered in depth in our units on the subjunctive:

⇨ See Unit 7 for coverage of **que** as a relative pronoun

Saben que hemos llegado.	They know (that) we've arrived.
Quiero que me ayudes.	I want you to help me.
Nos pidieron que asistiéramos.	They asked us to attend.

porque, como

The word *porque*, meaning 'because' (not to be confused with *por qué* – 'why' – and *el porqué*, meaning 'the motive'), works similarly to its English equivalent. Note, however, that the idea of *porque* is better expressed by *como* when it starts a sentence:

⇨ *For coverage of **como** + subjunctive, see Unit 16*

Te llamo porque quiero pedirte un favor.	I'm calling you because I want to ask you a favour.
Como no viniste, no pude darte el libro.	Because / since you didn't come, I couldn't give you the book. You didn't come, so I couldn't give you the book.

si

Spelt without an accent, the word for 'if' and 'whether' features in a wide range of conditional structures. These are a couple of basic examples:

Ven a mi casa si quieres.	Come to my house if you want.
No sabemos si han llegado.	We don't know whether they've arrived.

⇨ *For coverage on Conditional sentences, see Unit 16*

cuando

Not to be confused with the question word *¿cuándo?* ('when?'), *cuando* links two clauses to give the sense of 'at the time that':

Estabas cenando cuando llegamos.	You were having dinner when we arrived.

pues

Pues can equate to the rather old-fashioned English 'for' (e.g. 'He acted courteously, for he was a good man'), but is more commonly found as a filler roughly translatable as 'so', 'then' or 'well':

—Tengo sed. —Pues, bebe algo.	'I'm thirsty.' – 'Well, have something to drink.'
Pues, no sé.	Well, I don't know.

aunque

The general meaning of *aunque* is 'although', but its usage splits into two very different forms. When it means 'even though' (+ a fact), it takes the indicative; when it means 'even if' (+ a hypothesis), it takes the subjunctive. Both variants are covered in Units 14 and 21, but for now, here's an example of its simpler use:

Continuaba estudiando aunque era tarde.	S/he carried on studying even though it was late.

UNIT 8 — PREPOSITIONS AND CONJUNCTIONS

mientras

In time constructions requiring the meaning of 'while' (= 'during the time that'), *mientras* works straightforwardly with the indicative:

Hablaban de cosas raras mientras desayunaban. They talked about strange things while they were having breakfast.

⇨ There is an additional structure for **mientras**, which is dealt with in the Conditions section of Unit 21.

mientras que

Differently from the time-related use of *mientras*, *mientras que* carries the contrastive meaning of 'whereas':

A Pedro le gusta el italiano, mientras que Laura prefiere el griego. Pedro likes Italian, whereas Laura prefers Greek.

⇨ Other structures are covered elsewhere, for example **para que** (Units 14 and 21), **con tal de que** (Unit 21) and **siempre que** (Unit 21).

Split conjunctions

These occur when a pair of conjunctions work in tandem, each controlling a separate noun phrase. Here are the most common ones in Spanish. Notice the requirement to include *no* in one variant of the *ni ... ni ...* construction, and also that you mustn't try to say something like *ambos ... y ...* for the 'both ... and ...' structure:

Split conjunction	English equivalent	Spanish example	English
o ... o ...	either ... or ...	**Puedes coger o ciencias o humanidades.**	You can take either sciences or humanities.
ni ... ni ...	neither ... nor ...	**Ni Pepe ni Juan jugaron. / No jugaron ni Pepe ni Juan.**	Neither Pepe nor Juan played.
tanto ... como ...	both ... and ...	**Tanto mi hermana como yo fuimos a la fiesta.**	Both my sister and I went to the party.

PRACTICE

1 Correct the following sentences, each of which contains at least one error:

1. Después de cenando, salimos a dar una vuelta.

   ....

2. Cuando estabas a París, querías ir en España.

   ....

3. Es fácil de seguir este debate.

   ....

4. Consiste de tres partes.

   ....

5. Te conocí a la universidad.

   ....

2 Translate the following sentences into Spanish:

1. I'm against this law.

   ....

2. The station is fifty metres from the cathedral.

   ....

3. I'm the tallest woman in the group.

   ....

4. I live close to the university.

   ....

5. She's not Portuguese, but Italian.

   ....

6. We went by car.

   ....

7. Neither María nor Juan arrived on time.

   ....

PRACTICE

8 They stole my brother's bike from him.

....

9 We're going to help him with his studies.

....

10 I'm from Alicante but I've come from Valencia.

....

3 **Fill in the gaps in the following sentences with a suitable preposition:**

1. Voy a buscarte .... la estación.

2. Mercedes está .... misa.

3. La conocí .... el aeropuerto de Barajas.

4. Ten cuidado .... ese chico.

5. Estoy harta .... estudiar.

4 **How do you say the following in Spanish?**

1. on foot ....

2. little by little ....

3. five (degrees) below zero ....

4. at (the age of) fifty ....

5. at times ....

6. white coffee ....

7. in the shade ....

8. on time ....

9. according to her ....

10. under the dictatorship ....

PRACTICE

5 Fill each of the gaps with either *a*, *en*, *de* or *con*. Two of the gaps require nothing to be added!

1. He aprendido .... tocar la guitarra.

2. Amenazó .... romper la ventana.

3. Siempre he soñado .... hacerme futbolista.

4. Voy a tratar .... acabarlo.

5. Hemos quedado .... modificarlo.

6. Estaba pensando .... mi novia.

7. Intentamos .... aprenderlo rápidamente.

8. Huele .... humo.

9. Dependerá .... lo que quieras hacer.

10. He decidido .... no hacerlo.

6 Make any necessary corrections to the sentences below:

1. Os dije iba a venir hoy.

   ....

2. Mis hermanas se llaman Lidia y Isabel.

   ....

3. Es una mezcla de fruta y hielo.

   ....

4. De una manera o otra vamos a conseguirlo.

   ....

5. No viene hoy pero mañana.

   ....

PRACTICE

7 Translate the following sentences into Spanish:

1 You [*tú*] can watch either this film or the other one.

   ....

2 Both my brother and my sister have been to New York.

   ....

3 Neither Miguel nor his girlfriend have studied for the exam.

   ....

4 Last summer we didn't go to Catalonia, but to the Canary Islands.

   ....

5 Father and son drank seven or eight beers.

   ....

UNIT 9

Por / para and the personal *a*

> This unit begins with in-depth coverage of the differences between – and usages of – the prepositions **por** and **para**, including close focus on how to use them (and alternatives) in time structures. We then move on to look at the personal *a*.

Por versus *para*

This is one of the areas of most confusion among students of Spanish, as both prepositions can often translate as 'for'. The only reliable way to crack their usage is to practise each in great detail and get a feel for which applies in a given context. However, there are a couple of overarching observations which may be helpful. *Por* is generally used to express the cause of something, the reason behind it – so underlying notions such as 'due to', 'because of' or 'out of (e.g. sympathy)' are worth testing for compatibility as you weigh up your options. You can often tick the *por* box if you find that the situation responds to the question *¿por qué?* ('why?'). *Para*, on the other hand, usually indicates some sort of intention, destination or purpose, so if the meaning you are after matches 'intended for', 'for the benefit of' or 'in order to', there's a good chance *para* will be the one to opt for.

One circumstance in particular can cause headaches: when we talk about doing something 'for' someone. The 'for' here can theoretically be both *por* and *para*, and the temptation among students of French to choose *por* automatically (because of the unambiguous French *pour*) can be overwhelming. Let's look at a pair of sentences to try and clarify the matter:

Lo hice <u>por</u> un amigo. I did it for a friend.
Lo hice <u>para</u> un amigo. I did it for a friend.

In the first sentence, the feeling is that the object *lo* was done 'on behalf of', 'because of' the friend, who exists as the reason or motive of the action. It could, for example, refer to covering a work shift 'for' ('in the place of') the friend, or doing something like a charity run 'for' them ('in their honour', 'because of them').

The second sentence is more clear-cut. What is conveyed here by the *para* is that the action / item expressed by *lo* is 'intended for', 'aimed at' the friend. It could, for example, be some artefact or something to eat, a gift to give, etc.

There are, though, so many subtleties and areas of potential overlap that we need to look closely at each preposition in turn.

Por

After dealing with the tricky example shown above, we find that the remaining usages do, at least, lend themselves to some sort of categorisation. *Por* should be used in the following circumstances:

UNIT 9 POR / PARA AND THE PERSONAL A

1. When the meaning could also be conveyed by *a causa de*:

No salimos por la lluvia.	We didn't go out because of the rain.
Os quiero por vuestra sinceridad.	I love you for your sincerity.
Gracias por ayudarme / por el regalo.	Thanks for helping me / for the gift.

2. When the meaning is 'in exchange for', including sums of money paid:

Voy a cambiar este jersey por otro.	I'm going to change this jersey for another one.
Compramos la casa por medio millón de euros.	We bought the house for half a million euros.

3. In passive constructions with *ser*, *por* equates to the English 'by' in introducing the agent. Notice that this role can often be taken by *de* if the preceding verb is *estar*:

La novela fue leída por tres millones de personas.	The novel was read by three million people.
Los Juegos Olímpicos serán inaugurados por el presidente.	The Olympic Games will be opened by the president.
La solicitud debe estar acompañada de una foto reciente.	The application must be accompanied by a recent photo.

4. In expressions involving supporting, voting for, being in favour of, etc., (though you usually say *votar a un candidato*):

Tengo pensado votar por la independencia.	I intend to vote for independence.
Estamos por el cambio (a favor del cambio).	We're for change.

5. Meaning 'by' + means of transport, in the context of freight:

por avión	by airmail
por barco	by ship

6. Translating the English prepositions of 'along' (e.g. a path / road), 'through' (e.g. a tunnel) and 'around' (a place):

El coche iba por la carretera.	The car was travelling along the road.
Pasamos por el túnel sin poner los faros.	We went through the tunnel without putting the headlights on.
Dieron una vuelta por el centro.	They went for a stroll around the centre.
Lo encontraremos por aquí.	We'll find it around here somewhere.
Estarán por ahí.	They'll be out and about somewhere.

7. To express the relevant prepositions in the following English phrases denoting periods of the day. Notice what happens when a specific time is added:

por la mañana	in the morning
a las diez de la mañana	at ten o'clock in the morning
por la tarde	in the afternoon / evening
a las cuatro y media de la tarde	at half past four in the afternoon
por la noche	at night
a las once y cuarto de la noche	at quarter past eleven at night

POR / PARA AND THE PERSONAL A — UNIT 9

8. To refer to rates or frequencies (often equating to the English 'per'):

un diez por ciento	ten per cent
a diez kilómetros por hora	at ten kilometres per hour
veinte horas por semana / a la semana	twenty hours per week / a week
cien euros por persona	a hundred euros per person

9. To convey 'by' (and various other prepositions) in the sense of 'by means of', 'through' or 'via':

Tienen que llamarnos por teléfono.	They have to phone us ('call us by phone')
Lo van a transmitir por la radio.	They are going to broadcast it on the radio.
Nos enteramos por un contacto en el ministerio.	We found out through a contact at the ministry.
Preferimos la televisión por cable.	We prefer cable television.

10. In mathematics, 'multiplied by':

Cuatro por tres son doce.	Four times three equals twelve / Four threes are twelve.

11. To convey the meaning of 'as far as I'm (etc.) concerned':

Por mí, pueden quedarse.	As far as I'm concerned, they can stay.

⇨ See **para**, point 5

12. Meaning 'to judge by':

por lo visto	apparently / from what I (etc.) can see
por lo que he leído	from what I've read

13. There is a subtlety associated with *por* + infinitive ('to'), when it can sometimes be confused in meaning with *para* + infinitive ('to', 'in order to'). If the meaning is clearly 'with the intention of' or 'in order to', then *para* is needed; if a phrase such as 'from an urge to' or 'out of a desire to' can precede the infinitive and maintain the meaning, then *por* is required:

He montado la tienda por hacer algo.	I've opened the shop for the sake of doing something ('out of an urge to do something')
He traído la estatua para dártela.	I've brought the statue so as to give it to you.
Solo lo hacen por molestarme / para molestarme.	They only do it to irritate me (*por* for motive; *para* for intention – these two are actually very similar).
hablar por hablar	to talk for the sake of talking

Por also follows a number of common verbs:

Verb + *por*	Example	English
acabar por	Acabamos por romperlo.	We ended up breaking it.
comenzar por	Van a comenzar por el primer movimiento de la sinfonía número tres.	They're going to begin with the first movement of the third symphony.
disculparse por	Se han disculpado por hacerlo / por lo que hicieron.	They've apologised for doing it / for what they did.
empezar por	see *comenzar por*	
esforzarse por	Tendrás que esforzarte por terminarlo a tiempo.	You'll have to make an effort to finish it on time.
interesarse por	Se interesaba por mis libros.	S/he showed an interest in my books.
luchar por	Lucharon por hacerse oír / por la independencia.	They fought / struggled to make themselves heard / for independence.
optar por	¿Has optado por participar / por el rojo?	Have you chosen to take part / plumped for the red one?
preguntar por	Suelen preguntar por ti.	They usually ask after you.
preocuparse por / de	No te preocupes por todo eso.	Don't worry about all that.
terminar por	see *acabar por*	

Por in time phrases

There are three points to touch on here:

1   The meaning of 'in' / 'at' + a period of the day.

⇨ See point 7 on page 89

2   *Por*, as well as *en*, can mean 'in' when referring to a day, month, year etc. The rule is that *en* gives a straightforward usage, whereas *por* confers a rather vague, 'sometime during' idea:

Fue en agosto. It was in August.
Habrá sido por agosto. It must have been at some point in August.

3   To express 'for' + a period of time, *por* is permissible, but only when the period referred to is brief, and the shortness of the period is being emphasised. If you are in any doubt about translating 'for' in time expressions, *durante* will generally work as a safe alternative, or you can often omit the notion of 'for' altogether:

Lo necesito por cinco minutos. I need it for five minutes.
Quiero que me escuches (por) un momento. I want you to listen to me (for) a moment.

Para

There are fewer usages to consider for *para* than for *por*. Here are the main ones:

1. To denote purpose, destination or intention. This includes the common *para* ('in order to') + infinitive construction:

Esta habitación es para dos personas / para mí.	This room is for two people / for me.
Para abrirlo, tienes que girarlo hacia la derecha.	In order to open it, you have to turn it to the right.
¿Para qué los necesitas?	What do you need them for?

   > Confusion can sometimes arise as to the difference between *¿por qué?* and *¿para qué?* The former relates to a (previously established) cause: *¿por qué ocurrió el accidente?* ('For what reason did the accident happen?'; 'What was the cause of the accident?')
   >
   > The latter refers to intention: *¿para qué tenemos que ir a la reunión?* ('For what purpose / with what goal in mind do we have to go to the meeting?')

2. With verbs of motion, *para* can mean 'for', 'heading for', 'in the direction of':

Salimos para casa / para Salamanca a las dos.	We set off home / for Salamanca at two o'clock.
Va para directora.	She's on her way to becoming a director.

3. With an infinitive, *para* can equate to the English 'only to' in situations described with a note of sarcasm:

Tanto querer ser una mujer independiente, para luego acabar casándose con un hombre que la mantiene.	She went on and on about wanting to be an independent woman, only to end up marrying a man who keeps her.

4. To express advantage, disadvantage, usefulness etc. in expressions such as 'good for', 'bad for', 'vital for':

Beber alcohol es malo para el hígado.	Drinking alcohol is bad for the liver.
El entusiasmo es imprescindible para este puesto.	Enthusiasm is vital for this post.

5. Expressing opinions of the type 'in my view'. There is often a fine line between *por* and *para* in their respective meanings of 'as far as I'm concerned' and 'in my opinion', but with practice, the distinction does get clearer:

Para mi madre / Para mí, no vale la pena.	In my mother's / In my opinion, it's not worth it.

6. 'for' in the sense of 'in view of', 'considering':

Para un chaval tan corto, no juega mal al baloncesto.	He's not bad at basketball for a short lad.

Para in time phrases

There are three main usages:

1. To match the English 'by' or 'for' when referring to a deadline or specific point looked ahead to:

Estará listo para las cuatro y media.	It will be ready for / by half past four.
Habremos acabado para el lunes.	We will have finished by Monday.

2. Similar, but slightly less specific, is another use, equating to the English 'around':

Van a volver para la primavera.	They'll be back around springtime.
Esperan tenerlo hecho para finales de marzo.	They hope to have it done around the end of March.

3. With a specified period of time in the future (but not the markedly brief period triggering *por*), *para* is used to express the English 'for':

Querríamos alquilarlo para veintiún días.	We'd like to hire it for twenty-one days.
Lo voy a necesitar para dos semanas.	I'm going to need it for two weeks.

The personal *a*

The essential rule here is that when the direct object of a verb is a specific, identified person or familiar animal, *a* is placed immediately before it. Aside from the notion in itself – which is not used in other popular Romance languages – difficulties revolve around when a person is considered specific and identified, and how familiar (or cuddly) an animal has to be before it qualifies to receive the personal *a*. Here are some examples in which the personal *a* is used:

Quiero mucho a Laura / a mis primos.	I love Laura / my cousins a great deal.
He visto a la profesora en la plaza mayor.	I've seen the teacher in the main square.
Vamos a castrar al gato.	We're going to neuter the cat.

Conversely, if the person is not specifically identified, or the animal does not come within the range one would ordinarily keep as a pet (or would at least find loveable), the personal *a* may not be used, as in these examples:

Busco un intérprete que hable euskera. / Busco a un intérprete con el que trabajé el año pasado. He perdido su dirección.	I'm looking for an interpreter who speaks Basque [not a specific one]. / I'm looking for an interpreter I worked with last year. I've lost his address [a specific one].
Prefería deportistas a intelectuales.	She preferred sportsmen to intellectuals.
Maté la cucaracha.	I killed the cockroach.

The personal *a* before indefinite pronouns

The personal *a* is used before an indefinite pronoun referring to a person. Even though *alguien*, *cualquiera* and *nadie* don't refer to specific people (and hence appear to contradict the 'specifically identified' rule), they still need the personal *a*:

Han matado a alguien en la calle.	They've killed someone in the street.
Yo contrataría a cualquiera de ellos.	I'd employ any of them.
¿No conoces a nadie?	Don't you know anyone?
Aborrezco a ese chico.	I detest that boy.

The personal *a* before relative pronouns

The personal *a* can be used before a relative pronoun in the direct object position. The required forms become *a quien, a quienes / al que, a la que, a los que, a las que*:

Es el profesor al que / a quien más admiro.	He's the teacher (whom) I most admire.
Hay varias personas a quienes / a las que no aguanto.	There are several people (whom) I can't stand.

The personal *a* after *querer* or *tener*

When *querer* means 'to love', it takes the personal *a* and functions in keeping with the rules listed earlier:

Quiero mucho a ese hombre.	I love that man very much.
Nunca he querido a ninguna otra mujer.	I've never loved any other woman.

With its meaning of 'to want', however, it generally loses the personal *a*, unless you are being emphatic about someone specific:

Quiero un marido.	I want a husband.
Quiero a Pepe en mi equipo.	I want Pepe in my team.

In references to one's family, workmates, etc., *tener* does not generally take the personal *a*, though notice the contrast of the third example, below, where the man has, in effect, 'driven' his wife to bitterness. This is also an example of fluid word order in Spanish:

Tengo tres hermanas y un hermano.	I've got three sisters and one brother.
Tenemos un nuevo jefe.	We've got a new boss.
Tiene a su mujer amargada. / Tiene amargada a su mujer.	He's caused his wife to turn bitter / He's driven his wife to bitterness.

Notice the following uses, however:

Tenemos a Paco como ariete.	We're got Paco playing at centre forward.
Por lo menos te tengo a ti.	At least I've got you.

KEY POINT

The differences between *por* and *para* need to be studied closely until they are clear in the learner's mind. As with all elements of Spanish grammar, the real key to success is reading and practice. It's a good idea to choose at random a page of a Spanish-language newspaper, highlight all usages of both prepositions, and work out why either *por* or *para* is used on each occasion.

PRACTICE

1 Insert *por* or *para*, as appropriate:

1 .... ser una mujer tan joven, tiene muchos hijos.

2 Quiero darte las gracias .... tu generosidad.

3 ¿Por qué no cambiamos esta mesa .... otra nueva?

4 Una mesa .... cuatro personas, por favor.

5 El agua es buena .... la piel.

6 El diccionario fue escrito .... un grupo de académicos.

7 ¿Vas a votar .... la democracia?

8 Tendremos que salir .... la estación.

9 Siga usted .... este camino hasta el bosque.

10 .... mí, él ya no existe.

2 Translate the following sentences into Spanish, using a structure covered in this unit:

1 My grandmother asked after you yesterday.

   ....

2 I need your help to open the window.

   ....

3 We want to begin by reading a text.

   ....

4 He swore he had no money, only to buy a Porsche the following day.

   ....

5 I've apologised for what I said yesterday.

   ....

PRACTICE

3 **Are these sentences correct or incorrect? Make any necessary adjustments:**

1. Ocurrió a las once por la mañana.

   ....

2. Tenemos diez euros por persona.

   ....

3. Se vende por mil euros.

   ....

4. Me voy por casa.

   ....

5. Es útil por este trabajo.

   ....

4 **Fill in the gaps, where necessary, with *por* or *para*. Some gaps may not require a preposition!**

1. Lo tendremos listo .... las dos de la tarde.
2. .... ser inglés, habla muy bien español.
3. Queremos alquilar la casa .... tres semanas.
4. Llegamos ayer .... la tarde.
5. Lleva .... tres horas esperando.

5 **Insert the personal *a* where necessary. You may need to add pronouns in certain cases:**

1. Quiero .... personal motivado y dedicado a su trabajo.
2. Vamos a llevar .... la perra al veterinario.
3. Tenemos .... catorce primos.
4. He visto .... alguien que se parecía a ella.
5. Es la estudiante .... veo más a menudo.

UNIT 10 Numerals

This unit looks at ordinal numbers ('first', 'second', 'third') and cardinal numbers ('one', 'two', 'three'), how Spanish uses them, and how Spanish use compares with that of English. We also cover some practical applications such as telephone numbers, dates, percentages and fractions.

Ordinal numbers

'First' to 'tenth'

In general use, only the first ten ordinals are used in Spanish. They must agree in number and gender with the noun or noun phrase to which they refer, and almost always precede it. Notice that *primero* ('first') shortens to *primer* when it comes immediately before a masculine singular noun or noun phrase, and *tercero* ('third') becomes *tercer* in the same circumstance:

Mi hermano fue el primero. / Fui el primer hombre en hacerlo. / Fui la primera mujer en hacerlo.	My brother was the first. / I was the first man to do it. / I was the first woman to do it.
el segundo día / los segundos episodios	the second day / the second episodes
Juan acabó tercero. / el tercer libro de la colección / la tercera casa a la derecha	Juan finished third. / the third book in the collection / the third house on the right
Vivimos en el cuarto piso / en la cuarta planta.	We live on the fourth floor.
Miguel es el quinto ganador. / Laura y Lidia son las quintas ganadoras.	Miguel is the fifth winner. / Laura and Lidia are the fifth winners.
Será el sexto año consecutivo / la sexta victoria consecutiva.	It will be the sixth consecutive year / victory.
Julio es el séptimo mes del año. / Los séptimos somos tú y yo.	July is the seventh month of the year. / You and I are (the) seventh.
Es el octavo presidente del país. / Lo has hecho por octava vez.	He is the country's eighth president. / You've done it for the eighth time.
el noveno bloque a la izquierda / la novena ocasión	the ninth block on the left / the ninth occasion
Es el décimo campeonato. / Estas son las décimas jornadas shakesperianas.	It's the tenth championship. / This is the tenth conference on Shakespeare.

The numerical forms – such as the English '6th' – follow the format 6º (*sexto* – masc.) / 6ª (*sexta* – fem.). The shortened forms *primer* and *tercer* are numerically written 1er and 3er respectively.

There are occasions on which the ordinal comes after the noun. The most common of these is when referring to the title of a monarch or a pope. There are a few additional points to be made here – Spanish does not use the definite article, and English ordinals above 'tenth' are conveyed in Spanish by the cardinal number ('fourteen', 'twenty-three'). Also in the context of history, the cardinal number is more common in referring to a specific century (*el siglo tres / veintiuno* – 'the third / twenty-first century').

Juan Carlos Primero	Juan Carlos the First
Isabel Segunda	Elizabeth the Second
Enrique Octavo	Henry the Eighth
Luis Catorce	Louis the Fourteenth
Juan Veintitrés	John the Twenty-third

'Eleventh' and above

Spanish ordinals above 'tenth' are not widely used (e.g. *su quince aniversario* – 'his / her fifteenth birthday'), but there are occasions on which it is useful to say, specifically, 'for the fifteenth time' or (for fractions in maths) 'four thirteenths'. Spanish uses a dual system: one set of ordinals for general use (usually denoting a person, event or element's ranking or location in a series), and another set for fractions, generally found in contexts of maths or engineering. Here is a list of the ordinals in these categories you are most likely to see:

General use	Fraction	Meaning
undécimo / a	*onceavo / a*	11th
duodécimo / a	*doceavo / a*	12th
decimotercero / a	*treceavo / a*	13th
decimocuarto / a	*catorceavo / a*	14th
decimoquinto / a	*quinceavo / a*	15th
decimosexto / a	*dieciseisavo / a*	16th
decimoséptimo / a	*diecisieteavo / a*	17th
decimoctavo / a	*dieciochavo / a*	18th
decimonoveno / a	*diecinueveavo / a*	19th
vigésimo / a	*veinteavo / a*	20th
vigésimo / a sexto / a	*veintiseisavo / a*	26th
trigésimo / a	*treintavo / a*	30th
cuadragésimo / a	*cuarentavo / a*	40th
quincuagésimo / a	*cincuentavo / a*	50th
sexagésimo / a	*sesentavo / a*	60th
septuagésimo / a	*setentavo / a*	70th
octogésimo / a	*ochentavo / a*	80th
nonagésimo / a	*noventavo / a*	90th
centésimo / a	*centavo / a*	100th
milésimo / a	*milésimo / a*	1,000th
millonésimo / a	*millonésimo / a*	1,000,000th

UNIT 10 NUMERALS

Here are some illustrations of the usage of both types:

Cubrimos once doceavos de la distancia.   We covered eleven-twelfths of the distance.
Fue el decimocuarto presidente de la empresa.   He was the fourteenth president of the company.

Dieciseisavos, from the Fractions column, also features in the language of sports competitions in the term *dieciseisavos de final*, meaning 'the last 32' or 'round of 32' (32 teams; 16 matches), i.e. two rounds before the quarter finals (*los cuartos de final* – 8 teams; 4 matches), and one before 'the last sixteen' (*los octavos de final* – 16 teams; 8 matches).

In giving dates within a month, with the exception of 'the first' – where both *el primero de octubre* and *el uno de octubre* are possible – whereas English uses ordinals ('the fourteenth of January') Spanish uses cardinals (*el catorce de enero*).

Cardinal numbers

1–99

0	cero		
1	uno, un, una	21	veintiuno, veintiún, veintiuna
2	dos	22	veintidós
3	tres	23	veintitrés
4	cuatro	24	veinticuatro
5	cinco	25	veinticinco
6	seis	26	veintiséis
7	siete	27	veintisiete
8	ocho	28	veintiocho
9	nueve	29	veintinueve
10	diez	30	treinta
11	once	31	treinta y uno / treinta y un / treinta y una
12	doce	37	treinta y siete
13	trece	40	cuarenta
14	catorce	50	cincuenta
15	quince	60	sesenta
16	dieciséis	70	setenta
17	diecisiete	80	ochenta
18	dieciocho	90	noventa
19	diecinueve	99	noventa y nueve
20	veinte		

NUMERALS UNIT 10

A quick reminder of the basic rules for numbers:

1. Numbers 1-30 are written as one word; thereafter, all numbers are written as three words (e.g. *cuarenta y tres* – 43) except multiples of ten (e.g. *setenta* – 70), which are a single word. This is the point at which students of Italian must begin to take care to maintain the 'three-word' format.

2. *Dieciséis* (16), *veintiún* (21), *veintidós* (22), *veintitrés* (23) and *veintiséis* (26) are all written with an accent. Care is recommended when spelling 11-19, where ingrained 'schoolboy' French can sometimes be a hindrance, and throughout the 20s and 30s, where a common slip is to spell and pronounce -*ie*- rather than -*ei*-.

Once these rules have been mastered, the only really tricky issue is 'one' (*uno*) and numbers ending in 'one' (*cuarenta y uno* – 41, etc.). Any number ending in 'one' must be formed with care in Spanish, as the *uno* must agree in gender with whatever noun is being referred to. If the number is standing on its own (e.g. as a minimal answer to a question), but still relates to an underlying noun, the forms used are the following:

—¿Cuántos libros tienes? —Uno. / Veintiuno. / Ochenta y uno.	'How many books have you got?' – '1 / 21 / 81.'
—¿Cuántas nubes ves? —Una. / Veintiuna. / Ochenta y una.	'How many clouds can you see?' – '1 / 21 / 81.'

If the *uno* is followed by a masculine noun or noun phrase, it shortens to *un* (which is why 'a book' and 'one book' are rendered identically in Spanish). The feminine equivalent is straightforward:

Tengo un primo / veintiún primos / cuarenta y un primos.	I have 1 cousin / 21 cousins / 41 cousins.
Tengo una tía / veintiuna tías / cuarenta y una tías.	I have 1 aunt / 21 aunts / 41 aunts

However, one added (but, realistically, seldom encountered) difficulty, relates to an issue covered in Unit 2: that of having to use masculine articles before feminine singular nouns beginning with a stressed *a*- or *ha*- (e.g. *el agua* – 'the water', *un hacha* – 'an axe', *el águila* – 'the eagle'). When such a noun – singular or plural – is to be preceded by a number ending in 'one', the following must happen:

un hacha	1 axe
veintiún armas	21 weapons
cincuenta y un hayas	51 beech trees

100–199

Firstly, 'one hundred' (exactly) is *cien*, whether it stands on its own or is followed by a noun phrase:

—¿Cuántos/as tienes? —Cien.	'How many have you got?' – 'A hundred.'
cien hombres / cien gaviotas	a hundred men / seagulls

For 101-199, the full form of *ciento* is added in front of the relevant number from the 1-99 section. Note that the *y* between tens and units remains intact, but you should not try to replicate the English

UNIT 10 NUMERALS

'and' between hundreds and tens:

—¿Cuántos tienes? —Ciento uno.	'How many have you got?' – '101.' [masculine]
—¿Cuántas tienes? —Ciento una.	'How many have you got?' – '101.' [feminine]
ciento un libros / ciento una casas	101 books / houses
ciento ocho (libros / casas)	108 (books / houses)
ciento veinticinco (libros / casas)	125 (books / houses)
ciento cuarenta (libros / casas)	140 (books / houses)
ciento noventa y nueve (libros / casas)	199 (books / houses)

200–999

The words for 200, 300 … 900 have a masculine and feminine form, and these must be carefully applied depending on the gender of the noun to which the numeral refers. Notice that the words for 500, 700 and 900 have an 'irregular' stem. Once again, the forms we covered in the 1-99 section form the core of the number, with the *doscientos/as* (etc.) coming before them. Here are some examples of correct formation:

doscientos un coches / doscientas una bicicletas	201 cars [masculine] / 201 bicycles [feminine]
trescientos cuarenta y seis / trescientas cuarenta y seis	346
cuatrocientos veintiún coches / cuatrocientas veintiuna bicicletas	421 cars / bicycles
quinientos treinta y un rifles / quinientas treinta y un armas	531 rifles / weapons
seiscientos tres / seiscientas tres	603
setecientos diecisiete / setecientas diecisiete	717
ochocientos cincuenta / ochocientas cincuenta	850
novecientos noventa y nueve / novecientas noventa y nueve	999

1,000+

Let's take the example of 1,632. Again, we are helped in Spanish by being able to re-use the formation of 632 – which, in turn, is aided by re-using the formation of 32 – with a word for 'thousand' simply inserted at the beginning. The structure is straightforward, but now that we are into the larger numbers, there are a few traps tempting us to put *y* in the wrong place, to pluralise a word that should be left singular, and to forget our masculine / feminine distinction from the hundreds section.

The word for 'a thousand' or 'one thousand' is *mil*, 'two thousand' is *dos mil* and 'a / one hundred thousand' is *cien mil*. Note from this that – rather like the English 'two thousand' – the Spanish word does not pluralise (other than in the general usage *miles de personas*, where the number of thousands is not specified); however, unlike the English 'a / one thousand euros', *mil euros* does not have 'a' or 'one' at the beginning.

NUMERALS UNIT 10

Here are some examples incorporating 'thousand' and 'thousands'. It's a good idea to focus on how a large number has developed from right to left, e.g. 2 to 42, to 742 to 1,742 to 41,742. At the same time, keep an eye on issues like where y is located, and where (and why) the plurals and masculine / feminine distinctions are made. All the way up the scale, we're re-applying rules we've covered earlier on:

1,032	*mil treinta y dos*
1,021 books / houses	*mil veintiún libros / mil veintiuna casas*
1,100 (books / houses)	*mil cien (libros / casas)*
1,340 (books / houses)	*mil trescientos cuarenta libros / mil trescientas cuarenta casas*
2,501 books / houses	*dos mil quinientos un libros / dos mil quinientas una casas*
11,794	*once mil setecientos / as noventa y cuatro*
32,055	*treinta y dos mil cincuenta y cinco*
100,199	*cien mil ciento noventa y nueve*
142,981 books / houses	*ciento cuarenta y dos mil novecientos ochenta y un libros / ciento cuarenta y dos mil novecientas ochenta y una casas*

1,000,000+

Un millón is a masculine singular noun, and works rather like the unit *un kilo*, linking with the subsequent noun by *de* (though obviously it will always be followed by a plural noun). Compare the following, noting also the lack of an indefinite article in the Spanish for 'half a', and the loss of the accent in the plural *millones*:

un kilo de / medio kilo de / tres kilos de azúcar / naranjas	a kilo / half a kilo / three kilos of sugar / of oranges
kilos y kilos de jamón	kilos and kilos of ham
un millón de / medio millón de / tres millones de personas	a million / half a million / three million people
millones y millones de pobres	millions and millions of poor people

For high numbers other than an exact number of millions, once again we look to the formations learned in earlier sections, clamping *un millón*, *dos millones* (etc.) on at the beginning, and continuing to pay close attention to genders, plurals and location of *y*:

1,079,391 cars / houses	*un millón setenta y nueve mil trescientos noventa y <u>un</u> coches / un millón setenta y nueve mil trescien<u>tas</u> noventa y <u>una</u> casas*
16,452,900 cars / houses	*dieciséis millones cuatrocient<u>os</u> cincuenta y dos mil novecient<u>os</u> coches / dieciséis millones cuatrocien<u>tas</u> cincuenta y dos mil novecien<u>tas</u> casas*

Un billón (de) / dos billones (de) works identically to *un millón (de) / dos millones (de)*. It's worth noting that the American use of 'billion' is still *mil millones*, and that the Spanish language introduced the word *millardo* (adapted from the French) to convey it, but it has not really caught on.

UNIT 10 NUMERALS

Practical uses of numerals

Decimals

One important point to note is that the English-language conventions regarding the use of full stops (with decimals) and commas (with thousands) are reversed in Spanish. Note also the convention for pronouncing decimals of euros (which also applies to other currencies) and of temperatures:

Spanish written form	Spanish pronunciation	English written form	English pronunciation
6,4	seis coma cuatro	6.4	six point four
3.745	tres mil setecientos cuarenta y cinco	3,745	three thousand seven hundred and forty-five
4,25 euros	cuatro (euros) con veinticinco / cuatro (euros) veinticinco	4.25	four (euros) twenty-five
7,8°	siete con ocho grados / siete coma ocho grados	7.8°	seven point eight degrees

Times and dates

A quick reminder of how to give the time of day, plus an example of good usage in phrasing the date (note how Spanish differs from English in its inclusion / exclusion of *de* and *y*, and in how it structures the two years:

    1.25 / 11.50   *Es la una y veinticinco / Son las doce menos diez*

    12 August 1948 / 2012   *Es el doce de agosto de mil novecientos cuarenta y ocho / de dos mil doce*

Percentages

The trick here is to remember to include a definite or indefinite article in Spanish. It's a good opportunity to recap on decimals, too:

el cuarenta y cinco coma tres por ciento de los trabajadores	45.3% of workers
un dos por ciento	around / some two percent

Phone numbers

Spanish phone numbers are normally pronounced in pairs of digits, with those of an odd number being expressed as hundreds (or by a single digit) at the beginning. It is, however, perfectly permissible to recite a number in individual digits:

67–24–05	*sesenta y siete – veinticuatro – cero cinco*
925–11–32	*nueve – veinticinco – once – treinta y dos / novecientos veinticinco – once – treinta y dos*

PRACTICE

1 Write the following numbers in full in Spanish:

1. 16 ....
2. 22 ....
3. 23 ....
4. 26 ....
5. 30 ....

2 Express the following in Spanish:

1. King William the Fourth ....
2. Queen Elizabeth the First ....
3. Pope John Paul the Second ....
4. King Philip the Twelfth ....
5. Queen Victoria the Fifteenth ....

3 Translate the following into Spanish:

1. The third son ....
2. The ninth daughter ....
3. The tenth celebrations ....
4. The first episode ....
5. The second time ....

4 Write in full in Spanish:

1. 81 books ....
2. 21 keys ....

PRACTICE

3 41 weapons..

4 99 boys..

5 15 uncles...

6 100 people...

7 158 houses..

8 430 men..

9 578 women...

10 999...

5 Write the following in full, as they would be pronounced in Spanish:

1 10.4 degrees..

2 8.99 euros..

3 1.5...

4 [phone number] 23–01–44..

5 [phone number] 824–17–98..

6 Write the following numbers in full in Spanish:

1 1,234,567 cars..

2 2,654,321 houses...

UNIT 11

Indicative verb tenses

This unit offers an overview of the non-continuous indicative forms of the Spanish verb system, including focus on the main irregular verbs and the various radical-changing styles. Continuous forms are covered in the next unit.

The present tense

The present tense is used in the following ways in Spanish:

1 To express truths / facts that are timeless or habitual:

Hace calor en verano.	It's hot in summer.
Mi madre es irlandesa.	My mother is Irish.
Voy a la playa a menudo.	I often go to the beach.

2 It is much more common in Spanish than in English to use a non-continuous present tense to describe actions and states that are the case currently or are happening now:

Viven en Santander.	They live / are living in Santander.
Me parece que nieva.	I think it's snowing.
Estudiamos derecho.	We study / are studying law.

3 It is used in some cases where a different or more complex tense would be used in English. Here is a selection:

¿Te ayudo?	Shall I help you? [seeking consent]
Lorca nace en 1898.	Lorca was born in 1898. [historic present]
Tú te quedas aquí.	You stay here. [strong command – alternative to the imperative mood]
Te veo esta tarde.	I'll see you this afternoon. [present for future events]
Vivo aquí desde hace un mes. / Hace un mes que vivo aquí.	I've lived here / been living here for a month. [time expression – action or state still in progress]
Es la primera vez que hablo con ella.	It's the first time I've spoken to her. [another time expression]

Regular forms

The first table shows the regular forms of the present indicative of -*ar*, -*er* and -*ir* verbs. In this and other tables in this unit, the *vos* form – an alternative to *tú* used in certain Latin American countries, in particular Argentina – is listed, as is the *vosotros* form, which is limited to Spain (but is not widely used in the Canary Islands).

UNIT 11   INDICATIVE VERB TENSES

Infinitive	Meaning	yo	tú	vos	él, ella, usted	nosotros/as	vosotros/as	ellos/as, ustedes
hablar	to speak	hablo	hablas	hablás	habla	hablamos	habláis	hablan
comer	to eat	como	comes	comés	come	comemos	coméis	comen
vivir	to live	vivo	vives	vivís	vive	vivimos	vivís	viven

Radical-changing styles in the present tense

There are several types of verb whose stem alters for the four persons of the verb (*yo, tú, él/ ella/ usted, ellos/ ellas/ ustedes*) in which it is unstressed in the present indicative. The *vos, nosotros* and *vosotros* forms bear the 'logical' stem provided by the infinitive. In the table below, each example illustrates a different category of radical change. Some examples may seem superficially similar, but they are listed separately to maintain the distinction of conjugation (-*ar*, -*er*, -*ir*), to note the inclusion of an accentuated stem (as in four of the persons of *reír*) or because they exhibit more complex radical-changing properties in the preterite tense (as is the case with all four -*ir* verbs here). It's a good idea to make a note of each, and add new verbs to your lists as you come across them and ascertain which pattern they follow:

Style	Infinitive	Meaning	yo	tú	vos	él, ella, usted	nosotros/as	vosotros/as	ellos/as, ustedes
o>ue	costar	to cost	cuesto	cuestas	costás	cuesta	costamos	costáis	cuestan
e>ie	cerrar	to close	cierro	cierras	cerrás	cierra	cerramos	cerráis	cierran
u>ue	jugar	to play	juego	juegas	jugás	juega	jugamos	jugáis	juegan
o>ue	mover	to move	muevo	mueves	movés	mueve	movemos	movéis	mueven
e>ie	entender	to understand	entiendo	entiendes	entendés	entiende	entendemos	entendéis	entienden
e>i	pedir	to ask for	pido	pides	pedís	pide	pedimos	pedís	piden
e>i	reír	to laugh	río	ríes	reís	ríe	reímos	reís	ríen
e>ie	mentir	to lie (tell lies)	miento	mientes	mentís	miente	mentimos	mentís	mienten
o>ue	dormir	to sleep	duermo	duermes	dormís	duerme	dormimos	dormís	duermen

Irregular verbs

Aside from the radical-changing verbs, which are not strictly irregular, there are a number of genuinely irregular verbs (some of which are radical-changing too). In some cases, the present-tense irregularity is limited to a rogue -*g*- or -*z*- in the first person singular (e.g. *caer, conocer, hacer, parecer, poner, producir* – this nevertheless triggers irregularities in the subjunctive, as we'll see later). *Enviar* and *continuar* are not really irregular, but their accentuation is worthy of note. The important thing is

INDICATIVE VERB TENSES — UNIT 11

not to worry about sub-categories or extents to which a verb is irregular, but simply to learn its quirks and practise it until you are competent with its usage. Here is a list of the most commonly encountered verbs with some degree of irregularity in the present indicative:

Infinitive	Meaning	yo	tú	vos	él, ella, usted	nosotros/as	vosotros/as	ellos/as, ustedes
caber	to fit	quepo	cabes	cabés	cabe	cabemos	cabéis	caben
caer	to fall	caigo	caes	caés	cae	caemos	caéis	caen
conocer	to know	conozco	conoces	conocés	conoce	conocemos	conocéis	conocen
continuar	to continue	continúo	continúas	continuás	continúa	continuamos	continuáis	continúan
dar	to give	doy	das	das	da	damos	dais	dan
decir	to say, tell	digo	dices	decís	dice	decimos	decís	dicen
enviar	to send	envío	envías	enviás	envía	enviamos	enviáis	envían
estar	to be	estoy	estás	estás	está	estamos	estáis	están
haber	to have [auxiliary]	he	has	has	ha	hemos	habéis	han
haber	'there is / are'				hay			hay
hacer	to do, make	hago	haces	hacés	hace	hacemos	hacéis	hacen
huir	to flee	huyo	huyes	huís	huye	huimos	huís	huyen
ir	to go	voy	vas	vas	va	vamos	vais	van
oír	to hear	oigo	oyes	oís	oye	oímos	oís	oyen
parecer	to appear, seem	parezco	pareces	parecés	parece	parecemos	parecéis	parecen
poner	to put	pongo	pones	ponés	pone	ponemos	ponéis	ponen
producir	to produce	produzco	produces	producís	produce	producimos	producís	producen
saber	to know	sé	sabes	sabés	sabe	sabemos	sabéis	saben
salir	to go out	salgo	sales	salís	sale	salimos	salís	salen
ser	to be	soy	eres	sos	es	somos	sois	son
tener	to have	tengo	tienes	tenés	tiene	tenemos	tenéis	tienen
traer	to bring	traigo	traes	traés	trae	traemos	traéis	traen
valer	to be worth	valgo	vales	valés	vale	valemos	valéis	valen
venir	to come	vengo	vienes	venís	viene	venimos	venís	vienen
ver	to see	veo	ves	ves	ve	vemos	veis	ven

UNIT 11 INDICATIVE VERB TENSES

Ways of expressing the future

As we saw in point 3 of the introduction to the present tense, future actions can be conveyed in Spanish using the present tense, just as they can in English. This structure usually carries the suggestion that the action is prearranged:

El cursillo empieza el lunes que viene. The course starts next Monday.
Van a un restaurante esta noche. They're going to a restaurant this evening.

This usage aside, there are two main ways of expressing future actions in Spanish, one of which is very similar to the English.

Using *ir a* + infinitive

Just like its English counterpart, this structure states what one is 'going to do' at some point in the future. It is less formal than the conventionally formed, 'single-word' future tense (see below), and is by far the more common variant in spoken Spanish. It doesn't necessarily involve 'going' in any sense of movement, which is also the case in English. Here are some examples of how it works:

Te vas a enfriar. You're going to catch a chill.
Vamos a ganar. We're going to win.
Van a ayudarnos. They're going to help us.

⇨ See Unit 15 on the Imperative for use of **vamos a** as a command form

Using the single-word future tense

In its usage, this structure equates more to the English 'I shall / will begin', and can be used in such contexts. It is not as appropriate as the *ir a* method to talk about prearranged actions, and it is useful to bear in mind that – as in English – the present tense is often perfectly adequate for general future use. Its formation is based on a series of endings being added to the verb's infinitive. These endings are the same for all three conjugations, and five of the six have an accent – students of French should take care in this respect:

Infinitive	yo	tú, vos	él, ella, usted	nosotros/as	vosotros/as	ellos/as, ustedes
hablar	hablaré	hablarás	hablará	hablaremos	hablaréis	hablarán
comer	comeré	comerás	comerá	comeremos	comeréis	comerán
vivir	viviré	vivirás	vivirá	viviremos	viviréis	vivirán

INDICATIVE VERB TENSES — UNIT 11

A number of verbs are irregular in the future tense. The endings are still those given in the table of regular verbs, but the stem (ordinarily the infinitive) is somewhat contracted or otherwise modified in each case:

Infinitive	Meaning	Stem for future	yo	tú, vos	él, ella, usted	nosotros/as	vosotros/as	ellos/as, ustedes
caber	to fit	cabr	cabré	cabrás	cabrá	cabremos	cabréis	cabrán
decir	to say, tell	dir	diré	dirás	dirá	diremos	diréis	dirán
haber	'there will be'	habr			habrá			habrá
hacer	to do, make	har	haré	harás	hará	haremos	haréis	harán
poder	to be able	podr	podré	podrás	podrá	podremos	podréis	podrán
poner	to put	pondr	pondré	pondrás	pondrá	pondremos	pondréis	pondrán
querer	to want, love	querr	querré	querrás	querrá	querremos	querréis	querrán
saber	to know	sabr	sabré	sabrás	sabrá	sabremos	sabréis	sabrán
salir	to go out	saldr	saldré	saldrás	saldrá	saldremos	saldréis	saldrán
tener	to have	tendr	tendré	tendrás	tendrá	tendremos	tendréis	tendrán
valer	to be worth	valdr	valdré	valdrás	valdrá	valdremos	valdréis	valdrán
venir	to come	vendr	vendré	vendrás	vendrá	vendremos	vendréis	vendrán

This form has an additional usage, which is to express guesswork, approximations and suppositions – English can also use the future for this, but often uses alternative devices such as the adverb 'probably' or the verb 'must':

¿Dónde estarán?	Where are they, I wonder?
Ya estarán en Benidorm.	They'll be in Benidorm by now. / They're probably in Benidorm now.
¿Qué hora será?	What time is it, I wonder?
Serán las seis, me imagino.	It must be about six o'clock, I reckon.

⇨ See also the section on the future perfect tense

Finally, a word of warning for students of French and / or Italian. In time structures such as 'I'll retire when I'm 65', in Spanish the verb following 'when' must be expressed in the present subjunctive, not the future indicative (i.e. *cuando tenga 65 años*, not *cuando tendré 65 años*):

Cuando termines, me avisas, ¿vale?	When you finish, let me know, OK?
Te daré el dinero cuando me pague el jefe.	I'll give you the money when the boss pays me.

UNIT 11 — INDICATIVE VERB TENSES

The imperfect tense

This is the first of a trio of past tenses in Spanish whose usage must be studied carefully. It is used to describe a past event that was still 'in progress' or 'was the case' at the time being referred to. As such, it is very useful to describe things that 'were happening', actions that happened repeatedly or habitually, or that 'used to happen'.

⇨ See 'Combinations of Past Tenses' for coverage of how the imperfect can work with other tenses

⇨ The continuous form **estaba hablando** is studied in Unit 12

Hacía frío pero el sol brillaba.	It was cold but the sun was shining.
En 1990 tenía quince años.	In 1990 I was fifteen years old.
Cuando era pequeño tenía el pelo rubio.	When I was little I had fair hair.
Iba al gimnasio cada tres o cuatro días.	I went / used to go to the gym every three or four days.
Mi madre (siempre) decía que no le gustaba Madrid.	My mother (always) said / used to say that she didn't like Madrid.

There are some additional usages to note:

1 In certain time expressions, such as when English says 'it is / was the first / last time that ...', or when we say that something 'has / had been the case for' a period of time. Notice the difference in tense usage between Spanish and English:

Era la primera vez que hablaba con ella.	It was the first time I had spoken to her.
Vivía en ese piso desde hacía dos meses.	I had been living in that flat for two months.
Hacía mucho tiempo que trabajaba en la oficina.	I had been working in the office for a long time.

2 As a mark of courtesy when making an enquiry or asking for something. In this sense, it is used in place of the conditional tense. English can sometimes do a similar thing, in usages like 'I was looking for', 'I was hoping to', 'I was after', 'I wanted a word with', etc.:

Buscaba al señor Jiménez. ¿Está aquí hoy?	I was looking for Mr Jiménez. Is he here today?
Queríamos hablar con el encargado.	We'd like / we were wanting to speak to the person in change.

3 In informal speech, the imperfect is sometimes heard as a replacement for the conditional tense. This usage is not advisable for written Spanish:

Me prometiste que me lo dabas [imperfect] / que me lo darías [conditional].	You promised me that you would give me it.
Si pudiera, lo hacía [imperfect] / lo haría [conditional].	I would do it if I could.

Regular forms

The -ar conjugation has its own set of endings, of which only the *nosotros* form has an accent. The -er and -ir conjugations share a second set of endings, this time with six accents. Notice that the first and third persons share an ending in all cases. The context should make it clear who or what is the subject of the verb but if not, a subject pronoun can be added or the noun repeated:

Infin.	Meaning	yo	tú, vos	él, ella, usted	nosotros/as	vosotros/as	ellos/as, ustedes
hablar	to speak	hablaba	hablabas	hablaba	hablábamos	hablabais	hablaban
comer	to eat	comía	comías	comía	comíamos	comíais	comían
vivir	to live	vivía	vivías	vivía	vivíamos	vivíais	vivían

Irregular forms

There are only three commonly encountered irregular verbs in the imperfect tense in Spanish:

Infin.	Meaning	yo	tú, vos	él, ella, usted	nosotros/as	vosotros/as	ellos/as, ustedes
ir	to go	iba	ibas	iba	íbamos	ibais	iban
ser	to be	era	eras	era	éramos	erais	eran
ver	to see	veía	veías	veía	veíamos	veíais	veían

The perfect tense

Equating to the tense used in English to say 'I have eaten', but much wider in its scope the perfect tense in Spanish is used in the circumstances described below. A good rule to remember before we start, though, is that whenever English uses the perfect tense, Spanish does too. The reverse, unfortunately, is not always true. Here are some notes on its formation and usage:

1   The tense is formed with the present tense of *haber* + the past participle (e.g. *hemos terminado* – 'we have finished'). No pronoun, adverb or other word may be inserted between the part of *haber* and the past participle – in other words, they are inseparable. Within this formation, the past participle must remain in the masculine singular form, irrespective of the number and gender of the subject, whether or not the verb is reflexive, and whether or not there is a preceding direct object. Students of French and / or Italian will need to pay close attention to the Spanish form in the light of some or all of these factors:

    | *Han desayunado.* | They have had breakfast. |
    | *La hemos visto.* | We've seen her. |
    | *Mis hermanas ya se han levantado.* | My sisters have already got up. |

UNIT 11 · INDICATIVE VERB TENSES

2   Occasionally, you may come across a usage where *tener* is used instead of *haber*, to give the idea that someone has 'got something done', rather than just 'done' it. (Students of Portuguese should note that this is not the default formation of the perfect tense in Spanish.) In this case, the past participle does agree with the direct object in number and gender:

Las tareas ya las tengo hechas.	I've already got the tasks done.

3   With regard to usage, as has already been mentioned, the perfect is used in Spanish whenever it is used in English. In practice, this involves contexts of the following types:

An action completed recently that has relevance to the present:

He hecho la compra.	I've done the shopping.
Han abierto una nueva tienda en esta calle.	They've opened a new shop on this street.

An action completed further back but with a clear link to the present, often with the helpful inclusion of 'this...', 'always', 'never', etc.:

Te he querido siempre.	I've always loved you.
Lo han hecho esta semana.	They've done it this week.
He tenido dos infartos este mes / este siglo.	I've had two heart attacks this month / this century.

A reference to something that 'has happened' in history or in our lives so far:

Ha habido tres cambios de gobierno.	There have been three changes of government.
He estado dos veces en Estados Unidos.	I've been to the USA twice.
Se ha casado ocho veces.	S/he has been married eight times.

4   When talking about completed actions that we 'did' today, English generally prefers the simple past ('I woke up at eight o'clock this morning', 'I saw her five minutes ago'), whereas European Spanish tends to express such actions using the perfect tense if the speaker 'feels' that the action is close to, and connected with, the present:

Me he despertado muy pronto esta mañana.	I woke up very early this morning.
La he visto hace treinta minutos / segundos.	I saw her thirty minutes / seconds ago.

It's important to point out, however, that most Latin American countries, plus various areas of northern Spain (especially Galicia and Asturias), work like English, preferring to use the preterite in this circumstance. As such, it is a commonplace and by no means incorrect usage. It is recommended that students of Spanish be aware of the subtleties of this point, and use a tense to suit their surroundings.

La vi / la he visto hace treinta minutos.	I saw her thirty minutes ago.

5   The perfect tense is not generally used in Spanish to talk about single actions completed, e.g. 'yesterday', 'on Monday', 'last week', 'three years ago', 'in 2003'. French, Italian and German do use the perfect tense for this structure, but in Spanish we must be careful before saying something like *La hemos visto ayer / la semana pasada*, etc., a usage limited to the nuance of 'it was only yesterday (etc.) that we saw her'. A good rule to follow is that, if the period of time is over, it's safer for foreign learners to use the preterite (*La vimos ayer*, etc.).

Regular forms

The present tense of *haber* (*he, has, ha, hemos, habéis, han*) is used as the auxiliary, and is followed by the past participle (*hablado, comido, vivido*) to complete the form:

Han cenado.	They have had dinner.
Las hemos comido.	We have eaten them.
¿Has subido alguna vez al tejado?	Have you ever been up on the roof?

Irregular past participles

There are not too many irregular past participles in common use in Spanish. The main ones are shown below. Some of them have compounds using the same format (e.g. *poner > puesto; suponer > supuesto / cubrir > cubierto; descubrir > descubierto*):

Infinitive	Meaning	Past participle
abrir	to open	*abierto*
cubrir	to cover	*cubierto*
decir	to say, tell	*dicho*
escribir	to write	*escrito*
freír	to fry	*frito*
hacer	to do, make	*hecho*
imprimir	to print	*impreso*
morir	to die	*muerto*
poner	to put	*puesto*
romper	to break	*roto*
ver	to see	*visto*
volver	to return	*vuelto*

The preterite

The preterite (sometimes referred to as the 'simple past', 'past simple' or – perhaps unhelpfully – the 'past historic' in English), has the following main uses in Spanish:

1 To express single completed actions that happened yesterday or earlier (or – in the case of Latin America and northern Spain – earlier today):

Fuimos al supermercado a comprar leche.	We went to the supermarket to buy some milk.
Mi madre murió hace diez años.	My mother died ten years ago.
¿Dónde has estado? / ¿Dónde estuviste?	Where have you been?

UNIT 11 INDICATIVE VERB TENSES

2 In verbs of 'wanting', Spanish can use either the preterite or the imperfect, depending on the nuances of time-frames:

No quería ir con ellos.   He didn't want to go with them. [They hadn't gone yet]

No quiso ir con ellos.   He didn't want to go with them. [They had already gone, and the period of time and action had finished]

⇨ For more work on subtleties of this type, see Unit 18

3 For actions or states that happened or were the case for a defined period of time. In this circumstance, some confusion with the imperfect (one of whose roles is to describe something that happened over a period of time) is understandable, especially in usages relating to periods in a person's life. It's sometimes helpful to consider preterite use here as being correct for referring to such periods as 'chapters' (which opened and closed):

La Primera Guerra Mundial duró cuatro años.   The First World War lasted (for) four years.
En los años 80 vivieron en Nueva York.   In [throughout] the 80s they lived in New York.
La reunión fue todo un éxito.   The meeting was a complete success.

Regular forms

These are the formations of regular verbs. The *-ar* conjugation has its own endings; *-er* and *-ir* share a separate set. Persons 1 and 3 in all regular verbs have an accent (omission of which can cause confusion, in some cases, with other tenses), and care must be taken to ensure that the correct final vowel is used (especially among students of Italian). Don't be tempted to put an accent on the *vosotros* form:

Infin.	Meaning	yo	tú, vos	él, ella, usted	nosotros/as	vosotros/as	ellos/as, ustedes
hablar	to speak	hablé	hablaste	habló	hablamos	hablasteis	hablaron
comer	to eat	comí	comiste	comió	comimos	comisteis	comieron
vivir	to live	viví	viviste	vivió	vivimos	vivisteis	vivieron

Special forms

Verbs ending in *-car*, *-gar* and *-zar* undergo a spelling change in the first person singular (and that person only) of the preterite. From the second person onwards, the spelling reverts to the 'regular' form. These changes happen in order to preserve a hard sound in *-car* and *-gar*, and, in the case of *-zar*, because of the language's preference not to use the *-ze-* combination:

Infin.	Meaning	yo	tú, vos
buscar	to look for	busqué	buscaste
pagar	to pay (for)	pagué	pagaste
organizar	to organise	organicé	organizaste

Some verbs – the most common of which are *caer* ('to fall'), *creer* ('to believe / think'), *leer* ('to read') *oír* ('to hear') – have a -y- in the third persons singular and plural, and an accent on the first five forms. *Construir* also has the -y-, but accents only on persons 1 and 3:

Infin.	Meaning	yo	tú, vos	él, ella, usted	nosotros/as	vosotros/as	ellos/as, ustedes
caer	to fall	caí	caíste	cayó	caímos	caísteis	cayeron
creer	to believe, think	creí	creíste	creyó	creímos	creísteis	creyeron
leer	to read	leí	leíste	leyó	leímos	leísteis	leyeron
oír	to hear	oí	oíste	oyó	oímos	oísteis	oyeron
construir	to build	construí	construiste	construyó	construimos	construisteis	construyeron

A small number of verbs ending in *-ñir*, *-ñer* and *-llir* lose the *-i-* of the endings of the third persons singular and plural (e.g. in *gruñir* – 'to grunt' – *gruñió* and *gruñieron* become *gruñó* and *gruñeron*).

Radical-changing forms

Of all the radical-changing styles we studied in our section on the present tense, only those affecting verbs ending in *-ir* occur in the preterite tense. Note that this time, the persons affected are the third singular and third plural, and the nature of the change sometimes differs from that visible in the present tense:

Style in present	Style in preterite	Infin.	Meaning	yo	tú, vos	él, ella, usted	nosotros/as	vosotros/as	ellos/as, ustedes
e > ie	e > i	mentir	to lie (tell lies)	mentí	mentiste	mintió	mentimos	mentisteis	mintieron
e > i	e > i	pedir	to ask for	pedí	pediste	pidió	pedimos	pedisteis	pidieron
o > ue	o > u	dormir	to sleep	dormí	dormiste	durmió	dormimos	dormisteis	durmieron

Irregular forms

The following verbs are irregular in the preterite. A mastery of them (in addition to the regular, radical-changing and 'special forms', above) is particularly important because of the preterite's role in forming the imperfect subjunctive, which is covered in the units on the Subjunctive. Notice the tendency for fully irregular verbs not to have any accents in the preterite. Other potential areas of difficulty are a confusion of the forms of *dar/ decir* and *poder/ poner*, the issue of the *-z-* in *hizo*, the *-j-* in the forms of *traer* and *conducir* (and other verbs following their patterns), and the fact that some third person plurals end in *-eron* and others in *-ieron*. Close attention must be paid to all of these issues:

Infin.	Meaning	yo	tú, vos	él, ella, usted	nosotros/as	vosotros/as	ellos/as, ustedes
andar	to walk	anduve	anduviste	anduvo	anduvimos	anduvisteis	anduvieron
caber	to fit	cupe	cupiste	cupo	cupimos	cupisteis	cupieron
conducir	to drive	conduje	condujiste	condujo	condujimos	condujisteis	condujeron

UNIT 11 — INDICATIVE VERB TENSES

dar	to give	di	diste	dio	dimos	disteis	dieron
decir	to say, tell	dije	dijiste	dijo	dijimos	dijisteis	dijeron
estar	to be	estuve	estuviste	estuvo	estuvimos	estuvisteis	estuvieron
haber	'there was / were'			hubo			hubo
hacer	to do, make	hice	hiciste	hizo	hicimos	hicisteis	hicieron
ir	to go	fui	fuiste	fue	fuimos	fuisteis	fueron
poder	to be able	pude	pudiste	pudo	pudimos	pudisteis	pudieron
poner	to put	puse	pusiste	puso	pusimos	pusisteis	pusieron
querer	to want, love	quise	quisiste	quiso	quisimos	quisisteis	quisieron
saber	to know	supe	supiste	supo	supimos	supisteis	supieron
ser	to be	fui	fuiste	fue	fuimos	fuisteis	fueron
tener	to have	tuve	tuviste	tuvo	tuvimos	tuvisteis	tuvieron
traer	to bring	traje	trajiste	trajo	trajimos	trajisteis	trajeron
venir	to come	vine	viniste	vino	vinimos	vinisteis	vinieron
ver	to see	vi	viste	vio	vimos	visteis	vieron

Combinations of past tenses

It is quite possible for combinations of past tenses to work together in a sentence. In the table below, you will see examples of repetition and contrast, with indications of when the actions took place. The classic example for students to master is that of a preterite 'interrupting' an ongoing action described by an imperfect (of the type: 'while we were talking [imperfect] a bomb went off [preterite]'), but it's a good idea to study all the styles below, if only for reassurance:

Tenses used	Spanish example	English
Imperfect + imperfect	Mientras ella veía la televisión, yo planchaba las camisas.	While she was watching TV, I was ironing the shirts.
Perfect + imperfect	Ha salido hace una hora cuando yo hablaba por teléfono.	S/he left an hour ago when / while I was on the phone.
Imperfect + preterite	Cuando hablábamos anoche, estalló una bomba.	When / while we were talking last night, a bomb went off.
Perfect + perfect	Yo he preparado la paella y ella ha hecho la tortilla.	I (have) prepared the paella and she (has) made the omelette.
Perfect + preterite	Hoy lo has hecho bien, pero ayer lo hiciste muy mal.	Today you've done it well, but yesterday you did it very badly.
Preterite + preterite	Miguel ganó la carrera y Juan acabó tercero.	Miguel won the race and Juan finished third.

INDICATIVE VERB TENSES   UNIT 11

The pluperfect tense

The pluperfect (also known as the 'past perfect') tense coincides in usage in both languages in expressing actions that 'had happened' or 'had been the case' at or by a reference point in the past. It is formed by the imperfect tense of *haber* + the past participle.

⇨ For a list of irregular past participles, see the section on 'The perfect tense'

Esa luz la había encendido yo.	I had switched that light on.
Habías optado por no ir, ¿verdad?	You had chosen not to go, hadn't you?
Mi hermana ya había arrancado el coche.	My sister had already started the car up.
Habíamos bebido demasiado.	We had drunk too much.
Ya nos habíais comentado cuál era el problema.	You had already told us what the problem was.
No habían llegado a tiempo.	They hadn't arrived on time.

The conditional tense

This tense is recognisable in English as denoting what 'would happen' or 'would be the case' in certain circumstances. In Spanish it fulfils this role too:

Yo que tú, lo compraría.	If I were you, I would buy it.
Me gustaría tomar un café.	I would like ('it would please me') to have a coffee.
Sería una locura intentarlo.	It would be crazy to try.
Me dijeron que vendrían.	They told me they would come.

⇨ For full coverage of conditional sentences – 'if' clauses + another (main) clause – see Unit 16

Some extra usages

1 To make suppositions about events or experiences in the past – the English 'would have been' or 'must have been' sometimes equates to this usage:

Serían las ocho y media.	It must / would have been about half past eight.
Tendría unos diez años.	S/he must / would have been about ten years old.

2 With *poder*, it can be used to make suggestions:

Podríamos ir a la playa.	We could go to the beach.

3 With *deber*, it can be used to offer advice:

Deberías tener cuidado.	You ought to / should be careful.

UNIT 11 — INDICATIVE VERB TENSES

Regular forms

The conditional tense is formed by adding the *-er* / *-ir* imperfect endings to the infinitive of the verb, regardless of whether it is *-ar*, *-er* or *-ir*. Here are some examples:

hablaría	I would speak
empezarías	you would start
comería	he / she / you [*usted*] would eat
beberíamos	we would drink
decidiríais	you would decide
pedirían	they / you [*ustedes*] would ask for

Irregular forms

If a verb is irregular in the future tense, it is also irregular in the conditional, and the two tenses share an irregular stem for any such verb.

⇨ *A full list of irregular stems for the future tense can be found in 'Using the single-word future tense'*

Once we've got the irregular stem, the regular endings are used. Here are some examples of formation:

Infinitive	Future	Conditional
decir	diré	diría
hacer	haré	haría
haber [hay]	habrá	habría
querer	querré	querría
tener	tendré	tendría
venir	vendré	vendría

Here are some examples of usage:

Siempre te diría la verdad.	I would always tell you the truth.
Sé que lo harías por mí.	I know (that) you would do it for me.
En ese caso habría un problema.	In that case there would be a problem.
Querríamos leer los documentos.	We would like to read the documents.
Tendríais varias opciones.	You would have several options.
Dijeron que vendrían más tarde.	They said they would come later on.

The conditional of *querer* (*querría*) is sometimes replaced by the imperfect subjunctive *quisiera*, which fulfils the role of the conditional but lends it a slightly more formal air.

The future perfect tense

This tense equates to the English 'I will have eaten' (often with the detail of 'by' a particular point in time or deadline), and the Spanish form works very similarly, though it does have the additional nuance of supposition or perplexity:

Lo habré terminado para el lunes.	I will have finished it by Monday.
¿Por qué lo habrá dicho?	Why on earth did s/he say it?

Formation

The future perfect is formed by the future tense of *haber* + the past participle (with irregular forms of the latter borne in mind):

Habré visto doscientas películas.	I must have / will have seen two hundred films.
Habrás oído la noticia, ¿no?	You must have / will have heard the news, I imagine?
La póliza ya habrá vencido.	The policy will have matured by now.
Te lo habremos dicho diez veces.	We will / must have told you ten times.
Habréis cumplido con todos los criterios.	You will have fulfilled all the criteria.
Todos habrán recibido esta beca.	They will all have received this grant.

The conditional perfect tense

While the future perfect expresses 'will have done', the conditional perfect denotes 'would have done'. The general reference is to what somebody would have done if circumstances had been different. Again, there is a usage expressing a note of supposition or perplexity:

En esas circunstancias, yo habría hecho lo mismo.	In those circumstances, I would have done the same thing.
¿Lo habrían descubierto antes de la reunión?	Would / might they have discovered it before the meeting, I wonder?

Formation

To form this tense, we use the conditional tense of *haber* + the past participle:

Habría cobrado una cantidad parecida.	I would have charged a similar amount.
Habrías escrito más novelas.	You would have written more novels.
Mi hermana habría salido con él.	My sister would have gone out with him.
Habríamos abierto las ventanas.	We would have opened the windows.
Sin su ayuda, lo habríais pasado mal.	Without their help, you would have had a bad time.
Sin estas pastillas, habrían muerto antes.	Without these tablets, they would have died sooner.

PRACTICE

1   Translate the following sentences into Spanish:

1. They play cards, close the doors and sleep.
   ....

2. I know that you want to help me.
   ....

3. I'm a student – I go out on Fridays.
   ....

4. They're at the station – shall I send them a message?
   ....

5. We'll want to see her before going out.
   ....

6. Will I be able to swim in that pool?
   ....

7. They'll come here and then they'll go out.
   ....

8. It must be eight o'clock.
   ....

9. There will be a series of meetings.
   ....

10. I'm going to watch TV until ten o'clock.
    ....

2   Insert the correct form of either the imperfect or the preterite in each of the gaps below:

1. Ayer [ir, yo]......................al médico porque [tener, yo]......................el brazo hinchado.

2. Cuando [ser, yo].........................pequeña, el sol [brillar].........................todos los días.

PRACTICE

3 [Ver, ella].....................la tele cuando [haber].....................una explosión en la calle.

4 [Ser, ella].....................reina durante sesenta años hasta que [morir, ella].....................

5 [Pagar, yo].....................la cuenta cuando [estar, tú].....................en el servicio.

6 Mi primo [dormir].....................anoche en el jardín porque no [hacer]

.....................frío.

7 ¿Y por qué no se lo [decir, tú].....................al jefe cuando le [dar, tú]

.....................el regalo?

8 Mientras ella me [esperar]....................., [oír, ella].....................un ruido muy raro.

9 [Organizar, yo].....................una fiesta para mi amigo porque [querer, él]

.....................celebrar algo.

10 Cuando [terminar].....................el concierto, Laura [salir].....................a la calle.

3 Translate the following into Spanish. In some cases, there may be more than one solution:

1 It's the first time I've seen you.

....

2 I've been studying here for two years.

....

3 We'd been working here for a week.

....

4 I'd like to see more information, please.

....

5 If were you, I'd come at eleven o'clock.

....

PRACTICE

4   Translate the following sentences into Spanish:

1   She's written a letter to her mother and has told her the truth.

    ....

2   I've fried the onions and put them on a plate.

    ....

3   We've seen that you've broken the window.

    ....

4   Since you've returned, three people have died.

    ....

5   I've made the beds and printed the documents.

    ....

5   Using the verb *tener*, provide translations to reflect each of the tenses we have covered in this unit:

1   I have two sisters.

    ....

2   I am going to have two computers at home.

    ....

3   I will have problems.

    ....

4   I used to have a red car.

    ....

5   I have had moments of difficulty.

    ....

6   I had an accident.

    ....

UNIT 12

Other types of verb: continuous forms, the gerund, the infinitive, the past participle, reflexive verbs and *se*

All these types of verb will be covered in this unit. We'll look closely at how their usage differs from that of equivalent structures in English.

Continuous forms

In the previous unit, we looked at non-continuous indicative forms (e.g. 'I swim', 'I swam'), and made the point that in Spanish, these can cover the English-language notions of 'I am swimming' and 'I was swimming' – known as continuous forms because they emphasise the ongoing nature of the action. However, Spanish does have its own genuinely continuous forms, which we'll focus on now.

Formation

The continuous forms use the relevant tense of *estar* + the gerund (which in English is the '-ing' form of a verb). The gerund is formed by adding *-ando* (for *-ar* verbs) and *-iendo* (for both *-er* and *-ir* verbs) to the stem: *hablando, comiendo, viviendo*. There are a number of irregular gerunds, most of whose irregularities are allied to their parent verbs' radical changes. Here are the main ones:

Infinitive	Meaning	Gerund
caer	to fall	cayendo
construir	to build	construyendo
creer	to believe, think	creyendo
decir	to say, tell	diciendo
dormir	to sleep	durmiendo
freír	to fry	friendo
ir	to go	yendo
leer	to read	leyendo
morir	to die	muriendo
oír	to hear	oyendo
pedir	to ask for	pidiendo
poder	to be able	pudiendo
reír	to laugh	riendo
seguir	to follow, continue	siguiendo
sentir	to feel	sintiendo

UNIT 12   OTHER TYPES OF VERB

traer	to bring	*trayendo*
venir	to come	*viniendo*

Now let's see how the main continuous tenses look. The first example gives an illustration of the positioning of any associated object pronouns – notice that the first example requires an accent to maintain the stress on the correct syllable:

Tense	Formation	Example	English
Present continuous	Present of *estar* + gerund	*Estoy comentándolo con mi madre. / Lo estoy comentando con mi madre.*	I'm discussing it with my mother.
Future continuous	Future of *estar* + gerund	*A las diez y cuarto estaré cantando en la catedral.*	At 10.15 I will be singing in the cathedral.
	Present of *ir* + *a* + infinitive of *estar* + gerund	*A las diez y cuarto voy a estar cantando en la catedral.*	At 10.15 I'm going to be singing in the cathedral.
Preterite continuous	Preterite of *estar* + gerund	*Estuve dos horas cenando.*	I was having dinner for two hours.
Imperfect continuous	Imperfect of *estar* + gerund	*Estaba barriendo el suelo cuando llegaste.*	I was sweeping the floor when you arrived.
Perfect continuous	Perfect of *estar* + gerund	*He estado leyendo ese libro.*	I've been reading that book.
Pluperfect continuous	Pluperfect of *estar* + gerund	*Había estado preparando la comida.*	I had been preparing the meal.
Conditional continuous	Conditional of *estar* + gerund	*A esa hora estaría trabajando.*	At that time of day I would be working.
Future perfect continuous	Future perfect of *estar* + gerund	*Supongo que habrá estado escribiendo su novela todos estos meses.*	I guess he'll have been writing his novel all these months.
Conditional perfect continuous	Conditional perfect of *estar* + gerund	*El sospechoso lo habría estado planeando.*	The suspect would have been planning it.

Notes on usage

In each of the examples above, the idea is that the action is elongated and 'actually happening' at the time – emphasis is given to its ongoing nature, in contrast to the more specific timeframe of the non-continuous forms. It is generally considered that the imperfect tense and the imperfect continuous can often be interchangeable when referring to an event that 'was happening' at a point

OTHER TYPES OF VERB — UNIT 12

in time (*barría el suelo*, *estaba barriendo el suelo*), but in other tenses there is frequently a clear difference in meaning between the two forms:

Cantaré a las diez.	I will sing at ten o'clock [that's when my scheduled slot begins].
A las diez estaré cantando.	At ten o'clock I will be singing [presumably having already begun the recital some minutes or hours earlier].
He leído el libro.	I've read the book [i.e. finished it].
He estado leyendo el libro.	I've been reading the book [but might not have finished it, or might have just dipped in].

It's important to stress that although the English 'I am singing' and the Spanish *estoy cantando* are superficially very similar, there are some important differences:

1 Whereas 'they drink' and 'they are drinking' are different concepts in English, the Spanish *beben* can cover both. The continuous *están bebiendo* is available if you want to stress that they are actually drinking at the moment.

2 English uses the present continuous to express actions or events planned for the future, but Spanish cannot. Compare:

Se casan en junio.	They're getting married in June.
Llegan el jueves.	They're arriving on Thursday.

3 English happily uses the gerunds 'coming' and 'going', but the Spanish *viniendo* and *yendo* are less commonly found in this particular use. Notice also the reversal of verbs in the final example – when in English we say 'I'm coming' in response to being beckoned, Spanish uses *ir*:

Vienen por el camino. / Vienen pasado mañana.	They're coming along the path / They're coming the day after tomorrow.
Voy al cine. / ¡Ya voy!	I'm going to the cinema. / I'm coming!

4 Spanish does not use the continuous form to describe states or conditions, such as 'wearing' clothes or a posture, for example, or 'sitting down' (already being seated):

Lleva chaqueta.	S/he's wearing a jacket.
Estaba sentada.	She was sitting down.

The gerund – further usages

Aside from its main usage with *estar*, the gerund can feature with verbs like *ir* and *venir* to suggest an action proceeding gradually or slowly:

Iba anocheciendo.	It was gradually getting dark.
Venimos diciéndote la misma cosa.	We've been telling you the same thing over and over again.

UNIT 12 — OTHER TYPES OF VERB

As an alternative to the ways given in the previous unit to express that (e.g.) 'I have / had been living there for two years', the appropriate tense of *llevar* + the gerund can be used:

Hace dos meses que estudio aquí.	I've been studying here for two months.
Estudio aquí desde hace dos meses.	
Llevo dos meses estudiando aquí.	
Hacía tres semanas que vivía allí.	I had been living there for three weeks.
Vivía allí desde hacía tres semanas.	
Llevaba tres semanas viviendo allí.	

To convey the notion of 'still doing something', or to 'continue / go on doing something', Spanish can also use either *continuar* or *seguir* + the gerund:

¿Sigues fumando?	Do you still smoke? / Are you still smoking?
Continuó caminando.	S/he carried on walking.
Siguen estudiando todos los días.	They still study every day.
Continuaré haciéndolo hasta diciembre.	I'll carry on doing it until December.

Pasar + the gerund translates the idea of 'spending time doing something':

Pasamos la tarde charlando con ella.	We spent the afternoon chatting with her.
Pasé tres horas intentando solucionarlo.	I spent three hours trying to solve it.

With verbs of motion such as *ir*, *salir* and *entrar*, the gerund can be used to describe how an action happens. The literal translation of the first example below would be 'we went out running', more smoothly expressed as 'we ran out':

Salimos corriendo.	We ran out.
Entraron dando brincos.	They skipped in.
Iba cojeando.	S/he was limping along.

The Spanish gerund has a strong usage to express the English 'by doing':

Estudiando mucho aprobarás los exámenes.	You'll pass your exams by studying hard.
Hicieron sus millones vendiendo casas.	They made their millions by selling houses.

With verbs of perception (especially *ver* – 'to see'), Spanish can use either an infinitive or a gerund to describe the action perfomed by the object. Have a close look at these sentences and the accompanying notes:

Le vimos jugar al balonmano.	We saw him play handball [the whole match; his action was completed].
Le vimos jugando al balonmano.	We saw him playing handball [e.g. caught a glimpse of a game in progress; his action was ongoing].

OTHER TYPES OF VERB UNIT 12

English '-ing' but Spanish infinitive

This is a tricky area for English-speakers learning Spanish. It occurs in cases such as the following:

1   When the English '-ing' is the subject of a verb:

    Fumar es malo para la salud.   Smoking is bad for the health.
    Conducir no es fácil.   Driving isn't easy.

2   When the English '-ing' is the object of a verb – the following structure only works when the same subject does both actions (if two different subjects are involved, the subjunctive is required):

    Me gusta leer.   I like reading.
    Odiamos levantarnos pronto.   We hate getting up early.

3   When the English '-ing' comes after a preposition:

    Tenemos ganas de verla.   We're looking forward to seeing her.
    Lo consiguieron sin mover un dedo.   They managed it without lifting a finger.
    Le detuvieron por romper una ventana. He was arrested for breaking a window.
    Se fueron después de saludarnos.   They left after greeting us.

    ⇨ See also next section

The infinitive

We have already considered some of the uses of the Spanish infinitive: those equating to the English '-ing'.

Its main point of use, aside from being the basic 'dictionary' form of the verb, is to convey the English infinitive (e.g.) 'to eat'. Sometimes, it appears following another verb, without an interposed preposition – the verbs *querer*, *deber*, *poder*, *saber*, *dejar* and *hacer* are common examples of this:

   ⇨ See Unit 18 for further coverage

Quiero ir al parque.   I want to go to the park.
Deberías escucharle bien.   You should listen to him carefully.
¿Puedo ayudarle?   Can I help you?
No saben nadar.   They can't (don't know how to) swim.
¿Me dejáis abrir el regalo?   Will you let me open the present?
Nos hicieron sufrir.   They made us suffer.

UNIT 12   OTHER TYPES OF VERB

Other preceding verbs require a preposition before the infinitive, such as *a*, *de*, *con* or *por*. Lists of these verbs can be found in the relevant sections of the unit on Prepositions:

Aprendimos a bailar.	We learned to dance
Acabo de darme cuenta.	I've just realised.
Amenazan con quitarme la beca.	They're threatening to take my grant away.
Lucho por mantener mis derechos.	I'm struggling to maintain my rights.

The infinitive after an adjective or noun in combination with a preposition

This refers to examples such as the following, which feature the infinitive in Spanish – notice, once again, the English '-ing' in contrast:

Estaban hartos de vivir en esa ciudad.	They were sick of living in that city.
una máquina para juntar las piezas	a machine for joining the pieces together
una caja sin abrir	an unopened box

I want to do it / I want you to do it

This is a situation in which Spanish can differ radically from its English counterpart. Here is how it works in Spanish:

1   'I want to do it'

   Here, both verbs ('want' and 'do') are performed by the same subject, so the required structure is a straightforward infinitive, as in English:

   Quiero hacerlo.   I want to do it.

2   'I want you to do it'

   Here, the 'wanting' and the 'doing' are performed by two different people, i.e. there has been a change of subject. As such, Spanish no longer allows the infinitive construction, but now needs to alter the syntax, inserting *que* and bringing in the subjunctive:

   Quiero que lo hagas.   I want you to do it. [lit: 'I want that you do it']

   ⇨ *This concept is covered in more detail in Unit 14.*

al + infinitive

The neat and useful structure *al* + infinitive means the same as the English 'on doing' something, but English often finds a different way of expressing it:

Me caí al cruzar la calle.	I fell when / while I was crossing the street / on my way across the street ('on crossing the street').

The infinitive as a noun – further examples

More or less any Spanish infinitive can act as a noun, often equating to the English '-ing' form (*fumar* – 'smoking'). Such nouns are considered masculine, and they are sometimes used with a definite article:

Trocear la carne no me cuesta nada.	Chopping the meat up isn't a great hardship for me.
Miraba el ir y venir de la gente.	I was watching the people going to and fro.
con el pasar de los años	with the passing of the years

The infinitive used as an imperative

This phenomenon is found in various circumstances in Spanish:

1. It is a familiar alternative to the *vosotros* command (*hablad*, etc.), used mainly in the spoken Spanish of Spain:

   ¡Comer, que se os enfría la carne!   Eat up – your meat will be getting cold!

   ⇨ See Unit 15 on the Imperative for full coverage

2. More commonly, it is used to give instructions to the general public, either in public notices or in places like cookery books or technical manuals:

Respetar las plantas.	Please respect the plants.
No tocar.	Don't touch.
Cortar la cebolla y freírla a fuego lento.	Chop the onion and fry it on a low heat.

The past participle

Its basic use is to form compound tenses such as the perfect (*he hablado*) and the pluperfect (*había hablado*). There are, however, more roles it can perform.

⇨ *The use of the past participle with **ser** in the passive voice, and with **estar** to denote resultant states, is studied closely in Unit 19 on the Passive.*

As an adjective

Aside from the usages noted above, the Spanish past participle works commonly as an adjective, agreeing in number and gender with the noun it is describing:

una ventana rota	a broken window
con la cara cortada	with a cut face

As a noun

Closely allied to the adjectival usage, is that of the past participle functioning as a noun. With the addition of an article, demonstrative or possessive adjective, the adjective becomes a noun, often producing a far neater clause than the English equivalent:

El decano felicitó a todos los aprobados. The dean congratulated all those who had passed.

La detenida pidió la ayuda de un abogado. The arrested woman asked for the help of a lawyer.

Reflexive verbs and *se*

A quick reminder that reflexive verbs are actions that one does to oneself, such as getting up, showering, getting dressed, sitting down and going to bed. The reflexive format (in particular the pronoun *se*) has other uses, not all of which are strictly 'reflexive', which we'll explore at the end of the unit.

Formation

A reflexive verb is conjugated in the same way as a non-reflexive one, but a particular pronoun is added to each person to denote 'myself', 'ourselves', etc. These reflexive pronouns are valid across all tenses. Here is the basic formation, using the present tense of *lavarse* ('to wash oneself', 'to get washed') as the model:

yo	tú	vos	él, ella, usted	nosotros/as	vosotros/as	ellos/as, ustedes
me lavo	te lavas	te lavás	se lava	nos lavamos	os laváis	se lavan

With actions done to parts of the body or items of clothing, Spanish prefers to say things like *se secan el pelo* ('they dry themselves the hair' = 'they dry their hair') rather than using the possessive adjective, as English would.

Position of reflexive pronouns

1. In normal, finite usage, the pronoun goes before the verb:

   Mi primo se ducha. My cousin has a shower.

2. When a gerund is used and it doesn't follow another verb, the pronoun must go on the end of the gerund. Note the requirement for an accent, to keep the stress on the correct syllable:

   Cuidándote mucho, vivirás muchos años. By looking after yourself, you'll live a long time.

3. When a gerund is used and it follows another verb, the pronoun can go either on the end of the gerund, or before the preceding verb:

   Están vistiéndose. / Se están vistiendo. They're getting dressed.

OTHER TYPES OF VERB — UNIT 12

4   The same is true of infinitives, which follow the patterns outlined in points 2 and 3:

   Es importante acostarse temprano.   It's important to get to bed early
   Me voy a acostar. / Voy a acostarme.   I'm going to bed.

Some uses

Alongside the standard 'action done to oneself' usage, there are several other key uses of *se*:

1   *Se* as a passive substitute:

   In passive structures, English prefers to use a conventional passive – 'to be' + past participle – whereas Spanish employs a range of other devices to convey the same meaning. This is one of them. Notice that the verb matches the noun in number:

   El italiano se habla en Italia.   Italian is spoken in Italy.
   Se venden manzanas en este puesto.   Apples are sold at this stall.
   Se conocen varios casos de esta enfermedad.   Several cases of this illness are known.
   Este modelo se puso a la venta en 2010.   This model was put on sale in 2010.
   Las puertas se cierran a las ocho   The doors close (get closed) at eight o'clock.

   ➪ See Unit 19 on the Passive for fuller coverage

2   In reciprocal usages (where in English we might say 'each other'), the form moves away from the strictly reflexive ('they dress themselves' – i.e. each person dresses himself or herself) and expresses a form of mutual action ('they dress each other'):

   Evidentemente se quieren mucho.   They clearly love each other a great deal.
   Nos escribimos cada mes.   We write to each other every month.

3   The impersonal usage, traditionally expressed in English by the formal 'one' or the less formal 'you':

   Se puede jugar aquí.   One / you / people can play here.
   Eso no se dice.   That isn't said (You shouldn't say that).

4   The so-called 'accidental *se*', where an apparently reflexive action happens, to the detriment of a 'victim'. It's not as grim as it sounds. Essentially, Spanish builds a construction which translates as (for example) 'the keys have lost themselves to me', to express 'I've lost my keys'. Here are some examples:

   Se me han perdido las llaves.   I've lost my keys.
   Se te cayó la botella.   You dropped the bottle.
   Se nos había roto el sillón.   Our armchair had broken.

5   There is a quirky usage of the reflexive to suggest that one has done or consumed something in its entirety, or in a notable quantity. In most cases, the expression would work without the reflexive pronoun, but its inclusion adds a nice touch of emphasis:

   Me he comido dos pasteles enteros.   I've eaten two whole cakes.
   Nos hemos leído las obras completas de Cervantes.   We've read the complete works of Cervantes.
   Se ha bebido tres botellas de ginebra.   S/he's drunk three bottles of gin.

PRACTICE

1 Write the following sentences in Spanish, using a continuous verb form each time:

1 I'm reading it at this moment.

....

2 They're watching TV.

....

3 We're building a garage.

....

4 At this time tomorrow Miguel will be arriving in Madrid.

....

5 We had been asking them for help.

....

6 Laura was sleeping.

....

7 You [vosotros] have been waiting for us.

....

8 In January I will have been travelling around Asia for more than a year.

....

9 You [tú] would have been telling the truth.

....

10 I'm going to be frying the onions.

....

2 Say each of the following in Spanish in three different ways:

1 You've been writing a novel for six months.

....

2 We had been living in that house for two years.

....

PRACTICE

3 **Re-express each of the following, incorporating the verb given in brackets and using one of the structures covered in this unit:**

1. Charlé con ella durante tres horas. [pasar]

   ....

2. Todavía fumo. [seguir]

   ....

3. Amanecía poco a poco. [ir]

   ....

4. Si estudias, aprobarás los exámenes. [estudiar]

   ....

5. Cuando la vimos, jugaba al golf. [jugar]

   ....

4 **Make corrections to the following sentences, where necessary:**

1. Me gusta leyendo.

   ....

2. Bebiendo agua es bueno para el hígado.

   ....

3. Salió antes de saludando a los asistentes.

   ....

4. Debes a hacerlo.

   ....

5. Me hiciste para reír.

   ....

PRACTICE

5 Translate the following into Spanish:

1. They hate each other.

   ....

2. Beer is sold in this bar.

   ....

3. My mobile has broken.

   ....

4. You can't go into this building.

   ....

5. We've polished off a litre of cognac.

   ....

UNIT 13 | The subjunctive – 1

This unit covers mainly the formation of the subjunctive, not its usage. For usage, see Unit 14.

Notes on the subjunctive

The Spanish subjunctive is, in simple terms, a set of tenses running parallel to the indicative collection, and used for different purposes. It is often portrayed as something of a 'nightmare' for foreign learners of Spanish, but it needn't be. Rather than worrying about reasons why it is used, it's more effective to focus on the series of 'triggers' or situations which bring it into play. We'll look at these in detail in the next unit. With practice, we can develop a 'feel' for when a subjunctive is required.

Format

It's perfectly possible, as we shall see, for a subjunctive form to exist on its own in a sentence, but in the 'classic' format, the sentence comprises two halves: one (the main clause) with an indicative verb, the other (the subordinate clause) containing a subjunctive. The 'trigger' in the middle is usually *que*, but it can sometimes be *cuando* or another subordinator like *para que* ('in order that'), *sin que* ('without'), *a menos que* ('unless'), *antes de que* ('before') or *después de que* ('after').

Same subject / different subjects

This is one of the key factors affecting whether to use a subjunctive. We'll discuss and illustrate it in detail later on, but for now, we just need to note the difference between, for instance, 'I hope to win' – where both verbs ('hope' and 'win') are performed by the same subject – and 'I hope (that) you win' (where different subjects govern each of the verbs). In the first sentence, Spanish uses an infinitive – E*spero ganar* – as does English (and even if the English were expressed 'I hope I win', the subject is still the same and Spanish would still use the infinitive). In the sentence with the change of subject, Spanish says *Espero que ganes*, with the trigger *que* ushering in the subjunctive. That's just one example, but we need to keep the concept clear in our minds as we progress through this unit and the next one.

A word on the infinitive

The role of the infinitive in the example above is all very well, but there is another use featuring commonly in English sentences, which has a bearing on the Spanish subjunctive. Again, it involves a change of subject, but this time the English contains an infinitive which must not be transferred to the Spanish.

UNIT 13   THE SUBJUNCTIVE – 1

Spanish	English	Notes
Quiero ganar.	I want to win.	Same subject for both verbs, hence straightforward infinitive.
Quiero que ganes.	I want you to win [literally: 'I want that you win']	Change of subject, so the English infinitive must be replaced by *que* + subjunctive.

In the above table, we see an example of a classic English formation, which will always need to be reworked in Spanish (not just with the verb 'to want', but with other verbs such as 'to like', 'to prefer' and 'to ask'):

ENGLISH			
Subject	Verb	Object	Infinitive
I	want	you	to win
She	prefers	them	to help

Verb 1 (indicative)	Trigger	Verb 2 (subjunctive)
Quiero	que	ganes ['I want that you win']
Prefiere	que	ayuden ['She prefers that they help']

Of course, there may need to be extra words (named subjects, object pronouns, etc.) thrown in, but the basic difference in structure is something we need to bear in mind.

Tenses

The subjunctive exists in compound tenses (e.g. to express 'I hope you have enjoyed your meal'), but is more frequently found in two main simple tenses: the present and the imperfect – the latter with two sets of endings.

⇨ See 'Formation of the present subjunctive' and 'Formation of the imperfect subjunctive'

At every point of illustration in units on the subjunctive, it will be shown how each tense fits into the overall sentence structure.

Agreement of tenses

It's important to establish what tense of the subjunctive is triggered by particular tenses of the indicative. There are some grey areas and exceptions, but as a general rule we can adhere to the following pattern:

Verb in main clause	Tense of subjunctive
present, perfect, future, imperative	present
preterite, imperfect, pluperfect, conditional	imperfect

THE SUBJUNCTIVE – 1 — UNIT 13

Here are some examples reflecting this pattern outlined:

Quiero / querré que ganes.	I want / will want you to win. ['I want / will want that you win']
Hemos querido que estés cómodo.	We've wanted you to be comfortable ['We've wanted that you be comfortable']
Quería que ganaras / ganases.	I wanted you to win. ['I wanted that you won']
Habían querido que fuéramos / fuésemos a la fiesta.	They had wanted us to go to the party. ['They had wanted that we went to the party']

Formation of the present subjunctive

Regular forms

For regular verbs, the present subjunctive is formed by removing the *-o* from the first person singular of the present indicative, then adding a set of endings. For *-ar* verbs, these endings are: *-e, -es, -e, -emos, -éis, -en*. These bear a strong similarity to the present indicative of regular *-er* verbs, but note that the first person singular ends in *-e*. For *-er* and *-ir* verbs, the endings are: *-a, -as, -a, -amos, -áis, -an*. These bear a strong similarity to the present indicative of regular *-ar* verbs, but note that the first person singular ends in *-a*. In Latin American countries where the *vos* form is used, there is a subjunctive form for *vos*, but the tendency is for it to be overlooked (especially in positive usages) in favour of the *tú* form. As such, the *vos* form is not listed below:

Infin.	English	yo	tú	él, ella, usted	nosotros/as	vosotros/as	ellos/as, ustedes
hablar	to speak	hable	hables	hable	hablemos	habléis	hablen
comer	to eat	coma	comas	coma	comamos	comáis	coman
vivir	to live	viva	vivas	viva	vivamos	viváis	vivan

Radical-changing forms

Look carefully at how radical-changing verbs in the present indicative transfer over to the present subjunctive. The table includes a reminder of the first person singular of the present indicative – from which the present subjunctive is formed:

Infin.	Meaning	1st p. sing. indic.	yo	tú	él, ella, usted	nosotros/as	vosotros/as	ellos/as, ustedes
costar	to cost	cuesto	cueste	cuestes	cueste	costemos	costéis	cuesten
cerrar	to close	cierro	cierre	cierres	cierre	cerremos	cerréis	cierren
jugar	to play	juego	juegue	juegues	juegue	juguemos	juguéis	jueguen
mover	to move	muevo	mueva	muevas	mueva	movamos	mováis	muevan
entender	to understand	entiendo	entienda	entiendas	entienda	entendamos	entendáis	entiendan
pedir	to ask for	pido	pida	pidas	pida	pidamos	pidáis	pidan

UNIT 13   THE SUBJUNCTIVE – 1

reír	to laugh	río	ría	rías	ría	riamos	riáis	rían
mentir	to lie (tell lies)	miento	mienta	mientas	mienta	mintamos	mintáis	mientan
dormir	to sleep	duermo	duerma	duermas	duerma	durmamos	durmáis	duerman

Notice the pattern – familiar from our treatment of the present indicative of radical-changing verbs – of *nosotros* and *vosotros* escaping the radical change. However, verbs behaving like *pedir* and *reír* keep the same stem throughout, and *mentir* and *dormir* have a new peculiarity in the *nosotros* and *vosotros* forms. The forms of *jugar* feature a *-u-* in the endings, to keep the *-g-* sounding correct.

Irregular forms

You will remember that, in the present indicative, a number of verbs have a rogue *-g-* or *-z-* occurring only in the first person singular. Given that it is the first person singular which is used to form the present subjunctive, these same verbs maintain the *-g-* or *-z-* in the transition:

Infin.	Meaning	1st p. sing. indic.	yo	tú	él, ella, usted	nosotros/as	vosotros/as	ellos/as, ustedes
conducir	to drive	conduzco	conduzca	conduzcas	conduzca	conduzcamos	conduzcáis	conduzcan
conocer	to meet, know	conozco	conozca	conozcas	conozca	conozcamos	conozcáis	conozcan
decir	to say, tell	digo	diga	digas	diga	digamos	digáis	digan
hacer	to do, make	hago	haga	hagas	haga	hagamos	hagáis	hagan
poner	to put	pongo	ponga	pongas	ponga	pongamos	pongáis	pongan
salir	to go out	salgo	salga	salgas	salga	salgamos	salgáis	salgan
tener	to have	tengo	tenga	tengas	tenga	tengamos	tengáis	tengan
venir	to come	vengo	venga	vengas	venga	vengamos	vengáis	vengan

Additionally, there are six fully irregular verbs in the present subjunctive. Careful attention must be paid to the use of accents on particular forms of *dar* and *estar*: The two functions of *haber* – as the subjunctive of *hay* ('there is / are') and as the auxiliary verb for compound tenses – are listed separately:

Infin.	Meaning	yo	tú	él, ella, usted	nosotros/as	vosotros/as	ellos/as, ustedes
dar	to give	dé	des	dé	demos	deis	den
estar	to be	esté	estés	esté	estemos	estéis	estén
haber	'that there be'			haya			haya
haber	to have [auxiliary]	haya	hayas	haya	hayamos	hayáis	hayan
ir	to go	vaya	vayas	vaya	vayamos	vayáis	vayan
saber	to know	sepa	sepas	sepa	sepamos	sepáis	sepan
ser	to be	sea	seas	sea	seamos	seáis	sean

THE SUBJUNCTIVE – 1   UNIT 13

Formation of the imperfect subjunctive

The imperfect subjunctive is formed by removing the *-aron* or *-ieron* from the third person plural of the preterite indicative and adding either of the sets of endings shown below. Note the accent on the *nosotros* form throughout, but on no other person. Glancing at the first column of *hablar*, it will now be apparent why it is so important to place accents on the future indicative forms *hablará*, *hablarás* and *hablarán*. The forms for the Latin American *vos* are the same as those for *tú*. Of the two columns available in each conjugation (which are interchangeable in this usage), the *-ra* forms are more common. The *-ra* set has an additional meaning, in that *hubiera* can be an alternative to *habría*, the conditional of *haber*, but it's a good idea to use *habría* so as to avoid any pitfalls.

Regular forms

Person	*hablar* (to speak)		*comer* (to eat)		*vivir* (to live)	
	-ra form	*-se* form	*-ra* form	*-se* form	*-ra* form	*-se* form
yo	hablara	hablase	comiera	comiese	viviera	viviese
tú	hablaras	hablases	comieras	comieses	vivieras	vivieses
él, ella, usted	hablara	hablase	comiera	comiese	viviera	viviese
nosotros/as	habláramos	hablásemos	comiéramos	comiésemos	viviéramos	viviésemos
vosotros/as	hablarais	hablaseis	comierais	comieseis	vivierais	vivieseis
ellos/as, ustedes	hablaran	hablasen	comieran	comiesen	vivieran	viviesen

Special forms

Some common verbs receive a *-y-* in the third persons singular and plural of the preterite indicative.

⇨ See Unit 11 for discussion of this phenomenon

This letter is maintained in the imperfect subjunctive:

Infin.	Meaning	Form	yo	tú	él, ella, usted	nosotros/as	vosotros/as	ellos/as, ustedes
caer	to fall	-ra	cayera	cayeras	cayera	cayéramos	cayerais	cayeran
		-se	cayese	cayeses	cayese	cayésemos	cayeseis	cayesen
creer	to believe, think	-ra	creyera	creyeras	creyera	creyéramos	creyerais	creyeran
		-se	creyese	creyeses	creyese	creyésemos	creyeseis	creyesen
leer	to read	-ra	leyera	leyeras	leyera	leyéramos	leyerais	leyeran
		-se	leyese	leyeses	leyese	leyésemos	leyeseis	leyesen
oír	to hear	-ra	oyera	oyeras	oyera	oyéramos	oyerais	oyeran
		-se	oyese	oyeses	oyese	oyésemos	oyeseis	oyesen
construir	to build	-ra	construyera	construyeras	construyera	construyéramos	construyerais	construyeran
		-se	construyese	construyeses	construyese	construyésemos	construyeseis	construyesen

Radical-changing forms

Given this rule for forming the imperfect subjunctive, it follows that any verb with a radical change in the preterite indicative will carry this through to the imperfect subjunctive. Here is a selection of the most common verb-types affected in this way. Notice that all -ar verbs that were radical-changing in the present indicative and present subjunctive have now dropped out of the list. As they were not radical-changing in the preterite indicative, nor are they here:

Infin.	Meaning	Form	yo	tú	él, ella, usted	nosotros/as	vosotros/as	ellos/as, ustedes
dormir	to sleep	-ra	durmiera	durmieras	durmiera	durmiéramos	durmierais	durmieran
		-se	durmiese	durmieses	durmiese	durmiésemos	durmieseis	durmiesen
pedir	to ask for	-ra	pidiera	pidieras	pidiera	pidiéramos	pidierais	pidieran
		-se	pidiese	pidieses	pidiese	pidiésemos	pidieseis	pidiesen
reír	to laugh	-ra	riera	rieras	riera	riéramos	rierais	rieran
		-se	riese	rieses	riese	riésemos	rieseis	riesen
sentir	to feel	-ra	sintiera	sintieras	sintiera	sintiéramos	sintierais	sintieran
		-se	sintiese	sintieses	sintiese	sintiésemos	sintieseis	sintiesen

Irregular forms

Similarly, irregularities visible in the preterite are maintained in the imperfect subjunctive of the following verbs:

Infin.	Meaning	Form	yo	tú	él, ella, usted	nosotros/as	vosotros/as	ellos/as, ustedes
andar	to walk	-ra	anduviera	anduvieras	anduviera	anduviéramos	anduvierais	anduvieran
		-se	anduviese	anduvieses	anduviese	anduviésemos	anduvieseis	anduviesen
caber	to fit	-ra	cupiera	cupieras	cupiera	cupiéramos	cupierais	cupieran
		-se	cupiese	cupieses	cupiese	cupiésemos	cupieseis	cupiesen
conducir	to drive	-ra	condujera	condujeras	condujera	condujéramos	condujerais	condujeran
		-se	condujese	condujeses	condujese	condujésemos	condujeseis	condujesen
dar	to give	-ra	diera	dieras	diera	diéramos	dierais	dieran
		-se	diese	dieses	diese	diésemos	dieseis	diesen
decir	to say, tell	-ra	dijera	dijeras	dijera	dijéramos	dijerais	dijeran
		-se	dijese	dijeses	dijese	dijésemos	dijeseis	dijesen
estar	to be	-ra	estuviera	estuvieras	estuviera	estuviéramos	estuvierais	estuvieran
		-se	estuviese	estuvieses	estuviese	estuviésemos	estuvieseis	estuviesen
haber	to have [auxiliary]; imp. subj. of hay	-ra	hubiera	hubieras	hubiera hubiera	hubiéramos	hubierais	hubieran
		-se	hubiese	hubieses	hubiese hubiese	hubiésemos	hubieseis	hubiesen

hacer	to do, make	-ra	hiciera	hicieras	hiciera	hiciéramos	hicierais	hicieran
		-se	hiciese	hicieses	hiciese	hiciésemos	hicieseis	hiciesen
ir	to go	-ra	fuera	fueras	fuera	fuéramos	fuerais	fueran
		-se	fuese	fueses	fuese	fuésemos	fueseis	fuesen
poder	to be able	-ra	pudiera	pudieras	pudiera	pudiéramos	pudierais	pudieran
		-se	pudiese	pudieses	pudiese	pudiésemos	pudieseis	pudiesen
poner	to put	-ra	pusiera	pusieras	pusiera	pusiéramos	pusierais	pusieran
		-se	pusiese	pusieses	pusiese	pusiésemos	pusieseis	pusiesen
querer	to want, love	-ra	quisiera	quisieras	quisiera	quisiéramos	quisierais	quisieran
		-se	quisiese	quisieses	quisiese	quisiésemos	quisieseis	quisiesen
saber	to know	-ra	supiera	supieras	supiera	supiéramos	supierais	supieran
		-se	supiese	supieses	supiese	supiésemos	supieseis	supiesen
ser	to be	-ra	fuera	fueras	fuera	fuéramos	fuerais	fueran
		-se	fuese	fueses	fuese	fuésemos	fueseis	fuesen
tener	to have	-ra	tuviera	tuvieras	tuviera	tuviéramos	tuvierais	tuvieran
		-se	tuviese	tuvieses	tuviese	tuviésemos	tuvieseis	tuviesen
traer	to bring	-ra	trajera	trajeras	trajera	trajéramos	trajerais	trajeran
		-se	trajese	trajeses	trajese	trajésemos	trajeseis	trajesen
venir	to come	-ra	viniera	vinieras	viniera	viniéramos	vinierais	vinieran
		-se	viniese	vinieses	viniese	viniésemos	vinieseis	viniesen

Notice that, of the verbs in the table, *conducir, decir, ir, ser* (which shares its forms with *ir*) and *traer* all have *-era / -ese* rather than *-iera / -iese* as their endings, in consistency with their preterite form. Compounds of *traer* (*contraer, atraer*, etc.) and other verbs that end in *-ducir* (*producir, deducir*, etc.) behave in the same way.

Formation of compound tenses

The raw materials to form the perfect and pluperfect subjunctive are contained within the bounds of this unit. All we need now are some formation rules:

Tense	Formation rule	-ar example	-er example	-ir example
Perfect subjunctive	present subjunctive of *haber* + past participle	que haya hablado	que haya comido	que haya vivido
Pluperfect subjunctive	imperfect subjunctive of *haber* + past participle	que hubiera hablado / que hubiese hablado	que hubiera comido / que hubiese comido	que hubiera vivido / que hubiese vivido

UNIT 13 — THE SUBJUNCTIVE – 1

To put each into context, the following examples come in pairs – one showing the perfect subjunctive, the other the pluperfect subjunctive – and the three verb conjugations are covered. We'll stay with the small number of 'trigger verbs' encountered so far:

Espero que hayas tomado apuntes.	I hope you've taken notes.
Esperaba que hubieras / hubieses tomado apuntes.	I hoped you had taken notes.
Queremos que hayan comido antes de la fiesta.	We want them to have eaten before the party.
Queríamos que hubieran / hubiesen comido antes de la fiesta.	We wanted them to have eaten before the party.
El director prefiere que el candidato haya vivido en Francia.	The director prefers the candidate to have lived in France.
El director prefería que el candidato hubiera / hubiese vivido en Francia.	The director preferred the candidate to have lived in France.

KEY POINT

The aim of this unit has been to cover the basics of subjunctive formation, using a small number of structures to guide you through some essential points of usage. The main focus of usage comes in the unit 'The subjunctive – 2', where we look in detail at such issues as doubt, possibility and emotions. In the exercises in this unit, we concentrate mainly on the subjunctive forms themselves, checking radical changes, irregulars, etc., but a few 'real' structures – the same ones we've used for illustration – are included for context.

PRACTICE

1 **From memory, give the *yo*, *nosotros* and *ellos* forms of the present subjunctive of the following verbs:**

1. Estudiar..
2. Comprender..
3. Escribir...
4. Producir...
5. Decir..
6. Hacer...

2 **From memory, give the *tú* and *vosotros* forms of the present subjunctive of the following verbs:**

1. Encontrar...
2. Cerrar..
3. Morir..
4. Pedir..
5. Sentir...
6. Dar..

3 **Choose the correct form of the options given, to fill each gap:**

1. Esperan que el concierto............................éxito. [tengo / tiene / tenga / tendré]
2. Espero que............................bien. [has cenado / cenas / cenado / hayas cenado]
3. Mi hermana espera............................mañana. [veas / verte / vea / te ver]
4. Esperamos que............................suerte. [haya / hay / hayan / haber]
5. ¿Qué esperas que............................[ocurrir / ocurra / ocurre / ocurren]

PRACTICE

4 Change the following sentences into the past sequence, using the imperfect indicative followed by the imperfect subjunctive:

1 Quiero que tengas cuidado.

....

2 Quieren que leas el libro.

....

3 Queremos que duermas bien.

....

4 ¿Queréis que se lo diga?

....

5 Quieren que sea especial.

....

5 Translate the following pairs of sentences into Spanish. For any instances of 'you', use the *tú* form:

1 I prefer you to come at three o'clock. / I preferred you to come at three o'clock.

..../..

2 My mother prefers us to bring a bottle. / My mother preferred us to bring a bottle.

..../..

3 They prefer me to drive. / They preferred me to drive.

..../..

4 We prefer them to make the bed. / We preferred them to make the bed.

..../..

5 You prefer there to be food in the kitchen. / You preferred there to be food in the kitchen.

..../..

UNIT 14

The subjunctive – 2

> This unit covers some of the main usages of the subjunctive, including its functions with various 'types' of verb (hoping, thinking, requesting, forbidding, etc.), doubt and possibility, and sections on how it works in main and relative clauses.

Using the subjunctive

Following on from the previous unit, where we looked at the formation of the main tenses of the subjunctive and dipped our toes in some examples of usage, this unit covers the main usages of the subjunctive. Notable exceptions are its use in the imperative, conditional sentences and indirect speech, all of which are covered in separate units. In the majority of cases here, we will look at each structure in both the present and the past sequence, so as to illustrate the relevant tenses of the subjunctive. It's important to remember the discussion about changes of subject from the main verb to the subordinate clause – if the two subjects are the same, an infinitive will be used. Now let's have a look at the main structures involving the subjunctive in Spanish.

Statements – positive and negative, including denials

1. In a statement expressing that a subsequent action genuinely happened in the past, is happening (or habitually happens) now or will happen in the future, the verb in the subordinate clause is in the indicative:

    Es cierto que <u>ocurrió</u> / <u>ocurre</u> / <u>va</u> a ocurrir.   It's true that it happened / happens / is going to happen.

    Esto quiere decir que <u>es</u> verdad.   This means it's true.

2. If the statement opens negatively (e.g. 'it's not true that', 'this doesn't mean that'), the verb in the subordinate clause is in the subjunctive. This includes notions of denying that something is, was or will be the case:

    No es que <u>trabajen</u> mucho.   It's not that they work very much.
    No significa que <u>tengas</u> que sufrir.   It doesn't mean you've got to suffer.
    Niego que <u>sea</u> verdad.   I deny that it is true.
    Negaron que el dinero <u>fuera</u>/ <u>fuese</u> suyo.   They denied that the money was theirs.

Expressing a hope or wish

The most common verb used to express a hope in Spanish is *esperar*, whose basic usage we came across in our introduction to the subjunctive in the previous unit.

Esperamos que puedas asistir.   We hope you can attend.
Esperábamos que pudieras / pudieses asistir.   We hoped you could attend.

UNIT 14 THE SUBJUNCTIVE – 2

In a more informal setting, you can simply use *que* (without a preceding verb like *esperar*) and follow it with the subjunctive, to express your wishes to the person you're addressing:

Que apruebes el examen.	Hope you pass the exam.
Que no llueva.	Hope it doesn't rain. / It'd better not rain.

Verbs of wanting, preferring

The rationale and structure here are identical to those of *esperar*. You can use *querer*, or other verbs like *desear*, to express what you want someone to do; and *preferir* to suggest what you prefer to happen. Even if the main clause is negative (e.g. 'I don't want ...'), a subjunctive in the subordinate clause is still triggered. Again, bear in mind that if the person doing both the wanting / preferring and the subsequent action is the same, you must simply use an infinitive. Here's how *querer* and *preferir* work with the subjunctive:

(No) quiero que me des la oportunidad.	I (don't) want you to give me the opportunity.
(No) quise que me dieras / dieses la oportunidad.	I wanted (didn't want) you to give me the opportunity.
Prefieren que (no) vayamos.	They prefer us (not) to go.
Preferían que (no) fuéramos / fuésemos.	They preferred us (not) to go.

'To think that' and similar verbs

It's useful to divide this concept up into three scenarios:

1. If a verb giving a belief or opinion is expressed in a positive structure, the following verb (after *que*) is in the indicative. Students of Italian should pay close attention to this:

Creo que / Pienso que / Me parece que es justo.	I think it's fair.
Creía que / Pensaba que / Me parecía que era justo.	I thought it was fair.

2. If such a verb is asking a question about someone else's opinion, the following verb is also in the indicative. This is one for students of French to compare:

¿Crees que / Piensas que / Te parece que <u>vale</u> la pena?	Do you think it's worthwhile?
¿Creías que / Pensabas que / Te parecía que <u>valía</u> la pena?	Did you think it was worthwhile?

3. However, if the verb of thinking is negative, the verb after *que* must be in the subjunctive:

No creemos que / No pensamos que / No nos parece que haga falta.	We don't think it's necessary.
No creíamos que / no pensábamos que / no nos parecía que hiciera / hiciese falta.	We didn't think it was necessary.

THE SUBJUNCTIVE – 2   UNIT 14

Possibility and probability

The most commonly used units of possibility and probability in Spanish are, respectively, *es posible que* and *es probable que*, both of which must be followed by a subjunctive. This requirement is shared by related expressions such as *puede que* and *puede ser que* (both meaning 'it may be that', but see below for smoother translations), and *en caso de que* ('in the event that', 'in case'):

Es posible que vengan esta noche.	They may come tonight.
Era posible que el concierto empezara / empezase un poco tarde.	It was possible that the concert might start a bit late.
Puede (ser) que quieran participar.	They may / might want to take part.
En caso de que usted no quiera ir, por favor avise a mis compañeros.	Should you not wish to go, please let my colleagues know.

One important fact to point out when dealing with probability or likelihood (which are the same thing in terms of their rendering in Spanish) is that it is the circumstance that is likely, not the person / persons associated with it. We should not, therefore, attempt to construct a phrase in Spanish following the English syntax:

Es muy probable que Miguel nos visite la semana que viene.	Miguel is very likely to visit us next week.
Era poco probable que mis padres lo compraran / comprasen.	My parents were very unlikely to buy it.

There are a couple more useful expressions to note here. *Por si* ('in case') takes an indicative, and *por si acaso* ('just in case') can take either an indicative or a subjunctive:

Te he arreglado la habitación por si vienes a verme.	I've sorted your room out for you in case you come and see me.
Le sacaron una entrada para el concierto por si acaso quería / quisiera / quisiese ir.	They got him a ticket for the concert just in case he wanted to go.

Perhaps / maybe

There are usually ways of coping with 'perhaps' or 'maybe' in Spanish via the *es posible que* route, above. However, if you wish to use one of several other devices, do note the following:

1. If the verb linked to the 'perhaps' idea is happening in the present or has already happened, you can generally express it in either the indicative or the subjunctive, using *tal vez*, *quizá*, *quizás*, *acaso*, *posiblemente* or *probablemente*. There are some grey areas here, but generally speaking, the subjunctive will tend to indicate a slightly less likely situation:

Quizá está / esté enfermo.	Maybe he's ill.
Probablemente no querían / quisieran / quisiesen verte.	They probably didn't want to see you.

UNIT 14 THE SUBJUNCTIVE – 2

2. If the verb linked to the 'perhaps' idea is in the future, the use of the present subjunctive is more likely:

   Tal vez vengan mañana.   Perhaps they'll come tomorrow.

3. If you're in any doubt as to whether a subjunctive is required in a particular 'perhaps' situation, a good tip is to use *a lo mejor*, which always takes the indicative:

   A lo mejor terminamos mañana.   Maybe we'll finish tomorrow.

4. In informal usage in Spain, there are two other expressions you can use – *igual* and *lo mismo* – both meaning 'perhaps' and both taking the indicative:

   Igual vamos a algún sitio el domingo.   We might go somewhere on Sunday.
   Lo mismo te lo devuelven mañana.   Maybe they'll give you it back tomorrow.

Cuando

1. If the word for 'when' introduces a verb expressing something that either happens habitually, or has already taken place at the time of the main verb, the *cuando* verb must be in the indicative. The English 'whenever' sometimes features here to convey the notion of 'every time that':

   Cuando voy al supermercado, suelo tomar algo con mi amigo.
   When (whenever) I go to the supermarket, I usually have a drink with my friend.

   Cuando llegó a la estación, se digirió al punto de información.
   When she reached the station, she went to the information point.

2. If the *cuando* refers to a time which is (or was) still in the future, the subjunctive is used. Again, the English 'whenever' can feature when it means 'at whatever point in the future':

   Me jubilaré cuando tenga setenta años.   I'll retire when I'm seventy years old.
   Puedes venir a mi casa cuando quieras.   You can come to my house whenever you like.
   Dijeron que saldrían cuando hiciera / hiciese mejor tiempo.
   They said that they would go out when the weather improved.

   The last sentence is a complex example of reported speech.

   ⇨ *Reported speech and related structures are covered in Unit 17*

Antes de (que), después de (que), hasta (que)

Firstly, we need to point out that when the subject of the verb after the preposition is the same as the main verb, then the *que* is omitted and a straight infinitive used:

   Se lavaron las manos antes de empezar.   They washed their hands before beginning (before they began).
   Lo confirmé después de hablar con mi padre. I confirmed it after speaking (after I had spoken) to my father.
   Siguieron hasta aburrirse.   They carried on until they got bored.

THE SUBJUNCTIVE – 2 — UNIT 14

If the *que* is included, the following patterns must be observed:

Notes	Spanish	English
antes de que always takes a subjunctive	*Lo acabaré antes de que vuelvas.*	I'll finish it before you get back.
	Lo acabé antes de que volvieras / volvieses.	I finished it before you got back.
después de que + past action = indicative (though subjunctive is also possible)	*después de que murió (muriera / muriese) mi abuela*	after my grandmother died
después de que + action still in future = subjunctive	*después de que desmonten el andamio mañana*	after they('ve) dismantle(d) the scaffolding tomorrow
hasta que + past action = indicative	*Esperaron hasta que llegué.*	They waited until I arrived.
hasta que + action still in future = subjunctive	*Nos quedaremos aquí hasta que llame Juan.*	We'll stay here until Juan rings.

> If you're unsure about whether a subjunctive is needed in a 'before', 'after' or 'until' context, as discussed above, a useful trick is to find a relevant noun to use: *después de tu llegada* ('after your arrival'), *antes de su muerte* ('before his / her / its / their death'), *hasta mi nacimiento* ('until my birth'), etc.

Pedir and other requesting verbs

The use of *pedir* (and related verbs like *suplicar* and *rogar*) requires a few notes:

1. If the subject of both verbs is the same, an infinitive construction can be used:

   Pedimos hablar con el encargado.   We asked to speak to the person in charge.

2. Otherwise, *pedir* + *que* + subjunctive comes into play:

   Tengo que pedirte que me devuelvas ese dinero.   I have to ask you to give me back that money.
   Me pidieron que les diera una segunda oportunidad.   They asked me to give them a second chance.

3. However, an interesting contradiction can be seen in public notices:

   Se ruega no pisar el césped.   Please keep off the lawn.

UNIT 14 THE SUBJUNCTIVE – 2

Verbs of forbidding, allowing, ordering

The underlined verbs in the table below function either with an infinitive or with a *que* + subjunctive construction, as illustrated:

No te voy a <u>dejar</u> conducir (que conduzcas) mi coche.	I'm not going to let you drive my car.
Me <u>permitieron</u> entrar (que entrara / entrase) en el edificio.	They allowed me into the building.
Nos <u>hizo</u> ver (que viéramos / viésemos) la película.	S/he made us watch the film.
Les <u>mandaste</u> arreglar (que arreglaran / arreglasen) los asuntos.	You told them to sort things out.
Os <u>ordenaron</u> hacerlo (que lo hicierais / hicieseis).	They ordered you to do it.
Te van a <u>prohibir</u> presentarte (que te presentes).	They're going to forbid you to put yourself forward.
¿Por qué me <u>impides</u> entrar (que entre)?	Why are you stopping me from going in?

Personal value judgements

Earlier in the unit, we looked at the expression of opinions, saying for example *me parece que es justo*. If we now insert an adjective or adverb (e.g. *importante*, *bien*) after the *parece*, we are forming what is known in language analysis as a personal value judgement, and – where the subjects of the main verb and the verb after the *que* are different – Spanish requires us to put the latter in the subjunctive. If both subjects are the same, we use an infinitive. Here are some illustrations of how the structures work:

Me parece absurdo que digas eso.	I think it's absurd that you should say that.
Me parece absurdo decir eso.	I think it's absurd to say that.
Les parecía muy bien que el niño fuera / fuese a la piscina.	They considered it fine that the child should go to the pool.
Les parecía muy bien ir a la piscina.	They considered it fine to go to the pool.

Expressing emotions

A large number of verbs and structures can be used to express emotional reactions – for example, in English we can say 'I'm sorry that', 'I'm glad that', 'I like', etc. In Spanish, such reactions are generally expressed either with a following infinitive (if the subject of both verbs is the same) or the *que* + subjunctive formula if not. Here's a selection of the most common verbs:

Me alegro de estar aquí / de que estés aquí.	I'm glad to be here / that you're here.
Me gusta ir al gimnasio / que vayas al gimnasio.	I like going to the gym / I like you to go to the gym.
¿Te importa apagar la tele / que apague la tele?	Do you mind switching the telly off / if I switch the telly off?
Siento hacerte sufrir / que hayas sufrido.	I'm sorry to make you suffer / that you've suffered.

THE SUBJUNCTIVE – 2 — UNIT 14

You're probably familiar with the expression *lo siento*, meaning 'I'm sorry'. However, if you want to say 'I'm sorry that [something is the case]', don't forget to drop the *lo*, as the new information you're supplying after the *que* is a replacement for it:

Siento que estés enferma. I'm sorry that you're ill.

Expressing doubt

Here, the standard verb to focus on is *dudar*. The rule is that if the nature of the idea suggests that there is no doubt (e.g. *no dudo que* = 'I don't doubt that' = firm belief), the following verb goes in the indicative; if here is any doubt expressed, the following verb must go in the subjunctive:

No dudo que sabes hacerlo. I've no doubt that you know how to do it.
Dudo que sea posible. I doubt it's possible.

Being afraid that

1 The first scenario involves somebody fearing that, or being afraid that, something has happened, is happening or will happen. The existence of some genuine form of 'fear' is key. In this circumstance, we can use either *temer* ('to fear') or *tener miedo de que* ('to be afraid that'), both with a following subjunctive:

Tienen miedo de que no llegues a tiempo. They're afraid you won't arrive on time.
Temían que el plan saliera / saliese mal. They feared that the plan wouldn't work out.

2 However, if the 'being afraid' is not to do with fear but is said in the context of apologising or expressing regret, you can use the reflexive verb *temerse*, which is followed by an indicative:

Me temo que no queda comida. I'm afraid there's no food left.

Understanding, accepting, explaining that

➤ With the verbs *entender*, *comprender* (both 'to understand') and *aceptar* ('to accept'), there are two following structures:

1 If the verb is used in the general sense, followed by a fact (e.g. 'I understand that your parents are in town'; 'I accept that it's too late'), Spanish uses an indicative for the following verb:

Entiendo que vas a ayudarnos. I understand that you're going to help us.
Acepto que ya es demasiado tarde. I accept that it's now too late.

2 If the meaning in the main verb is one of sympathy with the action of the second verb, the latter must go in the subjunctive:

Comprendo que quiera alejarse de su familia. I can understand that he should want to get away from his family.

UNIT 14 THE SUBJUNCTIVE – 2

➤ The verb *explicar* ('to explain') has a similar duality:

1. In the straightforward sense of 'to state', it is followed by the indicative:

   Nos explicó que había estado en Australia.   He explained to us that he had been in Australia.

2. If the 'explain' carries the meaning of 'give the reason why', the following verb must be in the subjunctive:

   Esto explica que hayan tardado tanto.   This explains why they've taken so long.

Expressing purpose

Once again, we can differentiate between a circumstance where the subject of both verbs is the same – in which case the second one is in the infinitive – and where there is a change of subject, triggering a subjunctive. The classic set-up is *para* + infinitive ('in order to') for the former, and *para que* + subjunctive ('so that', 'in order that') for the latter:

Leemos para aprender.   We read in order to learn.
Te leo esto para que lo aprendas.   I'm reading this to you so that you learn it.

Alongside *para que* we find the pairing *de modo que* and *de manera que*, which merit their own brief analysis:

1. If the following verb shows a result, *de modo que* or *de manera que* (meaning, in effect, 'therefore') will take an indicative:

   Acabaron pronto, de modo que fueron a tomar algo.   They finished early, so went for a drink.

2. If aim or intention is implied – perhaps creating the meaning of 'in such a way that' – a subjunctive must follow:

   Lo hicieron de manera que el jefe no se enterara / enterase.   They did it in such a way that the boss wouldn't find out.

Without something happening

In normal use, *sin* can be followed by an infinitive when both subjects are the same, to convey 'without doing'. If there is a change of subject, we must use *sin que* + subjunctive:

Lograron salir del edificio sin que la policía los viera / viese.   They managed to get out of the building without the police seeing them.

THE SUBJUNCTIVE – 2 UNIT 14

Conditions and exceptions

A range of subordinators can be used in Spanish – all of which take the subjunctive – to express the imposing of conditions or the existence of exceptions. In English, we would think of 'provided (that)', 'so long as' or 'on condition that' as introducing a condition, whereas 'unless' might usher in an exception. Here are a few illustrations of each in Spanish:

Te lo dejo a condición de que me lo devuelvas mañana.	I'll give it to you on condition that you give me it back tomorrow.
Os dejaremos ir a la playa siempre que tengáis cuidado.	We'll let you go to the beach so long as you're careful.
Empezaremos a las nueve, a no ser que alguien no quiera.	We'll begin at nine o'clock, unless anyone doesn't want to.
A menos que nieve, saldremos mañana.	Unless it snows, we'll set off tomorrow.
Como te quejes, no te dejo ir con nosotros.	If you complain, I won't let you go with us.

Aunque

The usage of *aunque* – broadly meaning 'although' – divides into two:

1 If the meaning – or the implied meaning – is 'even though', followed by a fact, it is followed in Spanish by the indicative:

Aunque somos pequeños, nos gusta jugar al baloncesto.	Even though we're small, we enjoy playing basketball.
Aunque no teníamos comida, éramos felices.	Although we had no food, we were happy.

2 If the meaning is 'even if', followed by a hypothesis, it is followed in Spanish by the subjunctive:

Aunque venga a disculparse, no hablaré con él.	Even if he comes to apologise, I won't speak to him.
Aunque fuera / fuese verdad, no lo aceptaría.	Even if it were true, I wouldn't accept it.

The fact that

This can be a tricky area. We seem to be dealing with 'facts', which is usually a rock-solid case against requiring the subjunctive, but Spanish nevertheless divides up the usage of *el hecho de que*, *el que* and *que* (all of which can mean 'the fact that') into two areas:

1 If the main verb is one of knowing or perceiving, the subsequent verb (after the equivalent of 'the fact that') goes in the indicative:

Soy consciente del hecho de que has trabajado mucho.	I'm aware of the fact that you've put in a lot of work.

2. However, if there is any type of value judgement, emotional reaction, or any hint of influence or cause, the subjunctive must be used:

Que no te contesten lo dice todo.	The fact that they aren't replying speaks volumes.
Que hayas venido hoy no explica la ausencia de ayer.	The fact that you've come today doesn't explain yesterday's absence.

Whether ... or not

This structure uses a subjunctive (and an optional second subjunctive) in Spanish:

Lo voy a hacer, te guste o no (te guste).	I'm going to do it, whether you like it or not.
Contesten o no (contesten), voy a seguir llamando.	Whether they answer or not, I'm going to carry on phoning.

However (much) ... and similar

This is another structure whose use subdivides in Spanish, differentiating between the expressing of something that is / was / will be real, and something not. In either case, there are a handful of expressions equating to the English 'however much':

por mucho que + verb
por más que + verb
por mucho + noun + verb
por (muy) + adjective + verb

1. If the 'however much' expresses something that really happened / happens / will happen, the indicative is used in Spanish:

Por mucho que trabajaron, no lograron acabar el proyecto.	However much they worked, they weren't able to get the project finished.
Por más que como, no engordo.	However much I eat, I can't put on any weight.

2. If it refers to the build-up of something intangible or that didn't / doesn't / won't happen, the subjunctive is used:

Por mucho deporte que practiques, nunca llegarás a ser profesional.	However much sport you play, you'll never get to be a professional.
Por muy astuta que sea, a mí no me engañará.	However wily she may be, she'll never fool me.

The more ... the more ... / the less ... the less ...

These pairings (and crossover combinations of the two) can be easily dealt with in Spanish. The indicative versus subjunctive argument is exactly as detailed in the 'However (much) ...' section above. The key expressions are the following:

cuanto/a/os/as más ... más ...	The more ... the more ...
cuanto/a/os/as menos ... menos ...	The less ... the less ...

THE SUBJUNCTIVE – 2   UNIT 14

Here are some examples of usage. Note, where appropriate, the agreement of *cuanto*:

Cuanto menos hagas, menos podrás hacer. The less you do, the less you'll be able to do.
Cuantas más casas compraban, más querían comprar. The more houses they bought, the more they wanted to buy.
Cuanta más agua bebas, menos habrá para tu hermana. The more water you drink, the less there'll be for your sister.

Whichever one / the one that

This structure – which serves to refer to an as yet unidentified example of something – is rendered in Spanish by *que* or *el / la / los / las que* + the subjunctive:

Coge los libros que quieras. Take whichever books you want.
Podéis elegir la que os guste. You can choose the one you like.

Whoever / anyone who

Here we are talking about an unspecified person or persons who may fulfil a criterion (e.g. 'Whoever / anyone who laughs at me will regret it'). The Spanish equivalent requires a subjunctive and can be conveyed in any one of three ways:

Cualquiera que tenga sentido del humor lo entenderá. Anyone with a sense of humour will understand it.
El que quiera desafiarnos, que se atreva. Whoever wants to challenge us, let them dare.
Quien meta las narices aquí se va a pegar un susto. Anyone who sticks their nose in here will get a shock.

The subjunctive in relative clauses

We can find this occurring in several different circumstances:

1 To refer to someone or something as yet unidentified. Notice the contrast between the first example – where the object of the main verb is clearly identified, hence no subsequent subjunctive is needed – and the second example, where it's a case of 'anyone who happens to fit the category':

   Conozco a un profesor que tiene un coche muy caro. I know a teacher who has a very expensive car.
   Quiero conocer a alguien que tenga un coche muy caro. I want to meet someone who has a very expensive car.

2 To refer to a non-existent person or thing. In the Spanish equivalent of an English sentence like 'There is nobody who can take your place', the inexistence of a suitable candidate is taken as a trigger for a subjunctive:

   No hay nadie que hable tan bien como tú. There is nobody who speaks as well as you (do).
   Cuando se pone así no hay quien le tranquilice. When he gets like this nobody can calm him down.

UNIT 14 THE SUBJUNCTIVE – 2

3   Relative clauses in sentences where the main clause is in the future tense:

Será mi padre el que / quien pague la factura.   It'll be my father who pays the invoice.

The subjunctive in main clauses

There are three main scenarios in which this can happen:

1   The imperative

   ⇨ *The imperative is covered in Unit 15*

2   In a couple of structures used to express wishes (we came across the first of these earlier in the unit):

Que tengas suerte.   Good luck ('may you have luck').

Ojalá no llueva mañana / Ojalá fuéramos / fuésemos ricos.   Let's hope it doesn't rain tomorrow / If only we were rich.

3   In a handful of set expressions:

No tengo dinero, o sea que no te puedo invitar.   I've got no money, in other words I can't treat you.

Que yo sepa / recuerde, no hay dinero en esa cuenta.   As far as I know / remember, there's no money in that account.

PRACTICE

1 In each sentence, fill the gap with the correct form of the verb given in the infinitive in brackets:

1. No es verdad que mi hermano [TRABAJAR] .... en esa tienda.
2. Esperaba que vosotros [HACER] .... algo.
3. Los hombres negaron que el coche [SER] .... suyo.
4. No quiero hacer [TRABAJAR] .... al pobre chico.
5. Me parece que la película [IR] .... a empezar.
6. No creo que [HABER] .... muchos turistas este año.
7. No dudaba que el arquitecto [SABER] .... lo que hacía.
8. Temo que no [QUEDAR] .... gambas en la nevera.
9. Me vas a escribir siempre que [PODER] ...., ¿vale?
10. Me alegro de [VER] .... que estás bien.

2 Translate the following sentences into Spanish:

1. Pepe is very likely to arrive tomorrow.

2. Yesterday they asked me to make the bed.

3. Even if you want to be an artist, I'll work with you.

4. Before my brothers were ill, I went to visit them once.

5. When I was young I wanted to see the world.

6. When I see him tomorrow I'll tell him the truth.

PRACTICE

7 I'm sorry they've not eaten well.

....

8 It seems important to me that students have money for books.

....

9 I worked an additional day so that you had money for clothes.

....

10 We drank the wine without my parents seeing us.

....

3 **For each of the following sentences, give two possible translations, based on structures covered in the unit and centred round the verb given in brackets:**

1 They allow us to sleep here. [DEJAR]

..../..

2 We will let you study in our house. [PERMITIR]

..../..

3 I'm going to stop you from watching television. [IMPEDIR]

..../..

4 You ordered me to say it. [ORDENAR]

..../..

5 He has forbidden us to come here. [PROHIBIR]

..../..

4 **Correct any of the following verb forms that need attention:**

1 Por mucho que trabajas en los próximos meses, no estaré convencida ....

2 A menos que empieces muy pronto, no lo vas a acabar ....

3 Quiero vivir con alguien que está dispuesto a aguantarme ....

PRACTICE

4 Cuando tendré sesenta años mis nietos me querrán mucho...

5 Seguiremos aquí hasta que se pone el sol..

5 Re-write each of the following sentences, transposed into the past sequence, using the imperfect indicative followed by the imperfect subjunctive:

1 Dudo que las cajas quepan en el coche.

    ....

2 Es posible que no sepa qué hacer.

    ....

3 Prefiero que todo el mundo diga lo que quiera decir.

    ....

4 No quiero que conduzcas.

    ....

5 No es cierto que haya tantas personas en el aula.

    ....

6 Cada día te pido que me traigas el periódico.

    ....

7 Acepto que los políticos hagan lo que les dé la gana.

    ....

8 Tenemos miedo de que no salga bien.

    ....

9 Siempre sugiero que todos pongamos cien euros.

    ....

10 Tengo que esconder el dinero antes de que me vea mi padre.

    ....

UNIT 15: The imperative and how to express commands and invitations

Giving commands in Spanish

The first thing to point out, in starting to think about the use of the imperative, is the difference in cultural expectations in the English- and Spanish-speaking worlds. In English-speaking countries a command is restricted very much to moments when it is absolutely necessary (and carries the appropriate force); in other circumstances, speakers will 'soften' the message with devices such as 'could you please…?', 'could I ask you to…?' or 'would you mind…?' A simple imperative – 'do it!', 'give me them!' – can sound brusque and inappropriate. In Spanish-speaking countries, on the other hand, the use of the imperative is common – not always to order someone to do something: it has lighter tones too – although it is still important to use it with appropriate grace and tone, so as not to sound over-harsh. Context is everything.

To get a flavour of the range of structures we can find under this broad umbrella, have a look at these examples. They are not comprehensive, but hint at some of the devices to be studied. Each is expressed in the *tú* form, but could, of course, be adapted to other forms translating the English 'you':

Would you mind helping me?	*¿Te importaría ayudarme?*
Will you be quiet?	*¿Te quieres callar?*
Why don't you do it yourself?	*¿Por qué no lo haces tú?*
Let's get started!	*¡Vamos a empezar!*
Please sit down.	*Siéntate (por favor).*
Do it!	*¡Hazlo!*

This unit looks at the formation and use of the various types of Spanish imperative, outlining the mechanisms of positive and negative forms, which can differ from each other greatly. Just as importantly, it offers a selection of alternatives to the conventional imperative, which in some cases can come reassuringly close to the English 'would you mind…?', etc., quoted above.

Forms of the imperative

Just as indicative and subjunctive verb forms offer a variety of nuances for conveying the English 'you', the imperative offers the same range. As you'd expect, you can instruct a *tú*, a *vos* or an *usted* person to do (or not to do) something, and *vosotros* and *ustedes* situations (positive and negative) are covered, too. This differs markedly from English, where a simple 'speak!' and 'don't speak!' are the only true forms of the imperative. Students of French must be aware that the French *vous* embraces the Spanish *usted*, *vosotros* and *ustedes*, and Italianists should be careful when formulating positive and negative commands in Spanish (and deciding where to place the object pronouns).

Let's begin by focusing on each form in turn.

THE IMPERATIVE AND HOW TO EXPRESS COMMANDS AND INVITATIONS — UNIT 15

The *tú* form

Probably the most frequently used form, the rules for its formation are shown below:

Form	Rule for formation	*-ar* example	*-er* example	*-ir* example
positive	Remove the *-s* from the 2nd person singular, present indicative	¡habla!	¡come!	¡vive!
negative	*no* + 2nd person singular, present subjunctive	¡no hables!	¡no comas!	¡no vivas!

Some notes for us to be aware of at this stage:

1. You'll see that the negative form takes the subjunctive. This is a universal requirement across all negative imperatives in Spanish.

2. Naturally, there is scope to include object pronouns, so as to be able to say 'give him a chance' or 'pass it to me', etc.

    ⇨ See section on 'Using object pronouns with the imperative'

3. It's worth noting that the positive form of *estar* generally features as a reflexive – *estate* – as the regular *está* can be confused with the 3rd person singular of the present indicative. That aside, there are eight irregular forms of the positive *tú* imperative (plus a reflexive variant of one of them). Their negative forms are constructed conventionally, via the present subjunctive:

Infinitive	positive *tú* imperative	negative *tú* imperative
decir	¡di!	¡no digas!
hacer	¡haz!	¡no hagas!
ir / irse	¡ve! / ¡vete!	¡no vayas! / ¡no te vayas!
poner	¡pon!	¡no pongas!
salir	¡sal!	¡no salgas!
ser	¡sé!	¡no seas!
tener	¡ten!	¡no tengas!
venir	¡ven!	¡no vengas!

4. The reflexive form – you can see from the example of *irse* that in the positive form, the reflexive pronoun is added to the end of the imperative. In the negative form, the reflexive pronoun comes between the *no* and the imperative. These patterns are followed throughout the Spanish imperative system.

    ⇨ Help on the positioning of pronouns with the imperative can be found under 'Using object pronouns with the imperative' and 'Reflexive forms of the imperative'

UNIT 15 — THE IMPERATIVE AND HOW TO EXPRESS COMMANDS AND INVITATIONS

The *vos* form

The *vos* form of the imperative – for use in certain countries in Latin America – is formed as detailed in the table below. Whilst there is a recognised negative form, it is not commonly used, so the table shows the preferred negative variety:

Form	Rule for formation	-*ar* example	-*er* example	-*ir* example
positive	Remove final -*r* from infinitive; accentuate final vowel	¡hablá!	¡comé!	¡viví!
negative	*no* + 2nd person singular, present subjunctive	¡no hables!	¡no comas!	¡no vivas!

There is only one common irregular positive form: *ir* becomes ¡andá! or ¡andate!

⇨ See also section on 'Reflexive forms of the imperative'

The *vosotros* form

Remember that this form is only used in Spain, and even then not in the Canary Islands. Its formation – again with the subjunctive used for the negative forms – involves an unexpected -*d* in the positive form. In informal speech, it is quite common for this to be replaced by the infinitive.

Form	Rule for formation	-*ar* example	-*er* example	-*ir* example
positive	Replace the final -*r* of the infinitive with -*d*	¡hablad!	¡comed!	¡vivid!
negative	*no* + 2nd person plural, present subjunctive	¡no habléis!	¡no comáis!	¡no viváis!

⇨ See also section on 'Reflexive forms of the imperative'

The *usted* form

The *usted* form of the imperative is essentially a specific person of the subjunctive – there is no separate format, so there are no new forms to be learned! Notice that the positive and negative forms are identical, except that the negative forms carry the word *no*. We'll deal with the reflexive forms later in the unit.

Form	Rule for formation	-*ar* example	-*er* example	-*ir* example
positive	3rd person singular, present subjunctive	¡hable!	¡coma!	¡viva!
negative	*no* + 3rd person singular, present subjunctive	¡no hable!	¡no coma!	¡no viva!

The *ustedes* form

As you might expect, the *ustedes* form is identical to that of the singular *usted*, except that all endings carry the -*n* of the third person plural of the subjunctive. Reflexive forms come later in the unit.

THE IMPERATIVE AND HOW TO EXPRESS COMMANDS AND INVITATIONS UNIT 15

There is one important rule of usage to remember, which is that this form is used in place of *vosotros* in the Canary Islands and right across Latin American Spanish.

Form	Rule for formation	-*ar* example	-*er* example	-*ir* example
positive	3rd person plural, present subjunctive	¡hablen!	¡coman!	¡vivan!
negative	*no* + 3rd person plural, present subjunctive	¡no hablen!	¡no coman!	¡no vivan!

The *nosotros* form

The first person plural ('we') form has provision to issue imperatives in English, usually via the device 'let us (not)...' ('let's consider', 'let us pray', 'let's not worry about that', etc.). This can happen through an imperative form in Spanish too, with a similar effect, although it's worth pointing out that this usage is largely limited to formal variants of the written language, being generally sidestepped in spoken Spanish. There are alternative means of addressing the 'let's...' structure, which we'll discuss later in the unit.

Form	Rule for formation	-*ar* example	-*er* example	-*ir* example
positive	1st person plural, present subjunctive	¡hablemos!	¡comamos!	¡vivamos!
negative	*no* + 1st person plural, present subjunctive	¡no hablemos!	¡no comamos!	¡no vivamos!

Reflexive forms of the imperative

Reflexive verbs have a reasonably straightforward means of conveying instructions, but a little bit of care is needed to ensure that the reflexive pronoun is placed in the correct place, and there can sometimes be a need for an accent to be added.

Here is a table detailing the positive and negative imperative forms of regular -*ar* (*lavarse* – 'to get washed'), -*er* (*meterse* – 'to involve oneself') and -*ir* (*abrirse* – 'to open (oneself) up') verbs:

Form	Rule for formation	-*ar* example	-*er* example	-*ir* example
tú positive	non-reflexive imperative + *te* on end	¡lávate!*	¡métete!*	¡ábrete!*
tú negative	*te* inserted between *no* and subjunctive	¡no te laves!	¡no te metas!	¡no te abras!
vos positive	non-reflexive imperative (losing accent) + *te* on end	¡lavate!	¡metete!	¡abrite!
vos negative	*te* inserted between *no* and subjunctive	¡no te laves!	¡no te metas!	¡no te abras!
usted positive	non-reflexive imperative + *se* on end	¡lávese!*	¡métase!*	¡ábrase!*
usted negative	*se* inserted between *no* and subjunctive	¡no se lave!	¡no se meta!	¡no se abra!
nosotros positive	non-reflexive imperative (minus final -*s*) + *nos* on end	¡lavémonos!*	¡metámonos!*	¡abrámonos!*

UNIT 15 THE IMPERATIVE AND HOW TO EXPRESS COMMANDS AND INVITATIONS

nosotros negative	*nos* inserted between *no* and subjunctive	¡no nos lavemos!	¡no nos metamos!	¡no nos abramos!
vosotros positive	non-reflexive imperative (minus final *-d*) + *os* on end	¡lavaos!	¡meteos!	¡abríos!
vosotros negative	*os* inserted between *no* and subjunctive	¡no os lavéis!	¡no os metáis!	¡no os abráis!
ustedes positive	non-reflexive imperative + *se* on end	¡lávense!*	¡métanse!*	¡ábranse!*
ustedes negative	*se* inserted between *no* and subjunctive	¡no se laven!	¡no se metan!	¡no se abran!

Notes:

1 All the forms marked with an asterisk in the table above have received an accent which was not present in the corresponding non-reflexive form – i.e. on the positive *tú* imperative of the simple verbs *lavar* (*lava*), *meter* (*mete*) and *abrir* (*abre*). This is because of the requirement for the spoken stress to fall on the same syllable on which it fell before any pronoun was added. We'll see later on that this accentuation can occur when object pronouns are added to positive imperatives, too. General guidance on rules for the role and addition of accents can be found in the final unit.

2 As mentioned in the section on the *tú* form (note 4) earlier in the unit, the reflexive pronoun (*te, se, nos, os*) is glued to the end of a positive imperative, and comes between the *no* and the verb in negative forms.

3 In the *nosotros* positive form, the final *-s* of the non-reflexive form (e.g. *lavemos*) must be dropped before the reflexive pronoun *nos* is added on. There is one common irregularity, which comes with the verb *irse*: whilst the conventionally formed *vayámonos* exists and is sometimes found, in general use the truncated form *vámonos* is far more frequently used.

4 In the *vosotros* positive form, the final *-d* of the non-reflexive form (e.g. *lavad*) must be dropped before the reflexive pronoun *os* is added on. Notice that, in the *-ir* column, the 'i' receives an accent when the *-os* is added. There is only one verb which keeps its *-d* when the *-os* is added: again, this exception is *irse*, whose *vosotros* positive form is *idos*.

Using object pronouns with the imperative

Much of what we can note here also refers to the section on reflexive forms. One or, if need be, two object pronouns can be glued to the end of a positive imperative, but in the case of negative forms, any object pronoun(s) must go between the *no* and the verb. If you need to refresh yourself on object pronouns, have a quick look at Unit 6. In particular, if you are using two object pronouns with an imperative, they must come in the required order, as described in Unit 6: indirect first, then direct:

Da [imperative] + *me* [indirect object pronoun: 'to me'] + *lo* [direct object pronoun: 'it'] = ¡Dámelo!   Give it to me! / Give me it!

¡No me lo des!   Don't give it to me! / Don't give me it!

THE IMPERATIVE AND HOW TO EXPRESS COMMANDS AND INVITATIONS   UNIT 15

The note, under Reflexive forms of the imperative, about accentuation also applies here: the spoken stress must fall on the same syllable on which it fell before any pronoun was added. In other words we must, where necessary, add a written accent to keep the spoken stress wherever it was before anything was added to the 'raw' imperative form:

⇨ *Refer to Unit 23 for guidance on accentuation rules*

Raw form	Form with pronoun(s) added	Notes
da	*dame*	stress remains automatically on *da-* so no accent needed
da	*dámelo*	stress would logically fall on *-me-*, which is undesirable, so artificial accent added to keep stress on *da-* syllable

Further notes:

1. If the pronoun *nos* ('us', 'to us') is added to a positive *ustedes* command, we end up with what looks like a clash of two letter n's. This is not a problem, as Spanish allows for *-nn-*. The *-nn-* is actually essential, as if we were to drop one n, we would be left with the *usted*, rather than the *ustedes*, form:

    ¡Háblenos! [usted]   Speak to us!
    ¡Háblennos! [ustedes]   Speak to us!

2. However, if we need to add the indirect object pronoun *se* to a *nosotros* positive command, the resultant *-ss-* is not allowed, and has to be shortened to *-s-*:

    demos + se + lo = démosselo → ¡démoselo!   Let's give it to him / her / them.

The impersonal 'passive *se*' imperative

This is a reasonably common usage in formal written Spanish, often visible in instructions for filling in forms, assembling furniture, following recipes, etc. It consists of the third person singular or plural imperatives, with *-se* added, to allow an instruction like 'complete the following sections' to be rendered in a manner equating to 'let the following sections be completed'. It sounds less cumbersome in Spanish than it does in English! However, it isn't a usage that would be recommended in everyday speech, where an infinitive (one of our alternative techniques, below) would be far more appropriate. In the examples, notice how the singularity and plurality of the section(s) to be completed are matched in the verb forms:

Complétese la siguiente sección.   Complete the following section.
Complétense las siguientes secciones.   Complete the following sections.

UNIT 15 — THE IMPERATIVE AND HOW TO EXPRESS COMMANDS AND INVITATIONS

Other ways of expressing commands and invitations

As in English, there are various alternative means of issuing instructions and invitations. Here is an overview of the most common devices available in Spanish:

The infinitive as an imperative

The infinitive is commonly used as a form of imperative in three main contexts:

1. As an alternative to the positive *vosotros* command – e.g. *hablad > hablar*. This is restricted to informal settings, and to the Spanish of Spain:

   Bueno, recoger los trastos.   Right, collect your stuff.

2. Similarly, but in a nuance that can include the speaker, the infinitive, preceded by the preposition *a*, can be a way of urging something to be done:

   Es tarde, a dormir todos.   It's late – go to sleep, everyone.
   A trabajar, a ver si acabamos hoy.   Let's get to work – see if we can get finished today.

3. As a much more user-friendly alternative to the impersonal 'passive *se*' already discussed, in the same types of circumstance:

   Respetar las plantas.   Respect the plants.
   Cortar las zanahorias en tiras.   Cut the carrots into strips.

Use of a question form

Just as in the English 'will / would you…?' (etc.), Spanish imperatives can be converted into questions to lessen any sharpness that might otherwise have emerged:

   ¿Me decís cómo os llamáis?   Would you mind telling me your names?
   ¿Me das un cigarrillo?   Will you give me a cigarette, please?
   ¿Te corres un poco a la derecha para dejarme sentar?   Could you budge a bit to the right to let me sit down?

The verb *importar* – meaning, in this context, 'to mind' – can be very useful in questions of this type:

   ¿Te importa / te importaría cerrar la ventana?   Do you / would you mind shutting the window?

The present indicative as an imperative

In both languages, this structure can be used to convey a sense of brusqueness, giving the listener instructions in no uncertain terms:

   Entras ahora mismo en el jardín, recoges la pelota y le pides disculpas al señor.   You go into the garden right now, you get the ball and you apologise to the gentleman.

THE IMPERATIVE AND HOW TO EXPRESS COMMANDS AND INVITATIONS — UNIT 15

Use of the conditional of *poder* to soften an imperative

Equating to the English 'could you...?', this is a useful way of getting instructions across without resorting to a full imperative. The result is somewhere between a command and an invitation:

¿Puedes / Podrías dejar de gritar tanto? Could you stop shouting so much?

Remember that *poder* can also be used to issue an invitation of a friendlier variety:

Podemos / Podíamos / Podríamos ir a la playa. We could go to the beach.

Use of *querer*

This is like an emphatic use of the English 'will you...?', where a clear invitation to do something is intended:

¿Quieres callarte? Will you shut up?

A ver si...

Generally followed by the present indicative, this expression – literally meaning 'let's see if' – injects a note of firm suggestion into what is being said:

A ver si tienes más cuidado la próxima vez. Make sure you're more careful next time.

Use of *vamos a* + infinitive

This construction – meaning 'let's....' – can carry the nuance of either a gentle command or a suggestion / invitation, depending on context and intonation. It is an everyday structure, far less formal – and easier to form – than a *nosotros* imperative (which, for the examples below, would be *limpiemos* and *divirtámonos*):

Vamos a limpiar la cocina. Let's clean the kitchen.
Vamos a divertirnos. Let's have a good time.

KEY POINT

Remember that, while the forms of the imperative are important to learn and use, there are many other ways of expressing commands and invitations in Spanish!

PRACTICE

1 Using the imperative of the verb *decir* and the pronoun *lo*, offer appropriate translations of the English 'Say it!'/'Don't say it!' in each of the following forms:

1. *tú* positive..............................
2. *tú* negative............................
3. *usted* positive........................
4. *usted* negative......................
5. *vosotros* positive..................
6. *vosotros* negative................
7. *ustedes* positive...................
8. *ustedes* negative.................

2 Using the imperative of the verb *vestirse*, offer appropriate translations of the English 'Get dressed!'/'Don't get dressed!' in each of the following forms:

1. *tú* positive..............................
2. *tú* negative............................
3. *usted* positive........................
4. *usted* negative......................
5. *vosotros* positive..................
6. *vosotros* negative................
7. *ustedes* positive...................
8. *ustedes* negative.................

3 Re-express each of the following, using a *nosotros* imperative:

1. Vamos a verlo.

   ....

2. No vamos a pedírselo.

   ....

PRACTICE

3 Vamos a tener éxito.

   ....

4 Vamos a preocuparnos.

   ....

5 No vamos a secarnos.

   ....

4 Translate the following into Spanish, using an appropriate device from those covered in the unit. There may be several possibilities for each one! In each case of 'you', guidance is given as to which person is to be used:

1 When you [*tú*] reach the airport, do you mind calling me?

   ....

2 Do [*tú*] your homework after you've had a shower!

   ....

3 Wake up [*usted*]!

   ....

4 Let's play cards tonight.

   ....

5 Will you come [*vosotros*] here so that I can see you?

   ....

6 Don't fall asleep [*vosotros*] before ten o'clock.

   ....

7 Why don't you [*ustedes*] look at it one more time?

   ....

8 Don't be afraid [*ustedes*] of us coming in.

   ....

UNIT 16

Conditional sentences

> Conditional sentences are usually made up of two clauses: an 'if' clause and a main clause. In various ways, and using different combinations of tense and mood, they describe circumstances occurring if particular conditions are, were or had been met. These can range from the mundane ('if it rains I'll wear a coat') through the hypothetical ('if I were rich I'd buy a football club') to the regretful ('if I'd paid more attention at school I wouldn't have ended up on the dole'). Several sections in this unit focus on a different type of conditional sentence each, illustrating how the combinations work in Spanish.

A quick note on *si* ('if')

The primary rule associated with *si* is that it can never be followed by the present subjunctive. Otherwise, it can feature with a wide range of tenses in the indicative and subjunctive moods. It is used to convey the vast majority of 'if' clauses (see the final section of this unit for a couple of alternative structures).

Fulfilled conditions

Fulfilled conditions refer to sentences set entirely or partially in the past, where the matter suggested in the 'if' clause has been resolved. Typically, the 'if' element could also be expressed by phrases like 'whenever / every time that' or 'the reason why'. In Spanish, such sentences never use the subjunctive:

Si hacía frío me ponía el abrigo.	If (whenever) it was cold I used to put my overcoat on.
Si te contó eso, se habrá fiado de ti.	If she told you that, she must have trusted you.

Open conditions

An open condition usually starts off with an 'if' clause in the present tense, and is one that may or may not become 'fulfilled', i.e. the 'if' condition may or may not happen. There are several different sub-sets of structure, but these are more or less the same as the English equivalents. Again, there is no place for the subjunctive, other than in certain forms of the imperative used in the final variety:

If you work, you earn money

Here both clauses of the sentence are in the **present tense** and there is no complication. The sentence talks about a fact of life, and the 'if' clause may happen but isn't bound to do so. In Spanish, both clauses are rendered in the present indicative:

Si trabajas, ganas dinero. If you work, you earn money.

If you come to my house, I'll give you the money

The structure here is similar to that of the previous example, except that the main clause is in the **future tense**, to suggest that if the condition is fulfilled (if the listener does indeed come to the speaker's house), the result (the handing over of money) will happen. Spanish uses the same combination of tenses as English, and again there is no subjunctive:

Si vienes a mi casa, te daré el dinero. If you come to my house, I'll give you the money.

If you see her, call me

In this sentence, the first clause has the same structure as that of the previous example, but the main clause is an **imperative**. In Spanish, we need to be careful to determine which kind of 'you' is being spoken to, and to match that decision with the corresponding form of the imperative (which, in the case of *usted* or *ustedes*, involves the subjunctive). The indicative as an alternative structure is also possible, as shown in the final two examples in the table:

Si la ves, llámame. If you see her, call me.
Si la ve usted, llámeme. If you see her, call me.
Si la ves, me llamas. If you see her, you call me.
Si la ve usted, me llama. If you see her, you call me.

Remote conditions

In the 'if' clause of a remote condition, the reference is to something hypothetical: 'if I were rich' (but I'm not). The use of the English 'were' is helpful here in allowing us to determine which sort of condition is in play, but we can't always rely on it being present. The main clause is expressed in the **conditional tense** – the clause above might continue: 'I would buy a huge house'. In Spanish, the hypothetical nature of the *si* clause requires it to use the **imperfect subjunctive** (either form), and the main clause matches English in using the conditional. The use of the imperfect subjunctive in the *si* clause is vital, and we must not fall into the trap of using the imperfect indicative, which would turn the clause into a fulfilled condition. French uses the imperfect indicative for both of these structures, so students of that language should take extra care when forming remote conditions:

UNIT 16 CONDITIONAL SENTENCES

If I were rich, I'd buy a castle

The hypothesis here is clear: my genuine circumstances are contrary to those required for the main clause to take place – I'm not rich and probably never will be. Some more examples are added, for further illustration.

Si fuera / fuese rico, compraría un castillo.	If I were rich, I'd buy a castle.
Si no estuviera / estuviese casado, estaría contigo.	If I weren't married, I'd be with you.
Si me ayudara / ayudase Juan, acabaríamos antes.	If Juan helped me / were to help me, we'd finish sooner.

Unfulfilled conditions

Unfulfilled conditions typically take the following form: 'If I had (not) passed my exams, I would (not) have got a good job' / 'If we had (not) eaten the shellfish, we would (not) have been ill'. As can be seen, the sentences refer back to a past event and what did or didn't happen, and what influence that had on something subsequent. Positive and negative verbs can be mixed according to the circumstances. There are times when this conveys regret – 'if I had met her when I was sixteen, I would have married her', 'If I hadn't got married so young, I would have been happy'. Other times, the message is more mundane: 'If I'd seen your keys I would have picked them up'. In most cases, there is a feeling of 'what if...' hanging over the scenario, and it's useful for us to imagine the 'if' clause being followed by bracketed inserts like 'but I didn't'.

The Spanish formation involves the **pluperfect subjunctive** (e.g. *hubiera/ hubiese hablado*) for the *si* clause, and the **conditional perfect** (e.g. *habría hablado*) for the main clause. The latter can sometimes be expressed, in informal Spanish, as *hubiera hablado*, but the conventional *habría hablado* is recommended, partly because it is correctly gauged in more situations, but also because it helps us to keep the formation of the two clauses distinct in our minds.

Here is an example of this structure:

Si hubiera / hubiese visto tus llaves, las habría recogido.	If I'd seen your keys [but I didn't], I would have picked them up.

The next example illustrates the 'regretful' flavour this structure can carry. The negativity of the first verb invites us to conclude that the speaker did get married (that was the reality); only a non-marriage would have produced the desirable state – happiness, which in reality didn't happen – expressed in the main clause. It's useful to play around with sentences like this, for example swapping the negatives round: 'If I had got married so young [but I didn't], I wouldn't have been happy [but, on the contrary, I am]':

Si no me hubiera / hubiese casado tan joven, habría sido feliz.	If I hadn't got married so young [but I did], I would have been happy [but I'm not].

Expressing conditions without using *si*

There are a few circumstances in which the spirit of an English 'if' clause is conveyed in Spanish without using the types of *si* clause described above:

Use of *como* + subjunctive in open conditions

With the nuance of a threat, the *si* + present / future indicative of an open condition can be replaced by *como* + present subjunctive:

Como me vuelvas a hablar así, no te dejo / dejaré salir. If you speak to me like that again, I'll ground you.

Como Rosa no me preste el dinero, no voy a poder pagar el alquiler. If Rosa doesn't lend me the money, I'm not going to be able to pay the rent.

Use of *de* + infinitive

Whilst not common, this structure can be a useful alternative to the *si* clause in remote and unfulfilled conditional sentences:

Si clause	De + infin. alternative	Main clause	Full English sentence
Si no llegaran / llegasen a tiempo	De no llegar a tiempo	... perderían el discurso.	If they didn't arrive (were they not to arrive) on time, they would miss the speech.
Si no hubieran / hubiesen llegado a tiempo	De no haber llegado a tiempo	... habrían perdido el discurso.	If they hadn't arrived (had they not arrived) on time, they would have missed the speech.

PRACTICE

1. **To practise open, remote and unfulfilled conditions, look at the following sentences and choose the best of the three options given to fill each gap:**

    1. Si estudias los verbos, los .... sin problemas.

       (a) aprendas (b) aprenderás (c) aprendieses

    2. Si .... los verbos, los aprenderías sin problemas.

       (a) estudiarías (b) estudiabas (c) estudiaras

    3. Si .... los verbos, los habrías aprendido sin problemas.

       (a) hubieras estudiado (b) habías estudiado (c) habrías estudiado

2. **Translate the following fulfilled conditions into Spanish:**

    1. If it was sunny, I normally used to go to the beach.

       ....

    2. If we were at home, we watched television or read.

       ....

    3. If we went to Spain every year, it was because we had friends living there.

       ....

    4. If you were sad, you tended to cry.

       ....

    5. If they asked him a question, the teacher always came running.

       ....

3. **Translate the following open conditions into Spanish. One of them can be translated using the *como* construction:**

    1. If you go to the square at nine o'clock, I'll give you the letter.

       ....

    2. If we want to improve, we have to study more.

       ....

    3. If it rains, we won't go out.

       ....

PRACTICE

4 If this man asks you for information, don't say anything to him.

....

5 If it's possible, we'll do it.

....

4 Translate the following remote conditions into Spanish:

  1 If I brought you the book, would you read it?

  ....

  2 Were he to ask me to go with him, I'd do it.

  ....

  3 If we woke up late, we would miss the train.

  ....

  4 If you could, you would go to the moon.

  ....

  5 If you wanted me to help you, you would tell me.

  ....

5 Translate the following unfulfilled conditions into Spanish:

  1 If we hadn't met Juan, we wouldn't have been able to stay in Madrid.

  ....

  2 Had you told me the truth, I wouldn't have known what to do.

  ....

  3 If they had opted to study biology, they wouldn't have had the opportunity to live in Spain.

  ....

  4 If Laura hadn't written the letter, Juan wouldn't have received it.

  ....

  5 If you hadn't got dressed without putting the light on, you wouldn't have fallen over.

  ....

UNIT 17

Indirect speech

> Indirect speech – also known as 'reported speech' – occurs when someone refers to something said or written earlier, without quoting directly. An example in English would be 'she said she was tired', where the original utterance ('direct speech') would have been 'I am tired'. We can introduce indirect speech via a number of 'reporting verb' constructions, such as 'to say that', 'to ask if / whether', 'to tell [someone] to', and so on.
>
> This unit divides indirect speech up, according to the nature of the original utterance: a statement, a question (but not a request), a command, or a request. In each section, we will look at how Spanish deals with the constructions, including elements of flexibility and alternative renderings.

Reporting a statement

For the purposes of this unit, we consider a 'statement' to be something said or written that is not a question or a command.

How we report a statement depends on a number of factors, principally what was said / written, and when. For example, a person can say something in a variety of tenses, the choice of which – as we shall see – can affect the tense chosen to report it. Equally, the reporter may have to make choices regarding which verb and tense to use in opening the report (e.g. 'she says that', 'she's asking if', 'she's just mentioned that', 'she told me to').

Before we turn our attention to the relevant Spanish structures, let's look at some typical utterances of English statements, and think about how we might seek to report them:

Direct speech	Indirect speech	Notes
We are happy.	They say / are saying / have said they are happy. They said they are / were happy.	The choice of tense for the introductory 'reporting' verb is a matter of common sense, based on the level of immediacy the reporter wishes to convey. Then we need to decide which tense to use for the verb used by the original speakers. Are they still happy at the time of the reporting? In that case, 'are happy' is appropriate. If they were happy when they spoke but are not at the time of reporting, then 'were happy' is a more accurate choice. As you can see, there are plenty of possibilities, but as long as both verbs are pitched in a manner that makes the report clear, understanding will not generally be impaired.

INDIRECT SPEECH — UNIT 17

I am going to join the army.	She says / is saying / has said she is going to join the army. She said she is going / was going to join the army.	Similarly here, choices of tense need to be made at two points: the reporting verb and the verb used by the original speaker. Notice how the reporter relays the information in a way that tells us the timeframe both of when the utterance took place, and of the woman's intention to join the army: 'is going' can become 'was going' if the reporter wants to place the utterance in the past.
I have been to the supermerket	He says he has been to the supermarket. He said he had been to the supermarket.	When were the words uttered? In the first version of the report, it sounds very recent, so matching the man's original tense is appropriate. In the second version, a certain amount of time seems to have passed, so the report takes the tenses back a stage: notice how the direct speech 'has been' (perfect tense) becomes 'had been' (pluperfect) in reported speech.
We will do it tomorrow.	They say they will do it tomorrow. They said they would do it the following day.	Again, it's a question of how soon after the utterance it is being reported. If it's on the same day, then the word 'tomorrow' is still relevant, and can be kept in the report; if the utterance was last week, then 'tomorrow' has to become 'the next / following day'. The same thing can happen with 'this morning' becoming 'that morning', etc. Just as importantly, in the second version, notice that the future 'will do' turns into the conditional 'would do' in the reported style.

With so many possibilities, it's futile to make hard and fast rules about the sequence of tenses in these circumstances. However, the tense changes visible in the last two examples above are worth bearing in mind. Here are some examples of good practice in reporting statements in Spanish indirect speech, using the same sentences we discussed in the table above. The suggested reports are not comprehensive, but should offer a flavour of the sorts of combinations typically used. Remember that the conjunction *que* must be retained between the two clauses in Spanish, whereas its English counterpart 'that' can be dropped:

Direct speech	English	Indirect speech	English
Estamos contentos.	We're happy.	*Dijeron que estaban contentos.*	They said (that) they were happy.
Voy a alistarme.	I'm going to join the army.	*Ha comentado que va a alistarse. / Comentó que iba a alistarse.*	She said (that) she is / was going to join the army.
He ido al supermercado.	I've been to the supermarket.	*Mencionó que había ido al supermercado.*	He mentioned (that) he'd been to the supermarket.
Lo haremos mañana.	We'll do it tomorrow.	*Dijeron que lo harían al día siguiente.*	They said (that) they would do it the following day.

UNIT 17 — INDIRECT SPEECH

Extra care must be taken when the utterance in itself has particular linguistic characteristics that will lead to complexities in Spanish. Here's a potentially tricky example. Notice how the 'futureness' of the utterance – in this case with the *'cuando* + future idea' structure – must be accurately reported. Focus closely on the tenses used in the reported version:

Direct speech	English	Indirect speech	English
Saldré cuando haga mejor tiempo.	I'll go out when the weather improves.	*Dijo que saldría cuando hiciera / hiciese mejor tiempo.*	He said he would go out when the weather improved.

Reporting a question that is not a request

If you've mastered the concepts discussed in the sections above, you'll find that reporting questions is very similar to reporting statements, except that our reporting verbs will now be more like 'she asked whether' or 'they want to know if'. The same overlaps of tense apply here, depending on the extent to which the reporter feels the details of the utterance remain current. Here are some examples to illustrate how questions can typically be reported. The change of person (e.g. in the first example, from 'you' in the question to 'we' in the report; and in the second example, *conmigo* has to become *con ella*) can sometimes catch students out:

Direct speech	English	Indirect speech	English
¿Cómo estáis?	How are you [plural]?	*Nos preguntó cómo estábamos.*	He asked us how we were.
¿Quieres tomar un café conmigo?	Do you fancy a coffee?	*Me preguntó si quería tomar un café con ella.*	She asked if I fancied having a coffee with her.
¿Dónde han estado?	Where have they been?	*Quiso saber dónde habían estado.*	He wanted to know where they'd been.
¿Irás al teatro con nosotros esta semana?	Will you be going to the theatre with us this week?	*Me preguntó si iría al teatro con ellos esa semana.*	She asked me if I would be going to the theatre with them that week.

Reporting a command

Things get a bit trickier when the original utterance we want to report was a command. Here we're dealing with pairs such as 'Give me the money!' → 'He told / wanted / instructed me to give him the money'. Unsurprisingly, we need to work with the subjunctive and, in doing so, we need to make a choice of tenses based on the rule of thumb given in Unit 13. This structure does, however, serve as

INDIRECT SPEECH — UNIT 17

good revision for the subjunctive structures we cover and practise in Units 13 and 14. Let's have a look at some typical reporting of imperatives in Spanish:

Direct speech	English	Indirect speech	English
¡Cállate!	Shut up!	Me dice que me calle.	She's telling me to shut up.
		Le dice que se calle.	She's telling him / her to shut up.
		Me ha dicho que me calle.	She told me to shut up.
		Le ha dicho que se calle.	She's told him / her to shut up.
		Me dijo que me callara / callase.	She told me to shut up.
		Le dijo que se callara / callase.	She told him / her to shut up.
¡Pasadme el telemando!	Pass me the remote control!	Quiere que le pasemos el telemando.	He wants us to pass him the remote control.
		Quiere que le pasen el telemando.	He wants them to pass him the remote control.
		Quería que le pasáramos / pasásemos el telemando.	He wanted us to pass him the remote control.
		Quería que le pasaran / pasasen el telemando.	He wanted them to pass him the remote control.
¡Suban a la primera planta!	Go up to the first floor!	Les dijeron que subieran / subiesen a la primera planta.	They were told to go up to the first floor.
		Nos dijeron que subiéramos / subiésemos a la primera planta.	We were told to go up to the first floor.
¡No nos lo digáis!	Don't tell us (it)!	Nos dijeron que no se lo dijéramos / dijésemos.	They told us not to tell them (it).
		Les dijeron que no se lo dijeran / dijesen.	They told them not to tell them (it).

Reporting a request

Structurally, reporting a request in Spanish is similar to reporting a command, except that our introductory verbs will be things like 'he asked me to' rather than 'he told me to'. *Pedir* will be the key verb:

Direct speech	English	Indirect speech	English
¿Nos ayudas, por favor?	Will you help us, please?	Me piden que les ayude.	They're asking me to help them.
		Le piden que les ayude.	They're asking him / her to help them.
		Me han pedido que les ayude.	They've asked me to help them.
		Le han pedido que les ayude.	They've asked him / her to help them.
		Me pidieron que les ayudara / ayudase.	They asked me to help them.
		Le pidieron que les ayudara / ayudase.	They asked him / her to help them.

UNIT 17 INDIRECT SPEECH

¿Me abre la puerta, señora?	Would you open the door for me, madam?	Le pide a la señora que le abra la puerta.	He asks the lady to open the door for him.
		Le ha pedido a la señora que le abra la puerta.	He's asked the lady to open the door for him.
		Le pidió a la señora que le abriera / abriese la puerta.	He asked the lady to open the door for him.
¿Te puedo pedir un favor?	Can I ask you a favour?	Me ha pedido que le haga un favor.	He's asked me to do him a favour.
		Le ha pedido que le haga un favor.	He's asked him / her to do him a favour.

Sometimes we can get away with using a noun, such as in the first and third examples in the table:

Me pidieron ayuda.   They asked me for help.
Me ha pedido un favor. He's asked me a favour.

PRACTICE

1 'Report' the following utterances in indirect speech in Spanish, assuming them to have been spoken a week ago by a woman. Begin each of your reports with *Dijo que* …:

1 Acabo de ver esta película.

   ....

2 Me han confirmado que tengo que relajarme.

   ....

3 El accidente fue hace tres días.

   ....

4 Mi hija ya no me quiere.

   ....

5 Podré hacerlo mañana.

   ....

2 'Report' in Spanish the following questions, spoken by a man a few seconds ago. The person(s) to whom the question is directed should be the voice doing the 'reporting'. Your reports should use the verbs *preguntar* and *querer saber*:

1 ¿Sabéis jugar a las cartas?

   ....

2 ¿Cuánto dinero tienes?

   ....

3 ¿Hay agua en la nevera?

   ....

4 ¿Te lo puedo dar?

   ....

5 ¿Mi mujer y yo tenemos que salir hoy?

   ....

PRACTICE

3 **Translate the following commands and their corresponding 'reports' into Spanish. The original utterances were spoken by a woman last week. Assume all imperatives to be in the *vosotros* form, and the reporters to be *nosotros*:**

1 Wake up.

   ..../..

2 Open the book and read it.

   ..../..

3 Close the magazine and pass me it.

   ..../..

4 Don't fall asleep this afternoon.

   ..../..

5 Don't tell me a series of lies.

   ..../..

4 **Read the following 'reports' of questions and requests, and suggest what you think the original Spanish utterance was in each case:**

1 Mi amigo me ha pedido que le preste mis gafas.

   ....

2 Mi madre me pidió que le bajara la basura a la calle.

   ....

3 Mi abuelo me preguntó si me importaba cerrarle la ventana.

   ....

4 Mis hermanos me preguntaron si podía ayudarles.

   ....

5 Me pediste que te dejara diez euros.

   ....

UNIT 18
Expressing English modal auxiliary verbs in Spanish

> A modal auxiliary verb can be used in combination with another verb to give the latter a specific meaning. English modal verbs include 'should', 'ought to', 'may', 'might', 'can', 'could', 'will', 'shall', 'would', 'got to', 'do', 'need', 'have to' and 'must'. In Spanish, the usual format is for one of a small number of verbs (such as *deber* or *poder*) to be followed by an infinitive. The tense of the modal verb – and here, we will pay particular attention to the differences triggered by the use of the preterite, the imperfect and the conditional – is key to pinning down precise meaning.

Difference between *poder* and *saber*

Aside from its primary meaning of 'to know (a fact)', *saber* also means 'to know how to (do something)', in which usage it includes the notion of 'can do', and hence overlaps with *poder* in the mind of the English-speaking learner of Spanish. *Saber* is to do with 'being able' to do something in the sense of having undergone the training or possessing the skills to do it:

Sabes jugar al golf.	You know how to play golf.
Sabemos hablar francés	We can speak French.

Poder, on the other hand, relates to 'being able' in terms of:

1. circumstances:

    No podemos jugar al golf porque está lloviendo /   We can't play golf because it's raining /
    porque el campo está cerrado.   because the course is closed.

2. permission:

    No podemos hablar francés porque nuestros   We can't speak French because our parents
    padres quieren que practiquemos el español.   want us to practise Spanish.
    No se puede entrar.   Entry is prohibited. / You / we / one (etc.) can't go in.

3. possibility / suggestion:

    Podemos ir al cine si quieres.   We can go to the cinema if you like.

It's worth pointing out here that the preterite of *saber* moves away slightly from the notions of 'knowing' and 'knowing how to', and takes on the meaning of 'finding out' or 'becoming aware':

Supe la noticia al entrar en la iglesia.   I learned the news as I was going into the church.

UNIT 18 EXPRESSING ENGLISH MODAL AUXILIARY VERBS IN SPANISH

Use of *poder*

⇨ See Unit 14, under 'Possibility and Probability', for discussion of the structure **puede que**.

The first section of this unit, which distinguishes between the two verbs, details one of the main obstacles to mastering the use of *poder*. Also potentially tricky are the nuances associated with its use in the preterite, perfect, imperfect and conditional indicative tenses:

Poder in the preterite and perfect indicative

In the preterite and perfect tenses, *poder* takes on two very specific roles. In the first, it implies 'to succeed in [doing something]' or 'to manage to [do something]':

Pudieron salir a tiempo.	They managed to get out on time.
La ciencia ha podido demostrarlo.	Science has been able to prove it.

Confusingly, its use in the preterite and perfect can also mean 'could have done but didn't [do the following verb]'. Generally, the context will tell you which applies. Here are some examples:

Pude morir en ese accidente.	I could have died in that accident.
¡Has podido caerte por la ventana!	You could have fallen out of the window!

If the preterite or perfect is used in the negative form in any circumstance, the meaning is 'couldn't and didn't':

No pudimos comprarlo.	We weren't able to buy it.
No hemos podido comprarlo.	We haven't been able to buy it.

Note also this usage in a compound version of the preterite:

Pudo haberla matado.	He could have killed her [but luckily she survived].

Poder in the imperfect indicative

Use of the imperfect of *poder* implies the following, which will generally equate to the English 'could':

1 An (in)ability to do something over a period of time – contrasting with the more instantaneous usage of the preterite or perfect:

No podíamos salir porque estábamos enfermos.	We weren't able to / couldn't go out because we were ill.

2 As an alternative to the conditional – less common, but still valid – in making suggestions or stating possibilities:

Podíamos invitarle a casa.	We could invite him to the house.
Podía ser cierto.	It could be true.

EXPRESSING ENGLISH MODAL AUXILIARY VERBS IN SPANISH UNIT 18

3 In asking a favour or making a request, it can again be used as a less common alternative to the conditional:

¿Podía usted darles un mensaje, por favor?   Could you give them a message, please?

4 In issuing a rebuke – again, in place of the conditional tense:

Podías por lo menos disculparte.   You could at least apologise.

Poder in the conditional indicative

The conditional is the preferred tense for the usages outlined in cases 2, 3 and 4 of the section on *poder* in the imperfect, above:

Podríamos invitarle a casa.	We could invite him to the house.
Podría ser cierto.	It could be true.
¿Podrías darles un mensaje, por favor?	Could you give them a message, please?
Podrías por lo menos disculparte.	You could at least apologise.

Word order varieties in compound tenses of *poder*

In complex structures involving *poder*, such as the Spanish equivalent of 'you would have been able to do it', several word orders are permissible. Look closely at the options below, focusing in each case on which verb occurs in the infinitive and which in the past participle, and where the object pronoun *lo* can be positioned:

[conditional of **haber** + past participle of **poder** + infinitive]

Habrías podido hacerlo. / Lo habrías podido hacer.   You would have been able to do it / You could have done it.

[conditional of **poder** + infinitive of **haber** + past participle]

Podrías haberlo hecho. / Lo podrías haber hecho.

Use of *deber*

The primary use of *deber* + infinitive is as an equivalent to the English 'must' (in the sense of 'have the obligation to'). It plays a simlilar, but not always identical, role to *tener que*:

Deben hacerlo ya.   They must do it right now.

⇨ See section on **tener que**.

Just as we have seen with *poder*, *deber* also has a few subtleties depending on which tense is used.

UNIT 18   EXPRESSING ENGLISH MODAL AUXILIARY VERBS IN SPANISH

Deber in the preterite indicative

This tense of *deber* is used in the following circumstances:

1. As a means of saying that something 'should have been done' or 'ought to have been done' (or, in the case of the negative form, 'shouldn't have been done' or 'oughtn't to have been done'):

(No) debimos asistir.	We should (not) have attended.

2. Not fully recommendable, but commonly occurring, is the following usage, that of 'must have done' in the sense of guesswork / supposition. You will see that it treads on the toes of the function of *deber de* (and is considered unacceptable by many grammarians), so learners of Spanish can sidestep it to avoid confusion:

Debieron hacerlo ellos.	They must have done it (I imagine).
Debió hacerles gracia.	It must have tickled them / They must have found it funny.

   ⇨ See also section on ***deber de***.

Deber in the imperfect indicative

The imperfect use is quite straightforward in a normal, past-tense situation, as it simply means 'had to' or 'used to have to' do the verb in question:

Debíamos coger tres autobuses para ir al colegio.	We had to / used to have to take three buses to get to school.

It can also be used as an alternative to the conditional, to say that someone 'should do' or 'ought to do' the verb in question. See the section below for coverage of the role of the conditional:

Debías decirnos la verdad.	You should / ought to tell us the truth.

Deber in the conditional indicative

The conditional tense is the first port of call if we want to soften the present tense 'must' into a gentler 'ought to' or 'should'. Notice the difference in strength of obligation between the present and the conditional in the examples, below:

Debemos llegar a las nueve.	We must arrive at nine o'clock.
Deberíamos llegar a las nueve.	We should / ought to arrive at nine o'clock.

Word order varieties in compound tenses of *deber*

In complex structures involving *deber*, such as the Spanish equivalent of 'you ought to have done it', several word orders are permissible. Look closely at the options below, focusing in each case on

EXPRESSING ENGLISH MODAL AUXILIARY VERBS IN SPANISH UNIT 18

which verb occurs in the infinitive and which in the past participle, and where the object pronoun *lo* can be positioned:

Format (construction is given in brackets)	Alternative word order	Translation
Deberías haberlo hecho. [conditional of **deber** + infinitive of **haber** + past participle]	**Lo deberías haber hecho.**	You should have / ought to have done it.
Habrías debido hacerlo. [conditional of **haber** + past participle of **deber** + infinitive]	**Lo habrías debido hacer.**	

Use of *deber de*

Contrary to the function of *deber* for 'must of obligation', its sister verb *deber de* + infinitive is associated purely with 'must of assumption / guesswork':

Debe de ser muy bonito vivir en Italia.   It must be lovely to live in Italy.
Debió de abandonar la reunión antes de la conclusión.   He must have left the meeting before the conclusion.
Deben de haber pasado mucho calor.   They must have found it very hot (lit: experienced a lot of heat).

It's worth noting that in popular use there is a tendency to omit the *de* from this structure, thus creating a usage frowned on by many grammarians.

➪ See also point 2 of section 'Deber in the preterite indicative'

This has become acceptable in everyday usage, but it's still advisable to learn to distinguish clearly between the two structures.

Use of *tener que*

Tener que shares the sense of obligation denoted by *deber*, but in everyday Spanish it is the more likely verb to convey the English 'must'. Most of its tenses work – and translate into English – as you would expect:

Tienes que dedicarle más tiempo al proyecto si quieres concluirlo.   You have to devote more time to the project if you want to conclude it.
Tendremos que salir muy temprano.   We'll have to set off very early.
Si aceptara / aceptase el puesto tendría que mudarme.   If I accepted the job I'd have to move house.

There are a couple of points to make about its past tenses, which are outlined below.

Tener que in the imperfect indicative

The imperfect refers to what someone 'had to do' habitually or over a period of time:

Mi hermana tenía que levantarse pronto todos los días.   My sister had to get up early every day.

UNIT 18 EXPRESSING ENGLISH MODAL AUXILIARY VERBS IN SPANISH

It can also have the nuance that the listener won't necessarily know if the action the speaker 'had to do' was ever actually performed:

Tenía que pedir hora con el médico.	She had to make an appointment to see the doctor [but we don't know if she ever did].

This contrasts with one of the functions of the preterite.

⇨ See 'Tener que in the preterite indicative', second function

In addition, it shares a function with the conditional tense:

Tenías que haberlo hecho.	You ought to have done it [but didn't].
Tenías que haber salido antes.	You should have left earlier [but didn't, and missed the appointment].
No tenías que habérselo dicho.	You shouldn't have told him / her / them.

Tener que in the preterite indicative and perfect indicative

In this construction, the first role of the preterite and the perfect is to say, respectively, what someone 'had to do' and 'has had to do' spontaneously, quickly and as a single action:

Tuvimos que llevarla al hospital. / Tuvo que ser ingresada.	We had to take her to the hospital. / She had to be admitted.
Hemos tenido que llevarla al hospital. / Ha tenido que ser ingresada.	We've had to take her to the hospital. / She's had to be admitted.

Secondly, and in contrast to the second example in the 'Imperfect' section, the preterite implies that the action one 'had to do' was actually done. Note that this is also the case with the perfect tense:

Tuvo que / ha tenido que recoger a su suegra.	He had / has had to collect his mother-in-law [and he did so / has done so].

Word order varieties in compound tenses of *tener que*

In complex structures involving *tener que*, such as the Spanish equivalent of 'you ought to have done it', several word orders are permissible. Look closely at the options below, focusing in each case on which verb occurs in the infinitive and which in the past participle, and where the object pronoun *lo* can be positioned:

Format (construction is given in brackets)	Alternative word order	Translation
Tendrías que haberlo hecho. [conditional of **tener** + **que** + infinitive of **haber** + past participle]	**Lo tendrías que haber hecho.**	You should have / ought to have done it.
Habrías tenido que hacerlo. [conditional of **haber** + past participle of **tener** + **que** + infinitive]	**Lo habrías tenido que hacer.**	

Tener que as an alternative to deber de

Tener que also fulfils the 'must of supposition' role played by deber de, but it is generally considered to be rather more forceful:

Tiene que habérselo dicho a la profesora.	He's got to have (he must have) told the teacher.
Tienes que estar hasta las narices de tanto trabajo.	You've got to be (you must be) fed up to the back teeth with so much work.
Han tenido que pasarlo muy mal estos últimos años.	They must have had a really bad time these last few years.

Use of *haber que*

Hay que – and its equivalent in other tenses – is an impersonal, third-person-only structure which conveys what 'one' must do, what it is necessary for society to do, etc. It must never be applied to a particular person (e.g. 'my brother must', 'you all have to'): if this is required, *tener que* (*mi hermano tiene que*, *todos tenéis que*) or *deber* (*mi hermano debe*, *todos debéis*) will provide a solution. Here are a few examples:

Hay que pagar diez euros para ver la exposición.	It's necessary to (one has to, you have to) pay ten euros to see the exhibition.
Habrá que abrigarse este fin de semana.	People will need to wrap up this weekend.
Antes había que rellenar una hoja, pero ya no.	One (you) used to have to fill in a form, but not any longer.

The preterite is available to respond to actions that were spontaneously necessary and were carried out straight away:

Hubo que nombrar un sucesor en el acto.	A successor had to be named there and then.

Use of *haber de*

Haber de shares the 'obligation' and 'supposition' functions of *tener que*, but is far gentler and also far less commonly used, other than in written language, though it is frequently heard in Catalonia because of the influence of the Catalan *haver de*, which is the standard way of saying *tener que* in that language. Unlike *haber que*, *haber de* has a full complement of persons:

He de decirte que no me gustan los muebles.	I have to tell you I don't like the furniture.
Habían de desempeñar una gama de papeles.	They had to play a range of roles.

UNIT 18   EXPRESSING ENGLISH MODAL AUXILIARY VERBS IN SPANISH

Use of *querer*

In its meaning of 'to want', and taking an infinitive, *querer* is a very common and useful modal verb:

Quiero conocerla.	I want to meet her.
Querrán quedarse a dormir.	They'll want to sleep over.
Querríamos hablar con la encargada, por favor.	We'd like to speak to the woman in charge, please.

In sentences such as the last example, the conditional can often be replaced (without losing the conditional flavour) by the imperfect indicative *quería* or the imperfect subjunctive *quisiera*.

In the imperfect and preterite, there is sometimes a degree of ambiguity as to whether the action that the subject wanted to do actually took place. Context will generally shed light on the matter. Here are some examples:

Quería repetir la experiencia.	He wanted to repeat the experience [but we don't know if he managed to do so].
No querían verle.	They didn't want to see him [and we don't know whether they did].
Quisieron entrar.	They (decided spontaneously that they) wanted to come in [and they may or may not have done so].

The negative form of the preterite has two specific nuances:

1 The notion of 'refusing to':

Les pedí que participaran / participasen pero no quisieron.	I asked them to take part but they refused.

2 The sense of 'not meaning to', in seeking to mitigate a possible offence, etc.:

No quise molestarte.	I didn't mean to bother you.

Use of *soler*

Soler (radical change: *o >ue* in the present indicative) + infinitive can be jocularly referred to in English as the verb 'to usually', in that it serves to talk about what one tends to do, usually does, is in the habit of doing, etc. Realistically, its use is limited to the present (what I usually do) and imperfect (what I usually did) tenses:

Suelo trocear la carne antes de comerla.	I usually chop my meat up before I eat it.
Solíamos quedar los viernes por la mañana.	We tended to meet up on Friday mornings.

PRACTICE

1 Insert the most appropriate form of either *poder* or *saber* into each gap below:

1. Si .... tocar la guitarra, ¿me enseñarás a tocar a mí?

2. No creo que tú .... conducir con el brazo roto.

3. Si .... cocinar, te juro que te pasaría todas las recetas.

4. Te trataré como a un adulto cuando .... comportarte debidamente.

5. Me dijeron que cuando .... enviarme los documentos, lo harían.

2 Make any necessary changes to the verbs in the following sentences, so that each reads correctly:

1. Cuando tuve quince años no querría llegar a ser adulto.

   ....

2. Cuando tendré un poco de dinero lo poderé gastar en cosas importantes.

   ....

3. No solemos vernos muy a menudo porque no podamos dejar solos a nuestros hijos.

   ....

4. Le pedí que saliere conmigo pero no querió.

   ....

5. Sabía la noticia cuando por fin podía poner la radio.

   ....

3 Translate the following sentences into Spanish, using an appropriate form of *tener que*:

1. I had to do an exam last week, but I passed it.

   ....

2. We'll have to work if we want to buy this car.

   ....

PRACTICE

3. If you had to drink a litre of wine you would get drunk.

   ....

4. When I'm sixty-five I'll have to sell the house.

   ....

5. I had to spend time with a lot of friends when I was young.

   ....

4 Insert an appropriate form of either *haber que* or *tener que* into each of the gaps below:

1. El año que viene los vecinos .... pintar la fachada.

2. .... llamar a la policía cuando ocurrió el accidente.

3. Si vosotros .... aguantarlo, sabríais lo que siento yo.

4. .... pagar los impuestos, así es la vida.

5. Antes .... ir a misa cada domingo, pero la sociedad ya ha cambiado.

5 Using the same elements, re-express the following sentence in three alternative ways:
Lo deberían haber conseguido.

1. ....
2. ....
3. ....

UNIT 19

The passive and its alternatives

There are times when it's more appropriate or desirable to say not that someone performs or performed an action, but rather that the action <u>is perfomed</u> or <u>was performed</u>. Whilst we could meaningfully say 'The Normans <u>built</u> this castle' it would sound smoother to say 'This castle <u>was built</u> by the Normans'. Often we don't know the subject of the sentence, so this type of structure is the obvious one to use: 'The car was stolen last week'.

This turning-round of a structure, using the verb 'to be' and the past participle ('is made', 'will be achieved', 'was written', 'would have been changed', etc.) is known as the passive voice or, more commonly, the passive. In effect, the active sentence 'The Normans [subject] built [verb] this castle [object]' is inverted to give 'This castle [new subject] was built [passive verb] by the Normans [known as the 'agent' – the person(s) or thing(s) responsible for the action]'.

The passive in Spanish

The passive can be formed identically in Spanish, with *ser* and the past participle, using *por* ('by') to introduce the agent, if required:

Este castillo <u>fue construido</u> por los normandos.   This castle <u>was built</u> by the Normans.

When we studied the perfect tense in Spanish using the auxiliary *haber*, we learned not to make the past participle agree with the subject in either number or gender (*Pepe ha terminado*, *María ha terminado*, *ellas han terminado*). The passive with *ser*, however, is a structure where we must make it agree. Have a look at the following sentences, set out in both active and passive forms:

ACTIVE		PASSIVE	
El gobiero devaluó el peso.	The government devalued the peso.	*El peso <u>fue devaluado</u> por el gobierno.*	The peso was devalued by the government.
El ministro inaugurará la exposición.	The minister will open the exhibition.	*La exposición <u>será inaugurada</u> por el ministro.*	The exhibition will be opened by the minister.
El gobierno financió los Juegos Olímpicos.	The government funded the Olympic Games.	*Los Juegos Olímpicos <u>fueron financiados</u> por el gobierno.*	The Olympic Games were funded by the government.
Los guardas jurados abren las puertas cada mañana.	The security guards open the doors every morning.	*Las puertas <u>son abiertas</u> cada mañana por los guardas jurados.*	The doors are opened by the security guards every morning.

Estar and the past participle

If you come across *estar* with a past participle, what you've got is not a passive, but rather a description of the <u>resultant state</u> produced by an earlier action (which may or may not have been a passive). Have another look at one of the examples from the table:

Las puertas son abiertas cada mañana por los guardas jurados.

The doors are opened by the security guards every morning.

That's the action they perform (or that is performed by them) every morning: 'the doors <u>are opened</u> by someone'. But if a visitor arrives after the doors are opened, they will find them <u>open</u> (the resultant state):

Cuando llego al museo cada día, las puertas normalmente <u>están abiertas</u>.

When I get to the museum every day, the doors <u>are</u> normally <u>open</u>.

Notice that here too the past participle must agree in number and gender with the subject to which it is referring.

Other verbs used with the past participle in passive situations

Aside from *ser* (for genuine passives) and *estar* (to describe resultant states), a handful of other verbs can be very useful in providing a 'was done' style of passive in Spanish.

Quedar

Carrying something of the flavour of the English 'ended up' in passive structures, *quedar* + past participle refers to a state resulting from some kind of event, often an accident/catastrophe, or the implementation of something like a rule or a decision:

La moto quedó destrozada.

The motorbike was / ended up wrecked.

Las reglas del juego quedaron establecidas en 1850.

The rules of the game were fixed / agreed upon in 1850.

Resultar

Resultar is identical in structure to *quedar*, and similar in meaning – especially in referring to victims of accidents, etc. – although it can also veer slightly more towards the English 'turned out', as well as just 'ended up':

Cien personas resultaron heridas / muertas.

A hundred people were injured / killed.

Resultaron no saber nada.

They turned out not to know anything.

THE PASSIVE AND ITS ALTERNATIVES — UNIT 19

Verse

Often working with the past participle *afectado* ('affected'), the reflexive *verse* – literally 'to see itself', but in passive structures meaning simply 'to be' – is found in contexts such as describing the effects of the economy, statistics, etc.:

Los resultados se vieron afectados por la crisis bancaria.   The results were affected by the banking crisis.

Other ways of expressing an English passive in Spanish – avoidance techniques

So far, so good, but it's important to point out that Spanish isn't generally as keen on passives as English is. In fact, unless you're eager to point out by whom something was done (e.g. 'This castle was built by the Normans', as opposed to by someone else), there are a number of other devices – often preferred by Spanish – to convey the same information:

Leave the sentence active

There is usually a way, in both languages, of achieving this:

Los normandos construyeron este castillo.   The Normans built this castle.

If you want to keep the sentence active but give additional emphasis to who was responsible for the action, the following construction can be useful – note the seemingly redundant object pronoun *lo*, whose usage is discussed earlier in the book:

Este castillo lo construyeron los normandos.   The Normans built this castle.

The word order is rigid for this construction. Other examples of this type can be set up:

Esta lana la fabrica una empresa peruana.   A Peruvian company manufactures this wool / This wool is manufactured by a Peruvian company.

Las galletas las compró mi hermano.   The biscuits were bought by my brother / My brother bought the biscuits / It was my brother who bought the biscuits.

Use the third person plural of an active verb

We do this in English, too – often to talk about the mysterious 'they' people who go about society doing things: 'I see they've dug the road up', 'they should ban this type of event'. Spanish deals with

UNIT 19 THE PASSIVE AND ITS ALTERNATIVES

this structure very comfortably. In fact, there are times when Spanish prefers the third person plural to translate what would, in English, naturally be a passive:

<u>Echan</u> una película muy interesante en el cine.	<u>They're showing</u> a very interesting film at the cinema.
Veo que <u>han abierto</u> una nueva tienda en la calle principal.	I see <u>they've opened</u> a new shop on the high street.
<u>Han montado</u> una línea de asistencia.	A helpline has been set up. / They've set up a helpline.

Respectively, the examples above are avoiding the need to say 'is being shown' and 'has been opened', both of which are passives that would be very cumbersome if attempted literally in Spanish.

The impersonal *se* and the 'reflexive' construction

This is a bit like the generic English 'one' (meaning 'people in general', 'society at large') – considered by many to be excessively 'posh', but still a useful tool in modern English, even if just for humorous purpose: 'One likes to finish one's beer before going for one's kebab'.

The Spanish *uno* can serve this purpose, but far better is the use of an impersonal *se*:

Cuando se habla mucho es fácil meter la pata.	When you / people talk a lot, it's easy for you / them to put your / their foot in it.
Se dice que es terrorista.	S/he is said to be a terrorist / people say s/he is a terrorist.

If you see a structure like *estos coches se fabrican en España*, it doesn't necessarily mean that these cars manufacture themselves in Spain without human intervention! In fact, although it looks like a reflexive, the context will generally reassure us that it's really a device for us to express an English passive. Have a look at the following, and note in particular the plural verbs in the examples – verbs used in situations like these must agree with the subject (here *las patatas, las puertas*):

Eso no se hace.	That isn't done / shouldn't be done [= is naughty (etc.)].
'Vaca' se escribe con 'v'.	'Vaca' is written / is spelt with a 'v'.
Las patatas se fríen en un poco de aceite.	The potatoes / chips are fried in a little bit of oil.
Cuando se abren las puertas la gente entra en tropel.	When the doors are opened, people flood in.
El castillo se construyó en 1081.	The castle was built in 1081.

Going full circle back to the Normans building their castle, notice that when we use this *se* construction, we can't add the agent *por los normandos* ('by the Normans').

THE PASSIVE AND ITS ALTERNATIVES — UNIT 19

Misleading English 'passives'

We need to beware of an English usage that can land us in hot water when attempting a translation into Spanish. It happens when the passive is actually focusing more on the recipient ('once removed' from the object) of the action. Here's an example:

I was given a letter.

If you think about it, I wasn't the thing that was given: the letter was. To convert it into the type of sentence we've been dealing with, we'd have to say:

A letter was given to me.

This type of complication can arise with verbs that involve some kind of conveying (giving, telling, offering, passing etc.). If you have time on your hands to do some analysis, it's useful to practise rearranging such structures in English so as to make your job easier when constructing the Spanish equivalent:

She was told a joke.	= A joke was told <u>to her</u>.
I was offered a job.	= A job was offered <u>to me</u>.
They were handed a package.	= A package was handed <u>to them</u>.

To deal with such structures in Spanish, you can translate the modified version of the examples above:

Me fue ofrecido un trabajo.	A job was offered to me.
Alguien me ofreció un trabajo.	Someone offered me a job.

However, often the best thing is to use one of the 'avoidance devices':

Me ofrecieron un trabajo.

PRACTICE

1 Create a passive sentence using the preterite tense, based on the elements given in each case:

1 La casa / alquilar / un cantante / famoso

   ....

2 El incidente / ver / la policía

   ....

3 Sus novelas / leer / mucha gente

   ....

4 La ciudad / destrozar / los insurgentes

   ....

5 Los eslóganes / prohibir / el gobierno

   ....

2 Replace the underlined passive form with a relevant construction using *se*:

1 El libro <u>será escrito</u> en inglés.

   ....

2 Las reuniones <u>eran canceladas</u> a menudo sin previo aviso.

   ....

3 Los regalos <u>fueron enviados</u> el 20 de diciembre.

   ....

4 Estos platos <u>son preparados</u> a mano.

   ....

5 Las obras <u>serían realizadas</u> durante la noche.

   ....

PRACTICE

3 Translate the following sentences into Spanish using a construction other than the passive:

1. Thousands of cars are bought each month in Spain.

   ....

2. The cathedral will be completed by another architect.

   ....

3. The machine was stolen last week.

   ....

4. We were invited to visit the city.

   ....

5. It would be sold with some conditions.

   ....

4 Using *estar* + past participle of the verb in brackets, express the resultant state produced in the following scenarios – e.g. *La cocina se pintó el jueves, entonces cuando llegamos el viernes, ya <u>estaba pintada</u>*:

1. Van a apagar todos los electrodomésticos, entonces la televisión tampoco [encender]

   ....

2. Hacía mucho calor en la habitación porque las ventanas [cerrar] ....

3. ¿Habéis preparado todo? Muy bien, entonces la cena ya [preparar] ....

4. Si nos encierran, vamos a .... mucho tiempo [encerrar]

5. Ya son las nueve y entran los trabajadores, así que la oficina debe de [abrir] ....

PRACTICE

5 What are 'they' up to? Express the following in Spanish using a third person plural verb:

1 They've opened a cinema in the city centre.

....

2 They're going to change the plans.

....

3 They often organise exhibitions in the museum.

....

4 They used to spend a lot of money on roadworks.

....

5 They would close these buildings in the event of a fire.

....

6 Find a Spanish solution for each of the following English sentences, using the following formula: 'We were told the truth' → 'The truth was told to us' → *Se nos dijo la verdad / Nos dijeron la verdad*:

1 We will be given an opportunity.

....

2 They were told a joke.

....

3 He was awarded the gold medal.

....

4 You [tú] would be asked a question.

....

5 She was sold a car.

....

UNIT 20

Ser, estar and haber

> The two Spanish verbs *ser* and *estar* – both of which translate into English as 'to be' – are generally thought to constitute one of the trickiest aspects of Spanish grammar. Whilst it's true that there are some areas of overlap and apparent illogicality in their usage, with a bit of learning and a lot of practice it's not hard to keep them apart. A third verb, *haber*, joins the fray not so much because of its role – denoting existence – but more because its translation into English, starting with 'there is' and 'there are', appears to tread on the toes of the verb 'to be', and so particularly in compound tenses (e.g. 'there would have been'), learners can instinctively but erroneously opt for *ser* or *estar* when *haber* is required.
>
> This unit aims to distinguish, clarify and illustrate the uses of these three verbs, as well as guiding readers through areas of overlap and confusion.

Uses of *ser*

The generally recited rule – that *ser* is used for 'permanent' things – is a useful starting-point but, as we shall see, is not fully reliable. It's helpful to think of *ser* as addressing matters of a person or thing's nature or identity, including inherent physical characteristics and traits of personality. Here are some examples of this type, where *ser* is followed by a noun or pronoun:

Soy yo.	It's me.
Mi amiga es profesora.	My friend is a teacher.
Londres es la capital del Reino Unido.	London is the capital of the United Kingdom.
Es una lástima.	It's a pity.

In the second example above, remember the rule about not including the indefinite article before a job title, unless this is qualified by an adjective. The first example also brings up an important point: whereas in English we can readily mix third-person pronouns with first- and second-person ones in identifying people (e.g. 'it's me', 'was it you?', 'it's us'), Spanish is rigid in making subject pronouns correspond to the logical person of *ser* – respectively *soy yo*, *¿fuiste tú?*, *somos nosotros*.

Used with an adjective, *ser* again denotes something that is a characteristic or a permanent quality, such as a person or thing's nature, size, shape, height, colour or nationality. The table below includes some impersonal usages – typical of *ser* – in the second line:

Londres es inmensa.	London is huge.
Es importante / imposible / evidente / fácil.	It's important / impossible / obvious / easy.
La silla es redonda / cómoda.	The chair is round / comfortable.
Mi amiga es inteligente / alta.	My friend is intelligent / tall.
Todos sus coches son rojos / caros.	All their cars are red / expensive.
Mi madre es portuguesa.	My mother is Portuguese.

Ser in passive constructions

Ser is used to form the conventional passive in Spanish:

⇨ See Unit 19 for discussion

Los árboles fueron talados por el jardinero.	The trees were felled by the gardener.
La casa será vendida por las hijas del difunto.	The house will be sold by the daughters of the deceased.

Saying what time or what day it is, and when and where events happen

Ser is used to say what time or day it is. The fourth example reminds us that – irrespective of any urge to use estar for reasons of 'location' – ser is the correct verb to use if 'to be', referring to an event, actually means 'to take place' or 'to be held':

Son las ocho y media.	It's half past eight.
Hoy es lunes.	Today is Monday.
Van a llegar a las seis.	They're going to arrive at six o'clock.
La reunión es a las cinco: es en la sala 301.	The meeting is at five o'clock – it's in room 301.

Ser + de

When used with de, ser denotes origin, possession (but note the bracketed subtlety with the possessive mío, below), and can refer to the material from which something is made:

Mi novio es de Sevilla, pero los zapatos que lleva son de Roma.	My boyfriend is from Seville, but the shoes he's wearing are from Rome.
El coche es de mi padre (no es mío).	The car is my father's (it's not mine).
Esta camisa es de seda, ¿verdad?	This shirt is silk, isn't it?

Uses of estar

Use of estar is generally sub-divided into two main areas: location, and temporary states or conditions. The sections below seek to clarify these usages.

To denote location

With the exception of the 'location and timing of events' usage (see above), to say where a person or thing is, was, will be (etc.), in the sense of 'being located', we use estar. It's logical to have concerns about the second example, below – surely, you might think, with permanence in mind, Madrid is always in the middle of the country? – but we can take it as a rule in such circumstances that the geographical factor overrides the temporary / permanent argument. Furthermore, we can note that *ser* is always followed, in this usage, by a noun, pronoun or adjective:

Estamos en casa / en el bar / en Valencia / en España.	We're at home / in the bar / in Valencia / in Spain.
Madrid es la capital de España, está en el centro del país.	Madrid is the capital of Spain – it's in the middle of the country.

To refer to non-permanent conditions, appearances and states

This cluster of circumstances can be summed up by the difference between *soy inteligente* ('I'm intelligent' – deemed to be an innate characteristic, which therefore takes *ser*) and *estoy cansado* ('I'm tired' – a state of affairs that, all being well, will have changed or disappeared within a few hours or by tomorrow, hence *estar* is used). When you're pondering the use of the two verbs in a particular scenario, it's useful to weigh up the implications and reach of a particular adjective, as some can work with both verbs.

⇨ See section entitled 'Words whose meaning changes when used with *ser* or *estar*'

Consider the case of *guapo* ('good-looking'): *eres muy guapo* means 'you are [inherently] handsome', but *estás muy guapo* suggests that 'you're looking handsome today' – i.e. you've made an effort, have 'scrubbed up well'.

We use *estar* to refer to someone's health or mood:

Están enfermas.	They're ill.
Estoy triste.	I'm feeling sad.
Estamos deprimidos.	We're depressed.

It is also used to note that someone or something – as in the example of *guapo*, above – has undergone an unexpected change of condition, which seems to contradict their 'permanent' condition:

Estás muy delgada.	You're (looking) very slim [i.e. you've lost weight since I last saw you].

We noted in the introduction to this unit that the 'permanent' factor siding with *ser* does not always hold true:

Mis abuelos están muertos.	My grandparents are dead.

Estar with adverbs

An adverb such as 'well', 'badly', 'better' or 'worse' working with the verb 'to be', must be expressed in Spanish using *estar*, not *ser*:

Estamos muy bien / muy mal.	We're very well / in a very bad way.
Los / las pacientes están mejor.	The patients are (feeling / looking) better.
Estoy estupendamente, gracias.	I'm doing splendidly, thanks.

Any urge to use *ser* with an adverb or adverbial phrase must be resisted – this is particularly important for students of French to remember.

Estar + de

This combination can be used to describe someone's mood, situation or temporary job. In the third example, the normal rule of using *ser* for job titles is contradicted in the circumstance of a particular job one is 'doing at the moment':

Estaban de mal humor.	They were in a bad mood.
Estamos de vacaciones / de luto / de juerga.	We're on holiday / in mourning / out on the town.
Mi hermana está de monitora en un campamento de verano.	My sister's working as a monitor on a summer camp.

In continuous tenses

Estar, as we saw earlier in the book, is used as the auxiliary verb to form continuous verb tenses:

Estoy pensando.	I'm thinking.
Estaban desayunando.	They were having breakfast.

Estar + past participle

This usage is often linked to analysis of the passive by way of comparison. We use *ser* to form the pure passive:

La puerta fue abierta a las nueve.	The door was opened at nine o'clock.

Estar, on the other hand, is used to describe the resultant state:

Cuando llegué, la puerta estaba abierta.	When I arrived, the door was open.

Estar + past participle doesn't always come as a result of a passive construction, but it always relates the state a person or thing is in (or isn't in, or isn't yet in) in the light of some action or process:

Los documentos estaban preparados.	The documents were prepared / ready.
Las camas todavía no estarán hechas.	The beds won't be made yet.

Areas of overlap between *ser* and *estar*

Just as with the example of *guapo*, there are times when an adjective can mean either 'displaying this trait or characteristic as part of one's inherent physique or personality' (used with *ser*), or 'behaving or looking that way temporarily' (with *estar*). A few other areas touching on both verbs merit some notes:

Marital status

You are likely to hear both *ser* and *estar* used with words like *soltero/a* ('single'), *divorciado/a* ('divorced') and *viudo/a* ('widowed'). Strictly speaking, use of *ser* means that the marital-status word is being used as a noun – e.g. *es divorciada* ('she's a divorcee') – whereas *está divorciada* would be the adjectival, resultant-state use of 'she is divorced'. *Separado/a* ('separated') and *casado/a* ('married') tend to go with *estar*, but the others can be heard with either verb:

Espero que el hombre con el que sale sea / esté soltero.	I hope the man she's going out with is unmarried.
No quiero ser / estar viuda a los cuarenta años.	I don't want to be a widow at forty.

With adjectives denoting behaviour on a specific occasion

This usage refers to sentences like 'she was abrupt with me', 'they were very polite to the visitors', etc. *Ser* and *estar* are usually interchangeable in such situations:

Fue / estuvo muy brusca conmigo.	She was very abrupt with me.
Fueron / estuvieron muy corteses con los visitantes.	They were very polite to the visitors.
La fiesta fue / estuvo fenomenal.	The party was brilliant.

Words whose meaning changes when used with *ser* or *estar*

Some adjectives have one meaning when used with *estar*, but change their meaning when used with *ser*. The table below shows the most common examples of this phenomenon:

Adjective	Meaning when used with *estar*	Meaning when used with *ser*
aburrido	bored	boring
atento	attentive, alert, paying attention	courteous, thoughtful
bueno	tasty, 'fit' (good-looking)	good
cansado	tired	tiring
consciente	conscious (awake)	aware
fresco	cool, fresh	cheeky
guapo	looking handsome	good-looking by nature
interesado	interested	self-seeking
listo	ready	clever

malo	ill, 'off' (food, etc.)	bad
negro	fuming, irritated; also black in a 'temporary' sense – e.g. blackened by the effects of soot or smoke	black
orgulloso	proud (of a person, achievement)	proud (haughty, arrogant)
rico	tasty	rich
verde	unripe	green, 'dirty' (joke, etc.)
vivo	alive	lively, sharp, alert

Uses of *haber*

Our interest here is not in the role of *haber* as an auxiliary verb, but rather as the means of conveying the existential 'there is/are' in a variety of tenses.

The present tense existential form of *haber* – *hay* – conveys both the singular 'there is' and the plural 'there are'; there is no separate plural form available in this usage, and this fact remains the case across the tenses, though the English 'there' will always be attached to this construction, whether singular or plural:

Había un problema / Había varios problemas.	There was a problem / There were several problems.
Habrá un ayudante / tres ayudantes a vuestra disposición.	There will be a helper / three helpers at your disposal.

Care must be taken in analysing the nature of the English sentence to be translated, to ensure that *hay* is indeed the correct verb to be used in Spanish. In the term 'there is', we must be satisfied that we are talking about existence – are we sure that we could substitute the phrase 'there exists'? The word 'there' in this context must not be confused with the other 'there' (i.e. 'over there' – the opposite of 'here'), when *estar* would be used. Compare the following:

Hay diez libros en la mesa.	There are ten books on the table. ['There exist']
Allí están los libros que buscaba.	There are the books I was looking for. ['Over there ... are located']

As mentioned in the introduction to the unit, slips can sometimes occur in compound tenses of *haber* in its meaning of *hay*, stemming from the inclusion of the past participle 'been' in the English version:

Ha habido [not sido] *un accidente.*	There has been an accident.
Había habido [not sido] *catorce candidatos.*	There had been fourteen candidates.

The preterite of *hay* is *hubo*, and again we must remember that it only exists in the singular. It's also worth noting the shade of meaning in the preterite: *hubo un accidente* would give 'there was an accident' but we can see shades of 'there happened' or 'there occurred'.

Hay with direct object pronouns

Hay (in its variety of tenses) can take a direct object:

Hay un coche raro en la calle. There's a strange car in the street.
Hubo una explosión. There was an explosion.

When this direct object needs to be in the form of a pronoun, we can include it if the noun being replaced is countable – e.g. 'book(s)', 'boy(s)', 'problem(s)':

¿Tiendas de ropa? Las hay en varias calles del centro. Clothes shops? You can find them [literally: 'there are them'] in various streets in the centre.

If the noun is uncountable – e.g. 'flour', 'milk' – the pronoun is not used in Spanish:

—¿Hay harina en el armario? —Sí, hay. 'Is there any flour in the cupboard?' – 'Yes, there is.'

Potential confusion between *haber* and *estar*

There is sometimes a fine line between usages of *estar* (for location) and *hay* (for existence), and they can even occur in the same sentence. Focus closely on the use of each in the example below, to see the roles of location and existence in play:

No hay zapatos en la caja, pero los calcetines que mencionaste sí están. There are no shoes in the box [existence] but the socks you mentioned are here [location].

You'll notice that in the latter half of this example, *estar* is working with the definite article *los*. This is fine, but we must not use a definite article after *hay*:

Hay un parque muy bonito en el centro de la ciudad. There's a very pretty park in the city centre.
Si te interesa la cultura, está el Museo de Arte Contemporáneo. If you're interested in culture, there's the Museum of Contemporary Art.

PRACTICE

1 Insert the corresponding form of either *ser* or *estar* into each of the gaps:

1. El resultado del partido de hoy va a .... importante.
2. A ver si usted me puede orientar. No sé dónde .... la reunión.
3. La tortilla .... hecha, así que puedes tomar un pincho.
4. Los que lo hicimos mejor .... nosotros.
5. No creí que los chicos .... en el edificio.
6. ¿Vosotros .... bien si os dejo aquí?
7. Cuando yo .... mayor, no haré estas cosas.
8. Creo que en este momento Patricia .... de secretaria en una agencia.
9. París .... la capital de Francia; .... en el norte del país.
10. Cuando la vi .... muy delgada, lo que me sorprendió.

2 Translate the following sentences into Spanish, using the correct form of *ser* or *estar*:

1. The food is not prepared yet.

   ....

2. The house was bought by an Italian artist.

   ....

3. The door was open but the windows were closed.

   ....

4. I've read that your grandmother is in hospital but that she's much better.

   ....

5. They are always in a bad mood but they were polite to us on Thursday.

   ....

PRACTICE

3 **Use a suitable form of *haber* to fill each gap:**

1 .... una explosión ayer a las ocho de la mañana.

2 Cuando .... dinero en mi cuenta, te haré la transferencia.

3 Me han confirmado que .... dos intérpretes contigo mañana.

4 Solía .... una variedad de problemas.

5 Era posible que .... nieve en la carretera.

4 **Translate the following into Spanish, using *ser* or *estar* depending on the meaning of the adjective in each context:**

1 I'm alive, and I'm proud to be.

....

2 The class is boring, but Laura isn't bored.

....

3 I'm not aware of the problem, but I'm not clever like you.

....

4 As a student she's good, but she's a bit tired this morning.

....

5 This paella is very tasty, but I think the fish is off.

....

5 **Use your knowledge of *ser*, *estar* and *haber* to make any necessary corrections to the sentences below:**

1 Ahí hay la catedral, al final de esta calle. ....

2 Parece que ha sido un accidente en la carretera. ....

3 La casa estaba de mis padres; fue una ganga cuando la compraron. ....

4 Fue un golpe en la puerta cuando estaban cenando. ....

5 Me alegro de que eres tan delgado hoy en día. ....

UNIT 21 | More on syntax

This unit looks at areas of syntax, beginning with an overview of word order in different types of Spanish sentence, then consolidating some structures from earlier units: concession, condition and purpose.

Word order in Spanish

Generally speaking, word order is a far freer concept in Spanish than in English, but the two languages do share a 'basic', default structure of subject-verb-object:

Juan compra un helado.   Juan buys an ice cream.

There are many departures from this style in Spanish, usually either for reasons of emphasis, to focus on a particular element, or to keep the elements logical and unambiguous. For example, the following structure, with focus on the object and the addition of an object pronoun, exists to add emphasis:

El libro lo compró mi padre.   My father bought the book.

⇨ *See Unit 6 for detailed coverage of this point.*

This is a more emphatic means of stating the straightforward *mi padre compró el libro*. What we have done is to bring the direct object (*el libro*) to the beginning of the sentence, to turn it into the focus – or 'topic' – of the sentence. The importance of focusing clearly on a specific element in Spanish sentences is achieved more by word order than by the facility English can use of vocal emphasis – 'shouting' a particular word to make it stand out:

He gave ME the book.	*El libro me lo dio a mí.*
He gave me THE BOOK.	*A mí me dio el libro.*
HE gave me the book.	*Él me dio el libro.*

Word order in sentences containing a relative clause

English is fond of locating a relative clause in the middle of a main clause, as in this example – the relative clause is underlined, and the elements of the main clause 'the man lives here' can be seen sandwiching it:

The man <u>who sold me my motorbike</u> lives here.

In cases such as this, Spanish is keen to keep the elements of the main clause close to each other. To follow the English word order in Spanish in this case would not be wrong, but an inversion of the subject and verb makes the sentence sound a lot more elegant – and, crucially, is in keeping with preferred practice. The two versions of the sentence, below, have the subject and verb of the main clause underlined – notice that, when the two are inverted, they are satisfyingly closer together:

<u>El hombre</u> que me vendió la moto <u>vive</u> aquí.   [acceptable]
Aquí <u>vive el hombre</u> que me vendió la moto.   [preferred]

Relative clauses themselves can also read and sound more elegant in Spanish when the subject-verb word order is reversed. This time, the desire is for the verb to be as close as possible to the relative pronoun *que*:

los bocadillos <u>que</u> mi hermano <u>prepara</u>   [acceptable]   the sandwiches that my brother prepares
los bocadillos <u>que prepara</u> mi hermano   [preferred]

Activating these preferences, we can end up with an elegant Spanish sentence whose word order is radically different from that of its English equivalent:

Good Spanish	Literal English translation of Spanish	Good English
Sobresalió el cuadro que había presentado tu hermano.	Stood out the painting that had submitted your brother.	The painting your brother had submitted stood out.

Word order in questions with a question word

The order verb-subject must be observed in questions beginning with a question word – *¿cuándo?*, *¿cómo?*, *¿qué?*, etc. – and, in the case of indirect questions, in the clause following a question word:

¿Cómo <u>está tu madre</u>?   How's your mother?
Quieren saber cuánto <u>cobra mi hermano</u>.   They want to know how much my brother earns.

If there is a subject and a direct object in such a question or indirect question, Spanish looks at the relative length of each and sets the preferred word order accordingly, with the shorter element staying close to the verb:

Spanish	English	Preferred Spanish word order
¿Dónde coge flores tu prima?	Where does your cousin pick flowers?	verb-object-subject – object (*flores*) is shorter than subject (*tu prima*)
¿Dónde coge tu prima estas flores tan bonitas?	Where does your cousin pick such lovely flowers as these?	verb-subject-object – subject (*tu prima*) is shorter than object (*estas flores tan bonitas*)
¿Dónde coge Pepe flores / flores Pepe?	Where does Pepe pick flowers?	verb-subject-object / verb-object-subject – subject and object are same length, so either order possible

UNIT 21 — MORE ON SYNTAX

Word order in questions without a question word

Such questions (e.g. 'Are you happy?') are common in both languages. Spanish can use subject-verb word order (*¿Jorge está?* – 'Is Jorge there / in?') but needs to use rising intonation to denote that a question is being asked – this can happen in English, too. Far more elegant is to invert the verb and subject:

| *¿Está Jorge?* | Is Jorge there / in? |
| *¿Ha estado mi prima esta mañana?* | Has my cousin been around this morning? |

If a direct object is involved, Spanish employs the criterion of relative length of subject and object, which we met in the previous section. Again, the preferred order is to have the shorter element next to the verb:

Spanish	English	Preferred Spanish word order
¿Habla alemán tu vecino?	Does your neighbour speak German?	verb-object-subject – object (*alemán*) is shorter than subject (*tu vecino*)
¿Habla tu vecino más idiomas europeos?	Does your neighbour speak any more European languages?	verb-subject-object – subject (*tu vecino*) is shorter than object (*más idiomas europeos*)
¿Habla Marta alemán / alemán Marta?	Does Marta speak German?	verb-subject-object / verb-object-subject – subject and object are same length, so either order possible

Word order with adverbs and adverbial phrases

If we have in mind an English sentence involving an adverb or adverbial phrase – for example, 'often', 'never', 'until recently', 'no sooner', 'here' – the key in Spanish is to leave the adverbial phrase as close as possible to the verb to which it refers. Here are some examples of how Spanish would phrase different types of sentence falling into this category. Notice that in some cases, there is inversion of the subject and verb:

Apenas me hablaban los compañeros de clase.	My classmates hardly spoke to me.
Por aquí viven los futbolistas.	(The) footballers live around here.
Al final de la fiesta apareció una chica vestida de bruja.	At the end of the party a girl appeared dressed as a witch.
Condujo muy despacio el coche de su hermano.	He drove his brother's car very slowly.

Word order with prepositions

One notable difference between English and Spanish is – as we saw earlier in the book – that English prepositions can end a sentence, whereas Spanish ones absolutely cannot. A reworking may be necessary to change sentences like 'This is the house I live in' or 'He's the man I'm going out with' into Spanish-friendly phrasings:

Esta es la casa en la que vivo.	This is the house I live in / in which I live.
Es el hombre con el que / con quien salgo.	He's the man I'm going out with / out with whom I'm going.

In general – and in a relative clause in particular – Spanish must not separate a preposition from the noun or pronoun to which it refers. What this means is that Spanish needs to construct phrases of the 'in which' and 'out with whom' variety, in order for the sentence to be correct. Here are some more examples of usage – the English translations are given in both 'natural' and 'Spanish-friendly' forms:

Aquí está el biombo detrás del que estaba sentado.	Here's the screen I was sitting behind / behind which I was sitting.
la fiesta a la que íbamos	the party we were heading to / to which we were heading
Es un libro sin el que no podría vivir.	It's a book I couldn't live without / without which I couldn't live.

Word order with *haber* + past participle

Contrary to usage in English and French, in Spanish there must never be a word inserted between the auxiliary *haber* and the past participle working with it. Positions of adverbs and pronouns in structures like 'I've always thought it' and 'She's never visited me' must be dealt with in the following ways in Spanish – as you can see, there is some flexibility for adverbs, but the *haber* + past participle juxtaposition can not be broken:

Siempre lo he pensado / Lo he pensado siempre.	I've always thought it.
Nunca me ha visitado / No me ha visitado nunca.	She's never visited me.

Concession

The concessive conjunction *aunque* is followed by the indicative when it means 'even though' and refers to a fact, and by a subjunctive when it means the hypothetical 'even if':

Aunque estamos aquí, no vamos a hacer nada.	Even though we're here, we're not going to do anything.
Aunque me llamen mañana, no voy a hablar con ellos.	Even if they phone me tomorrow, I'm not going to talk to them.

⇨ See Unit 14 for further coverage.

The pair of sentences above are set in what we can call the present / future sequence. *Aunque* also works in the past sequence, saying respectively 'even though something was the case' and 'even if something were the case':

Aunque nevaba, salimos a la calle.	Even though it was snowing, we went outside (into the street).
Aunque no vinierais / vinieseis a verme, no dejaría de quereros.	Even if you didn't come to see me, I wouldn't stop loving you.

UNIT 21 — MORE ON SYNTAX

Don't be afraid to go a stage further back in time:

Aunque había terminado el partido, nos quedamos un rato en el estadio.	Even though the match had finished, we stayed on for a while in the stadium.
Aunque me lo hubieras / hubieses dicho ayer, no habría importado.	Even if you'd told me yesterday, it wouldn't have mattered.

Similar in meaning to *aunque*, and working very well with the subjunctive of hypothesis, are *aun cuando* and *así*:

Aun cuando haya algo que hacer cuando llegue, voy a leer un libro.	Even if there's something to do when I arrive, I'm going to read a book.
Así le amenacen, no se rendirá nunca.	Even if they threaten him, he will never surrender.

Also useful are the structures *por mucho que* and *por más que* (both meaning 'however much...' and both taking the indicative when referring to something factual, and the subjunctive when relating to something hypothetical), and *a pesar de que* – 'despite (something being the case)', which also takes the indicative when followed by a fact and can take the subjunctive when it precedes a hypothesis, though this is less common:

Por mucho que / Por más que insistías, no te creíamos.	However much you insisted, we didn't believe you.
Por mucho que / Por más que te esfuerces, no lo conseguirás.	However hard you try, you'll not make it.
A pesar de que eran amigos, no se hablaban mucho.	Despite their being friends, they didn't talk to each other very much.
A pesar de que todo parezca estar en orden, sigo bastante preocupado.	Despite everything seeming to be in order, I'm still pretty worried.

There is a structure in which subjunctives can be paired up, such as *sea como sea* ('be that as it may', 'however it works out') and *vengan o no (vengan)* – 'whether they come or not'.

⇨ See Unit 14 for further information.

Let's have a look at this structure working in the past sequence:

Me ofrecieran / ofreciesen lo que me ofrecieran / ofreciesen, no iba a aceptarlo.	Whatever they offered me, I wasn't going to accept it.
Se presentaran / presentasen o no (se presentaran / presentasen), íbamos a celebrar sus logros.	Whether they turned up or not, we were going to celebrate their achievements.

All these structures can be housed within indirect speech, adding another layer of complexity. Here's how such an example looks:

Me han dicho que aunque saque la mejor nota de la clase, no tendré derecho automático a la beca.	They've told me that even if I get the highest mark in the class, I won't have an automatic right to the grant.
Nos dijeron que aunque quisiéramos / quisiésemos seguir estudiando, no habría asignaturas que escogiéramos / escogiésemos.	They told us that even if we wanted to carry on studying, there wouldn't be any subjects we could choose.

MORE ON SYNTAX UNIT 21

Conditions

We can broadly divide the description of conditions in Spanish into positive (e.g. 'so long as') and negative ('unless') varieties.

⇨ See also Unit 16 for work on conditional sentences.

Positive conditions

There are several subordinators introducing positive conditions, including *mientras (que)*, *a condición de que*, *con tal (de) que* and *siempre que*, all of which mean 'on the condition that' and take the subjunctive in this context:

Mientras que me den el dinero prometido, haré lo que me pidan.	As long as they give me the money they promised me, I'll do whatever they ask of me.
Con tal de que no chilles, te enseñaré los insectos.	On the condition that you don't scream, I'll show you the insects.
Siempre que no haya voces en contra, todo se aprobará.	So long as there are no dissenting voices, it will all be approved.

Let's see how one of these would look in the past sequence, in indirect speech:

Me dijeron que con tal de que me gustara / gustase la carne, no habría problemas con el menú del día.	They told me that so long as I liked meat, there wouldn't be any problems with the set menu.

Negative conditions (exceptions)

All of the 'positive' subordinators, above, can work with *no* to form a negative construction, but a more authentic negative condition – or 'exception' – is provided by the following subordinators, both of which mean 'unless' and take the subjunctive: *a menos que*, *a no ser que*. Here are some examples of their use, in the past and present sequences:

A no ser que me traigan el documento mañana, no habrá contrato entre nosotros.	Unless they bring me the document tomorrow, there won't be a contract between us.
A menos que estuviera / estuviese borracho, no se comportaría así.	Unless he were drunk, he wouldn't behave like that.

In a sentence containing an indirect command, the structure would look like this:

Nos dijeron que nos fuéramos / fuésemos tranquilamente, a no ser que quisiéramos / quisiésemos que nos echaran / echasen.	They told us to leave quietly, unless we wanted to be thrown out.

UNIT 21 — MORE ON SYNTAX

Purpose

Let's have a broader look at the concept of stating purpose: doing one action in order to achieve something else. If the subjects of both verbs are the same, we can use *para* + infinitive. Alternatives to *para* here are *a fin de, con el fin de, con el objeto de* and *con el propósito de*. Remember that if the first verb is one of motion, *para* is normally replaced by *a*:

Leo libros para ampliar mis conocimientos.	I read books (in order) to broaden my knowledge.
He venido aquí a pedirte un favor.	I've come here to ask you a favour.
Lo debatimos con el objeto de llegar a un acuerdo.	We debated it with a view to reaching an agreement.

If there is a change of subject between the first and second verbs, the structure changes to *para que* + subjunctive. The subordinators *a fin de que, con el fin de que, con el objeto de que* and *con el propósito de que* all work the same way, taking the subjunctive:

Te doy este dinero para que compres algo que te guste.	I'm giving you this money so that you can buy something you like.
Nos castigaron para que aprendiéramos / aprendiésemos.	They punished us so that we would learn.
Os cuento esto a fin de que estéis al tanto.	I'm telling you this so that you're up to date / in the picture.
Me engatusaron a fin de que contribuyera / contribuyese cien euros.	They sweet-talked me into contributing / so that I would contribute a hundred euros.

Adding an extra layer of complexity, we can look at a statement of purpose of the above type, combining with a structure of indirect speech:

Nos dijeron que vendiéramos / vendiésemos el coche para que hubiera / hubiese dinero para ellos.	They told us to sell the car so that there was some money for them.

PRACTICE

1 Rearrange the elements of these sentences to produce a better Spanish word order:

1 La chica que trabajaba en la agencia donde ya trabajas tú vivía aquí.

   ....

2 El hombre en cuyo coche fuimos al concierto ya no conduce.

   ....

3 El plan que Diego propuso el otro día es bueno.

   ....

4 El poema que mi hermana mandó al concurso ganó.

   ....

5 El permiso que conseguí después de tres años de trámites ha caducado.

   ....

2 Ask a series of questions in Spanish, using the most appropriate word order, with the elements given:

1 ¿Por qué / el señor Ruiz / bebe / cerveza?

   ....

2 ¿Por qué / el señor Ruiz / bebe / esas cervezas tan exóticas?

   ....

3 ¿Ana / ha llegado?

   ....

4 ¿El hombre que conociste en la playa / ha llamado / te?

   ....

5 ¿El director de la empresa / escribió / ese informe anual / correctamente?

   ....

PRACTICE

3 Translate the following into Spanish, using an appropriate *aunque* construction:

1. Even though we were experts, we always had problems.

   ....

2. Even if you ask us to help you, we won't be willing to do so.

   ....

3. Even if they were to come now, it would be too late.

   ....

4. Even though he's intelligent, he makes mistakes.

   ....

5. They told me that even if I hadn't been tired, they would have left me in peace.

   ....

4 Translate the following into Spanish, using a structure with *con tal de (que)* or *a menos que*, as appropriate:

1. So long as you receive the documents, we'll be able to sign the contract.

   ....

2. So long as they gave me the opportunity, I'd be successful.

   ....

3. So long as I have the money, I'll make the transfer.

   ....

4. Unless you are ill tomorrow, I want you to come.

   ....

5. Unless they went to the bank, they wouldn't be able to pay for the meal.

   ....

PRACTICE

5 Translate the following into Spanish, using an appropriate structure with *para (que)*:

1 I'm studying these subjects so as to learn new things.

   ....

2 They work only so that Marta has money in her pocket.

   ....

3 They were with Miguel to organise the meeting.

   ....

4 We asked them to help us so that there were four people in the team.

   ....

5 I gave you the key so that you would drive the car.

   ....

UNIT 22 — Adverbs and time expressions

> This unit covers two areas. Firstly, it works on adverbs – words or expressions used to give additional information about the manner, place, time, etc. in which something is done; it then focuses on a variety of expressions of time, including how to deal with such concepts as 'yet', 'not yet', 'still', 'again' and 'for'.

Adverbs in Spanish

The standard adverb in Spanish ends in -*mente*, and goes after the verb (or immediately before it, if emphasis is required). However, as we shall see, there are other ways of constructing adverbs or adverbial phrases. This section looks at regular and irregular formation (including the retention of accents) and addresses limitations and degrees of intensity in adverbial use.

Adverbs ending in -*mente*

This is the 'classic' style, equating to the English adverb ending in '-ly'. It is formed by adding -*mente* to the feminine singular form of an adjective (which will either be distinct from, or the same as, the masculine singular, depending on the nature of the adjective). The case of *evidentemente* is included partly as a note to students of French that, in Spanish, the -*mente* suffix is added to the entirety of a feminine singular adjective – Spanish does not shorten any of its adjectives in this scenario:

Masc. sing. adj.	Fem. sing. adj.	Adverb	English
lento	lenta	lentamente	slowly
evidente	evidente	evidentemente	evidently
regular	regular	regularmente	regularly
normal	normal	normalmente	normally

Any written accent present in the feminine singular adjective is retained in the adverbial form. In pronunciation terms, this means that the adverb will be stressed at two points – on the accented vowel and on the -*men*- syllable (though the latter never bears a written accent):

fácil → fácilmente	easy → easily
cortés → cortésmente	courteous → courteously

There are restrictions regarding the use of the -*mente* adverb. Most importantly, if there is a potential build-up of two or more of them separated by a conjunction (*a*, *pero*, etc. – for example in a situation like the English 'quickly and efficiently'), all but the last one must drop the -*mente* suffix:

rápida, brutal y eficazmente	quickly, brutally and efficiently
lenta pero cuidadosamente	slowly but carefully

Equally, the English practice of one '-ly' adverb modifying another – for example, 'amazingly slowly' – must not be attempted in Spanish. More correct is to say the equivalent of 'with amazing slowness'.

ADVERBS AND TIME EXPRESSIONS — UNIT 22

Using a noun, as in this last example, is quite a common and neat way of expressing an adverbial idea.

⇨ *See 'Adverbs not ending in -mente' for exemplification.*

It is also considered bad style to have too many adverbs in *-mente* dotted around a paragraph. Spanish uses different strategies such as saying something works 'in a [+ adjective] way' or 'with [+ the corresponding noun]'.

⇨ *See 'Adverbs not ending in -mente' for exemplification.*

Adverbs not ending in *-mente*

These are mostly adverbs of manner – stating <u>how</u> something is done. Here is a selection of the most common:

bastante	fairly, quite
bien	well
demasiado	too, too much
deprisa / de prisa	quickly
despacio	slowly
igual	the same
mal	badly
mucho	a lot, very much
poco	little
pronto	quickly, soon
recién (+ past participle)	recently (+ past participle)

Spanish also uses a wide range of adverbial phrases – in effect, a phrase playing the role of an adverb. Many of these begin with a common preposition such as *a*, *de*, *en* or *con*:

a menudo / a mano	frequently / by hand
de golpe / de verdad	suddenly / really
en cambio / en el acto	on the other hand / on the spot (there and then)
con cuidado / con frecuencia	carefully / frequently

Another concept to note is the use of an adjective as an adverb – this is familiar to speakers of English, as we can say 'do it quick' (instead of 'quickly'), 'he sold it cheap' (for 'cheaply'), etc. This happens in Spanish, too, but it's vital to be aware that usage divides into two categories:

1. To work as an adverb, a small number of adjectives remain in the masculine singular form, regardless of who or what the subject is. Here is a selection of the most common adjectives that can function in this way – verbs typically working with them are provided for context:

hablar alto / volar alto	to speak loudly / to fly high
hablar bajo / volar bajo	to speak quietly / to fly low
venderse / comer barato	to sell / eat cheaply
verderse / comer caro	to sell / eat expensively

UNIT 22   ADVERBS AND TIME EXPRESSIONS

ir derecho	to go straight (on)
ir directo	to go direct [to a destination]
sentirse fatal	to feel awful
hablar fuerte / tirar fuerte	to speak loudly / to pull hard
respirar hondo	to breathe deeply
jugar limpio	to play fair
hacerlo rápido	to do it quickly

2 Other adjectives work in a way that would be better expressed by an adverb in English, but stay as conventional adjectives (agreeing with the corresponding noun in number and gender):

Las mujeres vivían tranquilas.	The women lived peacefully.
Me miró encantada.	She looked at me delightedly / in delight.

In a ... way / manner

If, to avoid awkwardness or proliferation of adverbs ending in -*mente*, a different style of adverb is required, you can usually draw upon the following formula, which equates to saying 'in a careful manner' instead of 'carefully' in English. *Modo*, *manera* and *forma* are more or less interchangeable here:

La crisis bancaria ha afectado de forma negativa los resultados.	The banking crisis has negatively affected (had a negative effect on) the results.
Lo dijo de manera muy graciosa.	He said it in a very funny way.
Lo importante es vivir de modo independiente.	The important thing is to live independently.

Intensifiers

Intensifiers are words like 'very', 'quite', 'extremely', etc., which serve to state or alter the strength of an adverb (or an adjective or verb). The most common intensifiers in Spanish are:

muy	very
extremadamente	extremely
bastante	quite, fairly
mucho	a lot
poco	little
algo	rather

It's useful to note that the English tendency to be extravagant with intensifiers – 'incredibly', 'amazingly', etc. – cannot really be replicated in Spanish, where a more sober adverb does the job perfectly well. Equally, it can sound very unnatural if we try to recreate, in Spanish, a sentence adverb such as 'incredibly' in a context such as 'Incredibly, he was only 15 when he released his first album'. Solutions are suggested below:

They did amazingly well.	*Lo hicieron muy, muy bien.*
Incredibly, he was only 15 when he released his first album.	*Por increíble que parezca, sólo tenía 15 años / Es increíble que sólo tuviera 15 años cuando sacó su primer álbum.*

ADVERBS AND TIME EXPRESSIONS — UNIT 22

Comparative and superlative adverbs

These – respectively equating to (e.g.) 'more attractively' and '(the) most attractively' in English – are formed similarly to comparative and superlative adjectives.

⇨ See Unit 4

Here are some examples of how they work in Spanish:

Este proceso se hace más fácilmente que el otro. This process can be done more easily than the other one.

Trabajas menos despacio que tu hermano. You work less slowly than your brother.

De toda la clase, Miguel es el que estudia más diligentemente. Of all the class, Miguel is the one who studies most assiduously.

Es mi prima la que viene con menos frecuencia. It's my cousin who comes least often.

There are a few common irregular forms:

Adverb	Meaning	Comparative	Meaning	Superlative	Meaning
bien	well	mejor	better	mejor	(the) best
mal	badly	peor	worse	peor	(the) worst
mucho	a lot	más	more	más	(the) most
poco	little	menos	less	menos	(the) least

It's also worth pointing out here the intensifying suffix *-ísimamente*. This equates to the *-ísimo* ending on adjectives, and comes to mean 'very [adverb]' or 'extremely [adverb]'. Here are some examples:

Vamos a evaluar rapidísimamente tu nivel. We're going to evaluate your level really quickly.

Lo hicieron lentísimamente. They did it incredibly slowly.

Adverbs of place

These, as the name suggests, refer to location. There are some subtleties attached to a few of them, which are addressed in the 'Notes' column in the table below:

Adverb	English	Notes
aquí	here	near to the speaker
acá	here	near to the speaker – more Latin American
ahí	there	near to the listener
allí	there	near to neither the speaker nor the listener
allá	there	more Latin American
dentro / adentro	inside	strictly speaking, *adentro* denotes movement, though usage is blurred
fuera / afuera	outside	strictly speaking, *afuera* denotes movement, though usage is blurred

UNIT 22 ADVERBS AND TIME EXPRESSIONS

abajo	down, downstairs	
arriba	up, upstairs	
encima	on top	
detrás	behind	
atrás	backwards, behind	used with movement for 'backwards', especially in phrases *hacia* atrás and *para* atrás
delante	in front, ahead	
adelante	forward(s), onward(s)	implies forward motion

Time expressions

This section looks at various structures associated with concepts such as duration, and how to say that something is still, already, again or not yet the case. Some of the terms will be familiar from other areas of grammar (e.g. *por, para, durante*), and a lot of the material could be classed as adverbial – and hence would have fitted into the first half of this unit – but it is sensible to give such an important and wide-ranging area of Spanish grammar its own space.

To have been doing something for… / since …

It's useful to recap on the ways in which this structure can be conveyed in Spanish:

1   To have been doing something <u>for</u> [a period of time]

   The present-tense verb is key in Spanish, regardless of the complex continuous tense used in English. Taken in isolation, <u>hace</u> *tres meses* means 'three months <u>ago</u>', but the combination <u>desde hace</u> *tres meses* – literally 'since three months ago' – takes on the 'for + period' role in structures like this:

Vivo aquí desde hace tres meses.	I have been living here (I have lived here) for three months.
Hace tres meses que vivo aquí.	
Llevo tres meses viviendo aquí.	

   To take things a stage further back and say that, at a particular point in time, I <u>had</u> been living here for three months, the structures work like this – notice that the Spanish imperfect tense now does the job of the English pluperfect continuous, and that *hacía* is, in effect, a past-sequence variant of *hace* ('ago' – though here it would come to mean 'previously'/'earlier'):

Vivía aquí desde hacía tres meses.	I had been living here (I had lived here) for three months.
Hacía tres meses que vivía aquí.	
Llevaba tres meses viviendo aquí.	

2 To have been doing something since [a point in time]

Here, the focus changes from a period (three months) to a point (e.g. since yesterday, since Tuesday, since March, since 2003):

Vivo aquí desde ayer / desde el mes pasado / desde 2010. I've been living here (I've lived here) since yesterday / since last month / since 2010.

Llevo desde ayer / desde el mes pasado / desde 2010 viviendo aquí.

To say that I had been living here since a point in time, we would change the verbs from present to imperfect:

Vivía aquí desde abril / desde el año anterior / desde 2005. I'd been living here since April / since the previous year / since 2005.

Llevaba desde abril / desde el año anterior / desde 2005 viviendo aquí.

Not to have done something for ... / since ...

Conceptually, this pairing is similar to that described immediately above, but the negative element triggers some changes in structure. Look closely at the tenses used in the following examples:

Hace dos meses que no la veo. I haven't seen her for two months.
No la veo desde hace dos meses.
Llevo dos meses sin verla.
No la veo desde abril. I haven't seen her since April.
Llevo desde abril sin verla.
Hacía dos meses que no la veía. I hadn't seen her for two months.
No la veía desde hacía dos meses.
Llevaba dos meses sin verla.
No la veía desde abril. I hadn't seen her since April.
Llevaba desde abril sin verla.

The '*hacer* + period of time + *que*' structure can be used in other tenses – often with a subsequent verb in the negative – to suggest guesswork or supposition. Pay close attention to the combination of tenses required, and what their English equivalents are:

Hará tres meses que no la veo. It must be three months since I've seen her / since I last saw her.

Haría tres meses que no la veía. It must have been three months since I'd (last) seen her.

UNIT 22 ADVERBS AND TIME EXPRESSIONS

More on 'for' in expressions of time

We've dealt with some examples of rendering the English 'for' in Spanish expressions of time, but there are more scenarios, which require different structures. Here is a selection of good practice:

1. When the period is completed and expressed with a past-tense verb.

   Here, we can simply omit any mention of 'for' in Spanish:

Estuve / trabajé un tiempo / seis meses en Madrid.	I was / worked in Madrid for a while / for six months.
Esperaron una hora en la estación.	They waited in the station for an hour.

2. Use of *durante*

   Durante + a plural noun can be used to mean 'for' – *durante años / siglos*, 'for years / centuries'.

   It is also useful to convey 'for' in the context of an action or state having taken place uninterrupted throughout a particular period. In this structure, the preterite continuous is generally used:

Estuvieron discutiendo durante cuatro horas.	They were arguing for four hours.

3. Use of *por*

   Por may be used to translate 'for' in expressions of time, but only when the period is very short, and is hinted at being so by the speaker. It may sometimes be omitted:

Por un momento, pensé que me estaba mintiendo.	For a moment, I thought s/he was lying to me.

4. Use of *para*

   Para works very well as 'for' in a time expression when it specifies a period of time in the future during which the action or state will be the case:

Vamos a reservar el piso para diez noches.	We're going to book the flat for ten nights.

Dentro de / en + period of time

The notion of 'in' + a period of time, when 'in' means 'after a period of' when looking towards the future, is best rendered by *dentro de*:

Voy a casarme dentro de quince días.	I'm getting married in a fortnight.
Dijo que iba a casarse dentro de quince días.	He said he was getting married in a fortnight.

If the 'in' means 'during a period of', the preposition *en* can work well:

Conseguimos acabarlo en veinte minutos.	We managed to get it finished in twenty minutes.

ADVERBS AND TIME EXPRESSIONS — UNIT 22

Again

There are two main ways of translating the adverb 'again' into Spanish:

1. With an adverbial phrase – *otra vez* is the obvious one, with *de nuevo* also possible:

   Te lo tuvimos que decir otra vez. We had to tell you again.

2. Slightly more stylish – and actually very commonly used – is the structure *volver a* + infinitive of the verb being repeated:

   Lo volveré a leer el año que viene. I'll read it again next year.
   Te he vuelto a ver en el cine. I've seen you in the cinema again.

To take (+ a period of time) to do something

This precise structure – where there's a second verb after the period of time – uses *tardar en* + infinitive:

Vamos a tardar dos horas en llegar al aeropuerto. We're going to take / It's going to take (us) two hours to get to the airport.
Tardó veinte minutos en descargarse. It took twenty minutes to download.

However, if it's just a question of something taking a period of time – without a second verb – use *durar*, which can be taken to mean 'to take' or 'to last':

El vuelo duró ocho horas. The flight took / lasted eight hours.

Still

The adverb 'still' can be translated into Spanish in the following ways:

1. With an adverb

   The Spanish adverbs for 'still' are *todavía* and (less commonly) *aún*. *Aún* must not be confused with the non-accented *aun*, meaning 'even'. (The latter features later in the unit, in our section on *hasta*.) Here are two examples, one of each adverb:

   Todavía vivimos en la misma casa. We still live in the same house.
   ¿Aún corres un kilómetro todos los días? Do you still run a kilometre every day?

2. Using *seguir / continuar* + gerund

   Giving the idea of 'still to be doing' some previously started or habitual activity, these two verbs – interchangeable, though *seguir* is more commonly used – take the gerund. Students of French should be careful not to use *continuar* + *a* + infinitive, which is not a Spanish construction:

   Sigo trabajando en la misma empresa. I'm still working in the same company.
   Continuaremos ensayando la escena hasta que nos salga bien. We'll carry on rehearsing the scene until we get it right.

UNIT 22 — ADVERBS AND TIME EXPRESSIONS

Yet / not yet

'Yet' features in the same cluster of adverbs as 'still' and 'already', but only features in question forms (e.g. 'Have they arrived yet?') and negative statements (e.g. 'They haven't arrived yet'). In the examples below, notice the specific roles played by *ya* and *todavía* in different types of sentence:

¿Ya han llegado?	Have they arrived yet / already?
Sí, ya están aquí.	Yes, they're (already) here.
No, no han llegado todavía.	No, they haven't arrived yet.
¿Todavía no has acabado el libro?	Have you still not finished the book? / Haven't you finished the book yet?
Sí, ya lo he acabado.	Yes, I've (already) finished it.
No, no lo he acabado todavía.	No, I haven't finished it yet.

Ya, ya no

Ya (most usually 'now' or 'already') has dozens of meanings and untranslatable quirks. Here we will just focus on a couple of the most common ones.

The positive *ya* conveys the sense of something 'already' having been done, even if the equivalent English sentence wouldn't necessarily carry 'already':

Veo que ya han empezado a colgar las banderitas en la calle.	I see they've (already) started hanging the bunting in the street.

Ya is also used as an urgent 'right now':

¡Hazlo ya!	Do it this instant!

The negative *ya no* equates to the English 'no longer', 'not ... any longer' or 'no more':

Ya no echan esa película en el cine.	That's film's no longer on at the cinema.
Mi hermana ya no estudia aquí.	My sister has stopped studying here.

Hasta

As well as being a preposition meaning, in spatial terms, 'up to' or 'as far as', *hasta* is equally commonly used in expressions of time to mean 'until':

hasta las ocho y media	until half past eight
hasta la guerra	until the war

It's worth pointing out the third meaning of *hasta*, as an adverb meaning 'even', in contexts like 'even a child of three knows that':

Hasta mi hermanito sabe que los cuchillos son peligrosos.	Even my little brother knows that knives are dangerous.

In this meaning, *hasta* is joined by its synonyms *aun* and *incluso*. Remember that *aun* must not be confused with *aún* (meaning 'still').

PRACTICE

1 Give the commonest form in Spanish of each of the following:

1. easily..
2. generally..
3. evidently..
4. economically and politically..
5. quickly but sincerely..

2 Translate the following into Spanish, using devices other than adverbs:

1. We're going to sell it cheap.

   ....

2. You'll have to speak louder.

   ....

3. The girls smiled innocently.

   ....

4. My brothers live peacefully on the island.

   ....

5. It's important to play fair.

   ....

3 Using a verb structure covered in this unit, find an alternative way of expressing each of these sentences in Spanish. Verbs you can use include the following: *tardar en* + infinitive; *volver a* + infinitive; *durar*; *seguir* + gerund:

1. Lo has perdido otra vez.

   ....

2. Has empezado a hacerlo a las tres y has terminado a las cinco.

   ....

PRACTICE

3 El viaje empezó a las siete y terminó a las once.

....

4 Todavía hago deporte.

....

5 Los vi hace seis meses y desde entonces no los he visto.

....

4 Translate the following sentences into Spanish:

1 Haven't you visited your grandmother yet?

....

2 Yes, I've already visited her.

....

3 No, I haven't visited her yet.

....

4 She doesn't live in that house any longer.

....

5 She's been living in Valencia for two years.

....

UNIT 23 | Spelling and the written accent

Spelling

There are relatively few problems associated with Spanish spelling, as the system works in a very logical way. However, there are a number of points worth discussing, most of them to do with altering the spelling of words to accommodate required sounds. In this sense, what Spanish does is a bit like the English addition of a 'k' to 'panic' in the forms 'panicked' and 'panicking' – it helps to keep the 'c' as a hard sound.

Maintaining the hard /k/ sound

When *c-* is followed by *-a*, *-o* or *-u*, there is no problem in maintaining the required hard /k/ sound (e.g. *caro*, *cola*, *cubo*). However, *ce-* and *ci-* are pronounced like the sounds in the English 'theft' and 'thief' respectively, so to produce a sound like the English 'kept' or 'kiss', Spanish needs to alter the *c-* to *qu-* (as seen in *queso* and *quito*). This is notable in verbs ending in *-car*, whose present subjunctive (in its entirety) and first person singular of the preterite indicative are affected:

bus<u>car</u>, bus<u>co</u>, bus<u>caste</u>	to look for, I look for, you looked for
Bus<u>qué</u> una solución.	I looked for a solution.
Quiero que me bus<u>ques</u> una solución.	I want you to look for a solution for me.

Maintaining the hard /g/ sound

Similar to the case of the hard /k/, above, is that of the letter 'g'. When it is followed by *-a*, *-o* or *-u*, there is no problem in maintaining the hard /g/ sound (e.g. *gato*, *gota*, *gusano*). However, *ge-* and *gi-* are pronounced using the guttural sound like that heard in the Scottish 'loch', so to keep the /g/ hard as in the English 'get' or 'gibbon', Spanish inserts a 'u', changing *ge-* to *gue-* (e.g. *guerra*) and *gi-* to *gui-* (e.g. *guisante*). This change is visible in verbs ending in *-gar*, whose present subjunctive (in its entirety) and first person singular of the preterite indicative are affected:

lle<u>gar</u>, lle<u>go</u>, lle<u>gaste</u>	to arrive, I arrive, you arrived
Lle<u>gué</u> a la una.	I arrived at one o'clock.
Prefiero que lle<u>gues</u> a tiempo.	I prefer you to arrive on time.

UNIT 23 SPELLING AND THE WRITTEN ACCENT

Maintaining the /gw/ sound

Again, this depends on which vowel follows the *gu-* combination. The groups *gua-* (as in *guapo*) and *guo-* (*averiguo*) are fine, but *gue-* and *gui-* are pronounced /g/ as in *guerra* and *guisante*, not as a /gw/. To achieve the /gwe/ and /gwi/ sounds, the letter 'u' receives what is known as a diaeresis – two dots on top, like a German umlaut:

aguar, aguo, aguaste	to water down, I water down, you watered down
agüé	I watered down
agüero, lingüística	omen, linguistics

Maintaining the European Spanish /th/ sound

The /th/ sound heard in the English 'think' is very common in the Spanish of mainland Spain and the Balearic Islands, but an eye must be kept on the spelling (which, of course, affects all countries where Spanish is used) of words containing this sound. The combinations in which it appears are the following:

za	*zapato, mostaza*
zo	*zorro, mozo*
zu	*zumo, concienzudo*
ce	*cerveza, avance*
ci	*cita, agencia*

In verbs ending in *-cer* or *-cir*, the *c-* must change to *z-* before any endings starting with *a-* or *o-*, otherwise a hard /k/ combination would be produced:

hi<u>ce</u>, hi<u>ciste</u>	I did / made, you did / made
hi<u>zo</u>	he / she / it / you did / made
zur<u>ces</u>	you darn
zur<u>zo</u>	I darn

Spanish prefers not to use the combinations *-ze-* and *-zi-*, so words you might expect to be spelt using them are rendered by *-ce-* and *-ci-* respectively (for example, the English 'zebra' is *cebra* in Spanish). A few exceptions do pop up now and then – *Nueva Zelanda* for 'New Zealand' is a common one, and *ázimo* (also spelt *ácimo*), meaning 'unleavened', rather less common.

Linked to this, verbs ending in *-zar* require a change from *z-* to *c-* before any endings starting with *e-*:

organizo, organizaste	I organise, you organised
organicé	I organised
Quiero que lo organicen ellos.	I want them to organise it.

SPELLING AND THE WRITTEN ACCENT UNIT 23

Maintaining the guttural sound of the Scottish 'loch'

This sound appears in the following combinations:

ja	jarra
jo	jota
ju	jugar
je	Jesús, jeringa
ji	jirafa, jinete
ge	general, gel
gi	Gibraltar, gitano

Although, as we can see in the table, *j-* can be followed by any of the five vowels, the combinations *je-* and *ji-* are less common than *ge-* and *gi-* (which, respectively, are pronounced the same as them). If you have ten minutes to spare, try and devise a system to remember the correct spelling of *jengibre* ('ginger')!

In verbs ending in *-ger* or *-gir*, the *g-* must change to *j-* before any endings starting with *a-* or *o-*, to avoid the production of a hard /g/ sound:

co*ger*, co*ges*	to take, you take
co*jo*, ¡có*jalo*!	I take, take it!
exi*gir*, exi*ges*	to demand, you demand
exi*jo*, ¡exí*jalo*!	I demand, demand it!

Spelling change in conversion from singular to plural

Earlier in the unit, we noted that Spanish is not keen on the combinations *-ze-* and *-zi-*. This concept features in the pluralisation of nouns and adjectives ending in *-z*, where the *-z* must be changed to *-c* before the plural *-es* is added:

Singular	Plural	Meaning
luz	luces	light(s)
vez	veces	time(s), occasion(s)
feroz	feroces	ferocious

The written accent

There are two useful things to remember before focusing on whether a word needs an accent:

1. A good approach to the concept of word stress in Spanish is to consider that the way a word is pronounced determines the way it is written – sound comes first, and the written form is a by-product.

UNIT 23 SPELLING AND THE WRITTEN ACCENT

2 There are two main 'norms' for the location of stress – by which we mean the most emphatically pronounced syllable – in Spanish words, which have a bearing on whether we need to add an accent.

Norms for where spoken stress falls on a Spanish word

1 If a word ends in a vowel, or in -*n* or -*s*, the norm is for its spoken stress to fall on the penultimate syllable:

pal*a*bra	word
ele*fan*te	elephant
*ca*si	almost
*li*bro	book
*tri*bu	tribe
*ha*blan	they speak
*ha*blas	you speak

2 If a word ends in any other consonant, the norm is for its spoken stress to fall on the final syllable:

co*ñac*	brandy
Ma*drid*	Madrid
re*loj*	watch, clock
ani*mal*	animal
ha*blar*	to speak
ma*mut*	mammoth
vi*rrey*	viceroy
albor*noz*	bathrobe

Addition of a written accent

If the established pronunciation of a Spanish word means that it contradicts the norm (see above) corresponding to how it is spelt – i.e. its final letter – then an accent is added to acknowledge this contradiction. Here are some examples from category 1, whose spoken stress does not fall on the penultimate syllable. As such, an accent has been added to the 'rogue' syllable where the stress does fall:

hablar*á* / *rá*faga	he (etc.) will speak / flash (of light, etc.)
comi*té* / *cé*lebre	committee / famous
ira*ní* / a*quí*	Iranian / here
eco*nó*mico / ha*bló*	economic(al) / he (etc.) spoke
hin*dú* / zu*lú*	Hindu / Zulu
an*dén* / cata*lán*	platform / Catalan
cor*tés* / ca*tás*trofes	courteous / catastrophes

SPELLING AND THE WRITTEN ACCENT — UNIT 23

Here are some examples from category 2, where the spoken stress does not fall on the final syllable. Again, an accent has been added to the 'contradictory' syllable:

c<u>é</u>sped	lawn
f<u>á</u>cil	easy
<u>á</u>lbum	album
alm<u>í</u>bar	syrup

Palabras esdrújulas

Several of the words included in these tables – *ráfaga, célebre, económico, catástrofe(s)* – are examples of the stress naturally falling on the antepenultimate (third from last) syllable. Naturally, given norms 1 and 2, these words need to receive an accent on the stressed syllable. It won't have escaped your attention that the word *esdrújulo* is an example of itself! We'll see more examples of this concept later in the unit.

Accents on monosyllabic words

Words of one syllable do not normally have a written accent. Exceptions occur where the accent is added to distinguish between two words which are pronounced the same but have different meanings.

⇨ See 'Accents used to distinguish two words pronounced the same' for a list of such words.

Also of interest is a recent official spelling change, whereby some words that could be pronounced as one syllable (as a diphthong) or two were standardised, and should now lose their accent. The clearest example of this is *guión*, which tends to be pronounced as two syllables in Spain and as a single syllable in Latin America. The preferred spelling in both styles of Spanish is now *guion*.

Accent needed in plural but not singular, and vice versa

If a noun or adjective ending in *-n* is unaccented in the singular, it receives an accent on the stressed syllable once the plural *-es* has been added:

Singular	Plural	Meaning
examen	exámenes	exam(s)
imagen	imágenes	image(s)
joven	jóvenes	young; young person / people
orden	órdenes	order(s)

Conversely, if a noun or adjective ending in -*n* or -*s* has an accent on the final syllable in the singular, this is lost in the plural:

Singular	Plural	Meaning
catalán	catalanes	Catalan(s)
opinión	opiniones	opinion(s)
autobús	autobuses	bus(es)
cortés	corteses	courteous
escocés	escoceses	Scottish; Scot(s)

Remember that there are three nouns whose singular / plural stress patterns and accentuation do not follow any rules:

Singular	Plural	Meaning
carácter	caracteres	character(s)
espécimen	especímenes	specimen(s)
régimen	regímenes	régime(s), diet(s)

Accents on infinitives, gerunds and positive imperatives

1   Infinitives

The rule here is that an infinitive must receive a written accent on its final syllable – which, by definition, is where its stress always falls – if <u>two</u> pronouns are added to the end:

Van a venderlo. [only one pronoun – no accent]   They're going to sell it.
Van a vendérnoslo. [two pronouns – accent]   They're going to sell it to us.

2   Gerunds

A gerund receives a written accent on its originally stressed vowel when <u>one or more</u> pronouns are added to the end:

Están ofreciendo [basic form – no accent]   They're offering
Están ofreciéndome algo. [one pronoun – accent]   They're offering me something.
Están ofreciéndomelo. [two pronouns – accent]   They're offering it to me.

3   Positive imperatives

Before we look at specific examples, a good rule to bear in mind here is that however many pronouns are added to a positive imperative, the spoken stress must continue to fall on the syllable on which it fell before they were added. An accent may need to be added to preserve the stress on the correct syllable.

SPELLING AND THE WRITTEN ACCENT — UNIT 23

If two pronouns are added, an accent is always placed on the syllable of the 'naked' imperative where the spoken stress originally fell:

¡Dámelo!	Give it to me!
¡Pásanoslos!	Pass them to us!
¡Ofrecédselo!	Offer [vosotros] it to him / her / them!

If one pronoun is added, the syllable where the spoken stress originally fell (before the addition of the pronoun) receives a written accent unless **(a)** the 'naked' imperative was monosyllabic, or **(b)** it is a *vosotros* command ending in -*d*:

¡Háblame! [tú]	Speak to me!
¡Tómelo! [usted]	Take it!
¡Cómprenlo! [ustedes]	Buy it!
¡Dilo! [tú – monosyllabic imperative]	Say it!
¡Deme! [usted – monosyllabic imperative]	Give me!
¡Bebedlo! [vosotros]	Drink it!

Accents on question words and exclamation words

An accent must be written on the question words *cómo, cuál, cuándo, cuánto, dónde, qué, por qué, para qué* and *quién* – in both direct and indirect questions, as illustrated below. Any of them used as exclamation words must also carry an accent:

¿Dónde / Cuándo naciste?	Where / when were you born?
Me preguntaron cuánto dinero había gastado.	They asked me how much money I had spent.
¡Qué sorpresa! ¡Cómo has crecido!	What a surprise! How you've grown!

Accents used to distinguish two words pronounced the same

Some Spanish words have two slightly different – or, in some cases, entirely different – meanings, and are distinguished by a written accent. Pronunciation is unaffected. Below is a list of the most common words falling into this category. Note that in the cases of *este, ese, aquel* and *solo*, current use dictates that the accent is only needed to avoid ambiguities. Such ambiguities would tend not to occur in conversation, but in the written form we can sometimes encounter a situation such as the following, where the accent plays a vital role:

Viajó solo por España.	He travelled around Spain on his own.
Viajó sólo por España.	He only travelled around Spain.

UNIT 23 SPELLING AND THE WRITTEN ACCENT

Without an accent		With an accent	
de	of	*dé*	give
el	the	*él*	he
este	this / this one / east	*éste*	this one
ese	that / that one	*ése*	that one
aquel	that / that one	*aquél*	that one
mas	but [either formal or old-fashioned]	*más*	more
mi	my	*mí*	me
se	himself, herself (etc.)	*sé*	I know / be!
si	if	*sí*	yes / oneself
solo	alone / only, solely	*sólo*	only, solely
te	you	*té*	tea
tu	your	*tú*	you

KEY POINTS

- Spanish spelling is fairly straightforward, but to master it fully, the key areas to focus on are the letters c, g, j and z.

- If you are unsure whether a particular consonant can double up in Spanish, check that it is contained within the helpful word CAROLINA. These four consonants are the only ones able to double up in Spanish.

- Spanish accentuation rules may seem a little tedious, but in fact they are finite and, with a bit of practice, the system does become second nature.

PRACTICE

1 Give the plural form of each of the following:

1. carácter..
2. albornoz..
3. espécimen..
4. capaz..
5. régimen..

2 Give the Spanish for each of the following, based on the infinitive supplied:

1. I organised [organizar]..
2. I take [coger]..
3. I looked for [buscar]..
4. I made [hacer]...
5. I arrived [llegar]...

3 Add an accent, if and where it is needed, to each of the following words. Meanings are given in brackets:

1. resumenes [summaries]...
2. dificil [difficult]...
3. politicos [politicians]...
4. origen [origin]..
5. sera [he / she will be]..

4 By stressing different syllables and adding accents as appropriate, give three different meanings for each of the following:

1. celebre...................................../...................................../...
2. continuo................................./...................................../...

247

PRACTICE

5 Add accents, where needed, to the following:

1. Voy a describirlo.

2. Leyendolo, aprenderas.

3. Hazme un favor.

4. Estaras defendiendome.

5. Ha intentado darmelo.

6. Ofrecedselo.

7. ¿Cuando nacio tu hermano?

8. Quiero mas te.

9. Tu me lo ibas a comprar a mi.

10. Se que sabes mas que el.

SOLUTIONS

SOLUTIONS

Unit 1

1.
  1. tía
  2. gata
  3. atleta
  4. economista
  5. estudiante
  6. dependienta

2.
  1. la madre
  2. la mujer
  3. la mujer / la esposa
  4. la reina
  5. la actriz
  6. la vaca

3.
  1. el
  2. la
  3. el
  4. la
  5. la
  6. el
  7. la
  8. el
  9. el
  10. el
  11. el

4.
  1. masc
  2. masc
  3. masc
  4. masc
  5. fem
  6. masc
  7. fem
  8. masc
  9. masc

5.
  1. conductora, conductores, conductoras
  2. catalana, catalanes, catalanas
  3. belga, belgas, belgas
  4. bailarina, bailarines, bailarinas
  5. anfitriona, anfitriones, anfitrionas

6.
  1. nietos
  2. mesas
  3. coches
  4. taxis
  5. tribus
  6. papás
  7. cafés
  8. pakistaníes
  9. hindúes
  10. menús
  11. autobuses
  12. imágenes
  13. orígenes
  14. luces
  15. portavoces

Unit 2

1.
  1. La paciencia es importante.
  2. Me encantan los perros.
  3. Los coches suelen ser caros.
  4. Los profesores no cobran mucho.
  5. Tengo hambre.
  6. La comida es a la una.
  7. La cerveza es fuerte.
  8. Mi color favorito es el rojo.
  9. Tienes los ojos azules.
  10. Me duele la pierna.

2.
  1. se, el.
  2. el, la.
  3. la, el.
  4. al, la.
  5. la.
  6. Blank.
  7. el, los.
  8. las, blank, la.
  9. Blank.
  10. el, blank, blank.

3.
  1. Incorrect: El italiano…
  2. Correct.
  3. Incorrect: en inglés.
  4. Incorrect: al español.
  5. Incorrect: en el Reino Unido.
  6. Incorrect: Francia.
  7. Incorrect: en la calle.
  8. Incorrect: el Barcelona, el Liverpool.
  9. Incorrect: Los catalanes.
  10. Correct.

4.
  1. Blank.
  2. Blank.
  3. Blank, un.
  4. unos.
  5. una.
  6. Blank.
  7. Blank.
  8. Blank.

SOLUTIONS

5 1 d.
   2 e.
   3 a.
   4 c.
   5 b.

Unit 3

1 1 alemanas, belgas.
   2 tercer, primero.
   3 capaces, azules.
   4 ningún, alguno.
   5 española, andaluza.
   6 fría, buena.
   7 ingleses, serio.
   8 gran, grande.
   9 gratis, mejores.
   10 realistas, iraníes.

2 1 La traductora catalana.
   2 Una intérprete canadiense.
   3 Una mujer descortés.
   4 La joven modelo.
   5 La colega andaluza.
   6 Unas chicas felices.
   7 Las policías trabajadoras.
   8 Unas niñas regordetas.
   9 Las agentes pakistaníes.
   10 Las reinas anteriores.

3 1 El antiguo profesor.
   2 Los coches nuevos.
   3 Las chicas pobres.
   4 Un hombre raro.
   5 Ciertas teorías.
   6 Un libro grande.
   7 La gran princesa.
   8 El pobre francés.
   9 Los muebles antiguos.
   10 Una nueva amiga.

4 1 tan.
   2 tanta.
   3 tan.
   4 tan.
   5 tantos.

5 1 las mejores.
   2 mejores.
   3 la mejor.
   4 el mejor.
   5 mejor.

6 1 de la que.
   2 que.
   3 de lo que.
   4 de.
   5 de los que.
   6 que.
   7 del que.
   8 de las que.
   9 que.
   10 de lo que.

7 1 baratísima.
   2 majísimos.
   3 jovencísima.
   4 cursilísima.
   5 amabilísimos.
   6 antiquísimas.
   7 grandísimo.
   8 simpatiquísimas.
   9 lejísimos.
   10 felicísimas.

Unit 4

1 1 ninguno.
   2 cualquier.
   3 nada.
   4 alguna.
   5 bastante.
   6 muchas.
   7 nadie.
   8 cada.
   9 poco.
   10 algún.

2 1 Tenemos el mismo sistema.
   2 Tengo tantas hermanas.
   3 No quiero hacer trabajo alguno.
   4 Ciertos hombres han llegado a la cárcel.
   5 Ningún chico debería comportarse así.
   6 Ambos (los dos) planes son excelentes.
   7 Tengo tres botellas de agua. ¿Quieres otra?
   8 Toda España quiere celebrar la victoria.
   9 Quiero mantequilla pero no hay.
   10 Nadie dijo nada.

3 1 Nadie ha venido.
   2 No me sorprende nada en esta ciudad.
   3 No lo entiende ninguno de los chicos.

SOLUTIONS

Unit 5

1
1. Este libro es mejor que ese.
2. Esas mujeres son más interesantes que estas.
3. Eso / aquello fue imposible.
4. Esta agua es más pura que esa.
5. Esto es útil.

2
1. Aquel chico.
2. Ese traductor.
3. Estos niños.
4. Aquellos canadienses.
5. Este francés.

3
1. Mis, los tuyos.
2. La nuestra.
3. mío.
4. tu, el suyo.
5. Sus, las mías.

4
1. Me duelen los pies.
2. Dame la mano.
3. Voy a ponerme la camisa. / Me voy a poner la camisa.
4. Me he roto el brazo.
5. Tuvimos que entregar la cartera.

Unit 6

1
1. ella.
2. él.
3. yo.
4. nosotros / nosotras.
5. ellos / ellas.

2
1. nosotros / nosotras, ellos / ellas.
2. yo, ella.
3. tú, ellos / ellas.
4. vosotros / vosotras, él.
5. tú, yo.

3
1. He escrito la carta y se la he enviado (a él).
2. Sí, las hemos escuchado.
3. ¿Te importaría dejárnoslos?
4. Le gusta mucho verlas.
5. Sí, se los han entregado (a ella) esta mañana.

4
1. enfrente de él.
2. para mí / por mí.
3. según ella.
4. delante de nosotros / nosotras.
5. conmigo.
6. entre tú (usted, etc.) y yo.
7. sin ellos / ellas.
8. gracias a ti, mi amigo / amiga / gracias a ti, amigo / a mío / a.
9. detrás de mí.
10. excepto / menos ella.

5
1. Voy a hacerlo. / Lo voy a hacer.
2. Se lo he dado.
3. Dánoslo cuando lo tengas.
4. ¿Después de pintarlo me lo enseñas? / ¿Me lo enseñas después de pintarlo?
5. Se las deberías entregar / Deberías entregárselas.

6
1. Nos lo dieron a nosotros.
2. Se los hemos pasado al abogado.
3. Os toca a vosotras hacerlo.
4. Les corresponderá a ellos realizarlo.
5. Te quiere a ti.

7
1. Le he comprado un reloj (a ella) para su cumpleaños.
2. Si quieres se lo puedes decir a tus padres / Si quieres puedes decírselo a tus padres.
3. ¿Pueden ir contigo mañana?
4. A mi primo le encantan las matemáticas.
5. Te lo voy a decir después de la reunión / Voy a decírtelo después de la reunión.

Unit 7

1
1. El chico con el que / con quien estudio.
2. La mujer cerca de la que / cerca de quien vivo.
3. El hombre al que / a quien le diste el documento.
4. Las calles en las que jugamos.
5. Las actrices sin las que / sin quienes.
6. Los franceses entre los que / entre quienes.
7. El edificio detrás del que.
8. La casa enfrente de la que.
9. Los exámenes durante los que.
10. La person contra la que / contra quien.

2
1. con cuyos hijos.
2. sin cuya ayuda.
3. en cuyo coche.

SOLUTIONS

    4 de cuyas hojas.
    5 debajo de cuyo jardín.

3   1 la que / quien.
    2 Los que / Quienes.
    3 El del.
    4 lo de.
    5 las de.
    6 lo que.
    7 los de.
    8 el que.
    9 la del.
    10 las que.

4   1 los que / quienes.
    2 la que / quien.
    3 el que / quien.
    4 las que / quienes.
    5 por el que.
    6 con la que / con quien.
    7 entre las que.
    8 por lo que.
    9 a la que.
    10 para los que / para quienes.

5   1 La chica con quien / con la que hablaste ayer está embarazada.
    2 Ese hombre en cuyo jardín hicimos una barbacoa ha muerto / Ha muerto ese hombre en cuyo jardín hicimos una barbacoa.
    3 La carta en la que me escribiste un poema es preciosa.
    4 Me interesó lo que me comentaste / Lo que me comentaste me interesó / Me comentaste algo que me interesó.
    5 Voy a llamar a mis primas sin quienes / sin las que estaría perdido.

Unit 8

1   1 Después de cenar.
    2 en París, a España.
    3 Es fácil seguir.
    4 Consiste en.
    5 en la universidad.

2   1 Estoy en contra de esta ley.
    2 La estación está a cincuenta metros de la catedral.
    3 Soy la mujer más alta del grupo.
    4 Vivo cerca de la universidad.

    5 No es portuguesa, sino italiana.
    6 Fuimos en coche.
    7 Ni María ni Juan llegaron a tiempo / No llegaron a tiempo ni María ni Juan.
    8 Le robaron la bici(cleta) a mi hermano.
    9 Vamos a ayudarle con los / sus estudios.
    10 Soy de Alicante pero vengo / he venido de Valencia.

3   1 a.
    2 en.
    3 en.
    4 con.
    5 de.

4   1 a pie.
    2 poco a poco.
    3 cinco (grados) bajo cero.
    4 a los cincuenta años.
    5 a veces.
    6 café con leche.
    7 a la sombra.
    8 a tiempo.
    9 según ella.
    10 bajo la dictadura.

5   1 a.
    2 con.
    3 con.
    4 de.
    5 en.
    6 en.
    7 blank.
    8 a.
    9 de.
    10 blank.

6   1 Os dije que iba …
    2 … Lidia e Isabel.
    3 [correct]
    4 … u otra …
    5 … sino mañana.

7   1 Puedes ver o esta película o la otra.
    2 Tanto mi hermano como mi hermana han estado en Nueva York.
    3 Ni Miguel ni su novia han estudiado para el examen.
    4 El verano pasado no fuimos a Cataluña sino a las Islas Canarias.
    5 Padre e hijo (se) bebieron siete u ocho cervezas.

SOLUTIONS

Unit 9

1.
   1. para.
   2. por.
   3. por.
   4. para.
   5. para.
   6. por.
   7. por.
   8. para.
   9. por.
   10. para.

2.
   1. Mi abuela preguntó por ti ayer.
   2. Necesito tu ayuda para abrir la ventana.
   3. Queremos empezar / comenzar por leer un texto.
   4. Me juró que no tenía dinero, para luego comprarse un Porsche al día siguiente.
   5. Me he disculpado por lo que dije ayer.

3.
   1. Incorrect – de la mañana.
   2. Correct.
   3. Correct.
   4. Incorrect – para casa.
   5. Incorrect – para este trabajo.

4.
   1. para.
   2. para.
   3. para.
   4. por.
   5. blank.

5.
   1. blank.
   2. a.
   3. blank.
   4. a.
   5. a la que / a quien.

Unit 10

1.
   1. dieciséis.
   2. veintidós.
   3. veintitrés.
   4. veintiséis.
   5. treinta.

2.
   1. El Rey Guillermo Cuarto.
   2. La Reina Isabel Segunda.
   3. El Papa Juan Pablo Segundo.
   4. El Rey Felipe Doce.
   5. La Reina Victoria Quince.

3.
   1. El tercer hijo.
   2. La novena hija.
   3. Las décimas celebraciones.
   4. El primer episodio.
   5. La segunda vez.

4.
   1. Ochenta y un libros.
   2. Veintiuna llaves.
   3. Cuarenta y un armas.
   4. Noventa y nueve chicos.
   5. Quince tíos.
   6. Cien personas.
   7. Ciento cincuenta y ocho casas.
   8. Cuatrocientos treinta hombres.
   9. Quinientas setenta y ocho mujeres.
   10. Novecientos noventa y nueva.

5.
   1. Diez con / coma cuatro grados.
   2. Ocho euros (con) noventa y nueve.
   3. Uno coma cinco.
   4. Veintitrés–cero uno–cuarenta y cuatro.
   5. Ocho veinticuatro–diecisiete–noventa y ocho / Ochocientos veinticuatro–diecisiete–noventa y ocho.

6.
   1. Un millón doscientos treinta y cuatro mil quinientos sesenta y siete coches.
   2. Dos millones seiscientas cincuenta y cuatro mil trescientas veintiuna casas.

Unit 11

1.
   1. Juegan a las cartas, cierran las puertas y duermen.
   2. Sé que quieres ayudarme / que me quieres ayudar.
   3. Soy estudiante, salgo los viernes.
   4. Están en la estación, ¿les envío / mando un mensaje?
   5. Querremos verla / La querremos ver antes de salir.
   6. ¿Podré nadar en esta piscina?
   7. Vendrán aquí y luego saldrán.
   8. Serán las ocho.
   9. Habrá una serie de reuniones.
   10. Voy a ver la tele hasta las once.

2.
   1. fui, tenía.
   2. era, brillaba.
   3. Veía, hubo.
   4. Fue, murió.
   5. Pagué, estabas.

SOLUTIONS

    6 durmió, hacía.
    7 dijiste, diste / dabas.
    8 esperaba, oyó.
    9 Organicé, quería.
  10 terminó, salió.

3   1 Es la primera vez que te veo.
    2 Estudio aquí desde hace dos años. / Hace dos años que estudio aquí. / Llevo dos años estudiando aquí.
    3 Trabajábamos allí desde hacía una semana / Hacía una semana que trabajábamos allí. / Llevábamos una semana trabajando aquí.
    4 Querría / Quería / Quisiera / Me gustaría ver más información, por favor.
    5 Yo de ti / Yo que tú, vendría a las once.

4   1 Ha escrito una carta a su madre y le ha dicho la verdad.
    2 He frito las cebollas y las he puesto en / sobre un plato.
    3 Hemos visto que has roto la ventana.
    4 Desde que has vuelto, tres personas han muerto / han muerto tres personas.
    5 He hecho las camas e impreso los documentos.

5   1 Tengo dos hermanas.
    2 Voy a tener dos ordenadores en casa.
    3 Tendré problemas.
    4 Tenía un coche rojo.
    5 He tenido momentos de dificultad.
    6 Tuve un accidente.

Unit 12

1   1 Estoy leyéndolo / Lo estoy leyendo en este momento.
    2 Están viendo la tele.
    3 Estamos construyendo un garaje.
    4 Mañana a estas horas Miguel estará llegando a Madrid.
    5 Les habíamos estado pidiendo ayuda / Habíamos estado pidiéndoles ayuda.
    6 Laura estaba durmiendo.
    7 Nos habéis estado esperando / Habéis estado esperándonos.
    8 En enero habré estado viajando más de un año por Asia.
    9 Habríais estado diciendo la verdad.
  10 Voy a estar friendo las cebollas.

2   1 Escribes una novela desde hace seis meses / Hace seis meses que escribes una novela / Llevas seis meses escribiendo una novela.
    2 Vivíamos en esa casa desde hacía dos años / Hacía dos años que vivíamos en esa casa / Llevábamos dos años viviendo en esa casa.

3   1 Pasé tres horas charlando con ella.
    2 Sigo fumando.
    3 Iba amaneciendo.
    4 Estudiando, aprobarás los exámenes.
    5 La vimos jugando al golf.

4   1 leer.
    2 beber.
    3 saludar.
    4 Debes hacerlo.
    5 Me hiciste reír.

5   1 Se odian.
    2 Se vende cerveza en este bar.
    3 Se me ha roto el móvil.
    4 No se puede entrar en este edificio.
    5 Nos hemos bebido un litro de coñac.

Unit 13

1   1 estudie, estudiemos, estudien.
    2 comprenda, comprendamos, comprendan.
    3 escriba, escribamos, escriban.
    4 produzca, produzcamos, produzcan.
    5 diga, digamos, digan.
    6 haga, hagamos, hagan.

2   1 encuentres, encontréis.
    2 cierres, cerréis.
    3 mueras, muráis.
    4 pidas, pidáis.
    5 sientas, sintáis.
    6 des, deis.

3   1 tenga.
    2 hayas cenado.
    3 verte.
    4 haya.
    5 ocurra.

4   1 Quería que tuvieras / tuvieses cuidado.
    2 Querían que leyeras / leyeses el libro.
    3 Queríamos que durmieras / durmieses bien.

SOLUTIONS

    4 ¿Queríais que se lo dijera / dijese?
    5 Querían que fuera / fuese especial.

5
1. Prefiero que vengas a las tres / Prefería que vinieras / vinieses a las tres.
2. Mi madre prefiere que traigamos una botella. / Mi madre prefería que trajéramos / trajésemos una botella.
3. Prefieren que conduzca (yo). / Preferían que condujera / condujese (yo).
4. Preferimos que hagan la cama. / Preferíamos que hicieran / hiciesen la cama.
5. Prefieres que haya comida en la cocina. / Preferías que hubiera / hubiese comida en la cocina.

Unit 14

1
1. trabaje.
2. hicierais / hicieseis.
3. fuera / fuese.
4. trabajar.
5. va.
6. haya.
7. sabía.
8. queden.
9. puedas.
10. ver.

2
1. Es muy probable que Pepe llegue mañana.
2. Ayer me pidieron que hiciera / hiciese la cama.
3. Aunque quieras ser artista, trabajaré contigo.
4. Antes de que mis hermanos estuvieran / estuviesen enfermos, fui a visitarlos (los fui a visitar) una vez.
5. Cuando era joven quería ver el mundo.
6. Cuando le vea mañana le diré la verdad.
7. Siento que no hayan comido bien.
8. Me parece importante que los estudiantes tengan dinero para libros.
9. Trabajé un día adicional para que tuvieras / tuvieses dinero para ropa.
10. Bebimos el vino sin que nos vieran / viesen mis padres.

3
1. Nos dejan dormir aquí. / Dejan que durmamos aquí.
2. Te permitiremos estudiar en nuestra casa. / Permitiremos que estudies en nuestra casa.
3. Te voy a impedir (Voy a impedirte) ver la televisión. / Voy a impedir que veas la televisión.
4. Me ordenaste decirlo. / Ordenaste que lo dijera / dijese.
5. Nos ha prohibido venir aquí. / Ha prohibido que vengamos aquí.

4
1. trabajes.
2. Correct.
3. esté.
4. tenga.
5. se ponga.

5
1. Dudaba que las cajas cupieran / cupiesen en el coche.
2. Era posible que no supiera / supiese qué hacer.
3. Prefería que todo el mundo dijera / dijese lo que quisiera / quisiese decir.
4. No quería que condujeras.
5. No era cierto que hubiera / hubiese tantas personas en el aula.
6. Cada día te pedía que me trajeras el periódico.
7. Aceptaba que los políticos hicieran / hiciesen lo que les diera / diese la gana.
8. Teníamos miedo de que no saliera / saliese bien.
9. Siempre sugería que todos pusiéramos / pudiésemos cien euros.
10. Tenía que esconder el dinero antes de que me viera / viese mi padre.

Unit 15

1
1. dilo.
2. no lo digas.
3. dígalo.
4. no lo diga.
5. decidlo.
6. no lo digáis.
7. díganlo.
8. no lo digan.

2
1. vístete.
2. no te vistas.
3. vístase.
4. no se vista.
5. vestíos.
6. no os vistáis.
7. vístanse.
8. no se vistan.

3
1. veámoslo.
2. no se lo pidamos.
3. tengamos éxito.
4. preocupémonos.
5. no nos sequemos.

4
1. Cuando llegues al aeropuerto, ¿te importa llamarme?
2. Haz los deberes después de ducharte.
3. Despiértese.
4. Juguemos / Vamos a jugar a las cartas esta noche.
5. Venid aquí a que / para que os vea. / ¿Queréis venir aquí a que / para que os vea?
6. No os durmáis antes de las diez.
7. ¿Por qué no lo miran una vez más?
8. No tengan miedo de que entremos / No teman que entremos.

Unit 16

1
1. b.
2. c.
3. a.

2
1. Si hacía sol, iba normalmente a la playa.
2. Si estábamos en casa, veíamos la televisión o leíamos.
3. Si íbamos a España todos los años, era porque teníamos amigos que vivían allí.
4. Si estabas triste, solías llorar / tendías a llorar.
5. Si le hacían una pregunta, el profesor siempre venía corriendo.

3
1. Si vas a la plaza a las nueve, te daré la carta.
2. Si queremos mejorar, tenemos que / debemos estudiar más.
3. Si llueve (como llueva), no salimos / saldremos.
4. Si este hombre te pide información, no le digas nada.
5. Si es posible, lo haremos.

4
1. Si te trajera / trajese el libro, ¿lo leerías?
2. Si me pidiera / pidiese que fuera / fuese con él (que le acompañara / acompañase), lo haría.
3. Si nos despertáramos / despertásemos tarde, perderíamos el tren.
4. Si pudieras / pudieses, irías a la luna.
5. Si quisieras / quisieses que te ayudara / ayudase, me lo dirías.

5
1. Si no hubiéramos / hubiésemos conocido a Juan, no habríamos podido quedarnos en Madrid.
2. Si me hubieras / hubieses dicho la verdad, no habría sabido qué hacer.
3. Si hubieran / hubiesen optado por estudiar biología, no habrían tenido la oportunidad de vivir en España.
4. Si Laura no hubiera / hubiese escrito la carta, Juan no la habría recibido.
5. Si no te hubieras / hubieses vestido sin poner / encender la luz, no te habrías caído.

Unit 17

1
1. Dijo que acababa de ver esa película.
2. Dijo que le habían confirmado que tenía que relajarse.
3. Dijo que el accidente había sido (fue) hacía tres días / tres días antes.
4. Dijo que su hija ya no la quería / quiere.
5. Dijo que podría hacerlo al día siguiente.

2
1. Pregunta si sabemos jugar a las cartas.
2. Quiere saber cuánto dinero tengo.
3. Pregunta si hay agua en la nevera.
4. Pregunta si me lo puede dar.
5. Quiere saber si su mujer y él tienen que salir hoy.

3
1. ¡Despertaos! / (Nos) dijo que nos despertáramos / despertásemos.
2. ¡Abrid el libro y leedlo! / (Nos) dijo que abriéramos / abriésemos el libro y lo leyéramos / leyésemos.
3. ¡Cerrad la revista y pasádmela! / (Nos) dijo que cerráramos / cerrásemos la revista y se la pasáramos / pasásemos
4. ¡No os durmáis esta tarde! / (Nos) dijo que no nos durmiéramos / durmiésemos esa tarde.
5. ¡No me digáis una serie de mentiras! / (Nos) dijo que no le dijéramos / dijésemos una serie de mentiras.

4
1. ¿Me prestas tus gafas?
2. ¿Me bajas la basura a la calle?
3. ¿Te importa cerrarme la ventana?

4 ¿Nos puedes ayudar? / ¿Puedes ayudarnos?
5 ¿Me dejas diez euros?

Unit 18

1 1 sabes.
   2 puedas.
   3 supiera / supiese.
   4 sepas.
   5 pudieran / pudiesen.

2 1 tenía, quería.
   2 tenga, podré.
   3 solemos, podemos.
   4 saliera / saliese, quiso.
   5 supe, pude.

3 1 Tuve que hacer un examen la semana pasada pero lo aprobé.
   2 Tendremos que trabajar si queremos comprar este coche.
   3 Si tuvieras / tuvieses que beberte un litro de vino te emborracharías.
   4 Cuando tenga sesenta y cinco años tendré que vender la casa.
   5 Tenía que pasar tiempo con muchos amigos cuando era joven.

4 1 tendrán que.
   2 hubo que.
   3 tuvierais que / tuvieseis que.
   4 hay que.
   5 había que.

5 1 Deberían haberlo conseguido.
   2 Lo habrían debido conseguir.
   3 Habrían debido conseguirlo.

Unit 19

1 1 La casa fue alquilada por un cantante famoso.
   2 El incidente fue visto por la policía.
   3 Sus novelas fueron leídas por mucha gente.
   4 La ciudad fue destrozada por los insurgentes.
   5 Los eslóganes fueron prohibidos por el gobierno.

2 1 El libro se escribirá en inglés.
   2 Las reuniones se cancelaban a menudo sin previo aviso.
   3 Los regalos se enviaron el 20 de diciembre.
   4 Estos platos se preparan a mano.
   5 Las obras se realizarían durante la noche.

3 1 Se compran miles de coches cada mes en España.
   2 Otro arquitecto completará la catedral.
   3 Robaron [preferred] / Se robó [possible] la máquina la semana pasada.
   4 Nos invitaron [preferred] / Se nos invitó [possible] a visitar la ciudad.
   5 Se vendería con algunas condiciones.

4 1 estará apagada.
   2 estaban cerradas.
   3 está preparado.
   4 estar encerrados.
   5 estar abierta.

5 1 Han abierto un cine en el centro de la ciudad.
   2 Van a cambiar los planes.
   3 Organizan exposiciones a menudo en el museo.
   4 Gastaban mucho dinero en obras en la carretera.
   5 Cerrarían estos edificios en caso de incendio.

6 1 Se nos dará una oportunidad / Nos darán una oportunidad.
   2 Se les contó un chiste / Les contaron un chiste [preferred].
   3 Se le concedió la medalla de oro / Le concedieron la medalla de oro.
   4 Se te haría una pregunta / Te harían una pregunta.
   5 Se le vendió (a ella) un coche [possible] / Le vendieron (a ella) un coche [preferred].

Unit 20

1 1 ser.
   2 es.
   3 está.
   4 fuimos (somos).
   5 estuvieran / estuviesen.
   6 estaréis (estáis).
   7 sea.
   8 está.
   9 es, está.
   10 estaba.

SOLUTIONS

2
1. La comida todavía no está preparada.
2. La casa fue comprada por un artista italiano / por una artista italiana.
3. La puerta estaba abierta pero las ventanas estaban cerradas.
4. He leído que tu abuela está en el hospital pero que está mucho mejor.
5. Siempre están de mal humor pero estuvieron / fueron muy corteses con nosotros el jueves.

3
1. hubo.
2. haya.
3. habrá.
4. haber.
5. hubiera / hubiese.

4
1. Estoy vivo/a, y estoy orgulloso/a de estarlo.
2. La clase es aburrida, pero Laura no está aburrida.
3. No soy consciente del problema, pero no soy listo/a como tú.
4. Como estudiante es buena, pero está un poco cansada esta mañana.
5. Esta paella está muy buena / rica, pero creo que el pescado está malo.

5
1. Ahí está.
2. ha habido.
3. La casa era.
4. Hubo un golpe.
5. de que estés.

Unit 21

1
1. Aquí vivía la chica que trabajaba en la agencia donde ya trabajas tú.
2. Ya no conduce el hombre en cuyo coche fuimos al concierto.
3. Es bueno el plan que propuso Diego el otro día.
4. Ganó el poema que mandó mi hermana al concurso.
5. Ha caducado el permiso que conseguí después de tres años de trámites.

2
1. ¿Por qué bebe cerveza el señor Ruiz?
2. ¿Por qué bebe el señor Ruiz esas cervezas tan exóticas?
3. ¿Ha llegado Ana?
4. ¿Te ha llamado el hombre que conociste en la playa?
5. ¿Escribió correctamente ese informe anual el director de la empresa?

3
1. Aunque éramos expertos, siempre teníamos problemas.
2. Aunque nos pidas que te ayudemos, no estaremos dispuestos a hacerlo.
3. Aunque vinieran / viniesen ahora, sería demasiado tarde.
4. Aunque es inteligente, comete errores.
5. Me dijeron que aunque no hubiera / hubiese estado cansado/a, me habrían dejado en paz.

4
1. Con tal de que recibas los documentos, podremos firmar el contrato.
2. Con tal de que me dieran / diesen la oportunidad, tendría éxito.
3. Con tal de tener el dinero, haré la transferencia.
4. A menos que estés enfermo/a mañana, quiero que vengas.
5. Aunque fueran / fuesen al banco, no podrían pagar la comida.

5
1. Estudio / estoy estudiando estas asignaturas para aprender cosas nuevas.
2. Trabajan solamente / sólo / solo para que Marta tenga dinero en el bolsillo.
3. Estaban con Miguel para organizar la reunión.
4. Les pedimos que nos ayudaran / ayudasen para que hubiera / hubiese cuatro personas en el equipo.
5. Te di la llave para que condujeras el coche.

Unit 22

1
1. fácilmente.
2. generalmente.
3. evidentemente.
4. económica y políticamente.
5. rápida pero sinceramente.

2
1. Vamos a venderlo barato / lo vamos a vender barato.
2. Tendrás que hablar más fuerte / más alto.
3. Las chicas sonrieron inocentes.
4. Mis hermanos viven tranquilos en la isla.
5. Es importante jugar limpio

SOLUTIONS

3
1. Lo has vuelto a perder / Has vuelto a perderlo.
2. Has tardado dos horas en hacerlo.
3. El viaje duró cuatro horas.
4. Sigo haciendo deporte / Continúo haciendo deporte.
5. Hace seis meses que no los veo / No los veo desde hace seis meses / Llevo seis meses sin verlos.

4
1. Todavía no has visitado a tu abuela?
2. Sí, ya la he visitado.
3. No, no la he visitado todavía.
4. Ya no vive en esa casa.
5. Vive en Valencia desde hace dos años / Hace dos años que vive en Valencia / Lleva dos años viviendo en Valencia.

9. Tú me lo ibas a comprar a mí.
10. Sé que sabes más que él.

Unit 23

1
1. caracteres.
2. albornoces.
3. especímenes.
4. capaces.
5. regímenes.

2
1. Organicé.
2. Cojo.
3. Busqué.
4. Hice.
5. Llegué.

3
1. resúmenes.
2. difícil.
3. políticos.
4. origen.
5. será.

4
1. celebre [present subjunctive of *celebrar*] / celebré [I celebrated] / célebre [famous].
2. continuo [continuous] / continúo [I continue] / continuó [he / she / it / you continued].

5
1. [none needed]
2. Leyéndolo, aprenderás.
3. [none]
4. Estarás defendiéndome.
5. Ha intentado dármelo.
6. Ofrecédselo.
7. ¿Cuándo nació tu hermano?
8. Quiero más té.

INDEX

INDEX

a (personal *a*) 44, 100-1
a (preposition) 15, 75-8, 84, 174
accentuation 2, 8, 9, 23-4, 26, 28, 33, 48, 49-50, 58-9, 89, 107, 109, 114, 116, 119, 122, 123, 132, 138, 146, 147, 170, 171, 172, 173, 228, 235, 241-6
adjectives, agreement of 23-8
adjectives, comparative and superlative of 30-3
adjectives, demonstrative 29, 48-9, 138
adjectives, indefinite 29, 37-42
adjectives, invariable 25-6, 28, 38
adjectives, possessive 14, 29, 50-2, 138, 210
adjectives, short forms of 26-7, 50, 52
adjectives, word order with 29-30
adverbs 16, 18, 31, 38, 39, 40, 44, 45, 117, 119, 158, 211-12, 220, 221, 228-32, 235, 236
adverbs, comparative and superlative of 231
agent in passive structures 96, 201, 204
agua, gender and use of article 14, 49, 107
al + infinitive 76, 136
algo 42-3, 44, 230
alguien 42-3, 44, 100-1
alguno 26, 37-8, 42-3
ambiguity 50, 51, 53, 56, 95, 198, 218, 245
ambos 29, 37-8, 90
animals, feminine of 3-4
animals, personal *a* with 100
apocopation – see 'adjectives, short forms of'
article, definite 13-7, 42, 51, 52-3, 104, 110, 137, 215
article, indefinite 14, 18-9, 109, 110, 209
Asturias 120
aunque 89, 161, 221-2

bastante 37-8, 229, 230

cada 29, 37, 38-9, 43
Catalan, confusion with 197
cleft sentences 70
colour, adjectives of 26
commands – see 'imperative'
como 31-2, 57, 89, 90, 161, 181
comparisons of equality 31-2
compound nouns 5, 9

compound tenses 137, 144, 146, 149-50, 193, 194-5, 196, 209, 214
comprar 76
con 62, 79, 110, 229
concession 221-2
condition 161, 223
conditional sentences 178-81
conditional tense 118, 125-6, 175, 179, 185, 191, 193, 194, 195, 196, 198
conditional perfect tense 127, 180
contra 80
conjunctions 87-90
conjunctions, split 90
continuar + gerund 134, 235
countries, article with 16
countries, gender of 7
cualquiera 27, 37, 39, 42-3, 100-1, 163
cuando 89, 117, 143, 156, 186
cuyo 68

dar 115, 123-4, 146, 148
dates 106, 110
de 80-1, 181, 210, 212
de, usage between adjective and infinitive 81
deber 58, 125, 135, 193-5
deber de 194, 195, 197
decimals 110
demasiado 37, 39, 229
desde hace, desde hacía 113, 118, 134, 232-3
diphthongs 243
donde 68-9
doubt 159
dudar 84, 159
durante 83, 98, 232, 234

e – see 'y'
emotions 29, 150, 158-9, 162
en 83-4, 234
ese v. aquel 48
estar 59, 80, 96, 115, 124, 131-2, 146, 148, 169, 202, 209, 210-15

French, confusion with 7, 24, 32, 84, 95, 107, 116, 117, 119, 120, 154, 168, 179, 212, 221, 228, 235
future perfect tense 127
future tense 116-7, 126, 127, 164, 179

Galicia 120
gerund, accent on 59, 138, 244
gerund, as adjective 26
gerund, versus infinitive 74, 78, 135

gerund, with object pronoun 59-61
grande 27, 30, 31

haber 18, 58, 115, 117, 119-21, 124, 125-6, 127, 146, 147, 148, 149, 201, 209, 214-5, 221
haber de 58, 197
haber que 197
hace, hacía in time structures 113, 120, 134, 232-3
hasta 57, 85, 156-7, 236
hoping, verbs of 143-4, 150, 153-4
hypothesis 89, 161, 179-80, 221-2

imperative (command) 113, 137, 144, 153, 164, 168-75, 178-9, 187, 244-5
imperfect tense 118-9, 122, 124, 132-3, 179, 191, 192, 194, 195, 196, 198, 232-3
indirect speech 153, 156, 184-8, 222, 223, 224
infinitive 58, 74, 81, 99, 114, 116, 135-7, 143-4, 160, 170, 174, 175, 181, 193, 198, 224, 235
intensifiers 32, 230
invitations 174-5
ir 58-9, 76, 115, 116, 119, 124, 131, 132, 133, 146, 149, 169, 170
-*ísimamente* 231
-*ísimo* 32-3, 40, 231
Italian, confusion with 7, 48, 107, 117, 119, 120, 122, 154, 168

job titles, article with 18, 209, 212
job titles, feminine of 2-3
jugar a 15

languages, verbs and articles with 16
Latin American Spanish 50-2, 56, 58, 113, 120, 121, 145, 147, 170-1, 231, 243
llevar + gerund 134
lo, direct object pronoun 57-9
lo, neuter article 17-8
locuciones preposicionales 75, 78
loísmo, laísmo, leísmo 60
lo que / lo cual 17, 31, 68, 69

mismo 30, 37, 40
modal auxiliary verbs 191-8
modified – see 'qualified statements'
mucho 37, 40, 42, 44, 229, 230, 231

INDEX

nada 42, 44
nadie 42, 44, 100-1
nationalities, spelling of 24
nominalisers 69-70
nouns, abstract 13, 19
nouns, gender of 1-7, 31, 108
nouns, number of 8-9, 31
numerals, cardinal 104-9
numerals, ordinal 104-6

o, ó 88, 90
oír 76, 115, 123, 131, 147
otro 18, 37, 41, 42, 45

para 76, 83, 95, 97, 99-100, 101, 160, 224, 232, 234
para que 143, 160, 224
pasar + gerund 134
passive voice 96, 139, 173, 174, 201-5, 210, 212
past participle 17, 119-21, 125, 127, 137-8, 139, 149, 193, 195, 196, 201-5, 212, 214, 221, 229
past perfect tense – see 'pluperfect tense'
percentages 15, 104, 110
perfect tense 119-21, 124, 137, 144-5, 192, 196, 201
permission 158, 191
pero v. sino 88
personal *a* – see '*a* (personal *a*)'
personal value judgements 29, 158, 162
phone numbers 104, 110
pluperfect tense 125, 137, 144, 185
poco 37, 41, 42, 45, 229, 230, 231
poder 58, 117, 123-4, 125, 131, 135, 149, 175, 191-3
por 15, 95-8, 136, 201, 204, 232, 234
Portuguese, confusion with 7, 120
possibility and probability 155, 191
practicar 15
prepositions 13-6, 44, 57, 62, 66-70, 74-87, 95-101, 135-6, 156, 174, 220-1, 229, 234, 236
present tense 113-5, 116, 119, 123, 145, 169, 174, 175, 178-9, 194, 232
preterite tense 114, 120, 121-4, 144-5, 147-9, 191-8, 239
primer(o) 27, 33, 84, 104-6, 118
pronouns, after prepositions 62, 86
pronouns, demonstrative 48-50
pronouns, direct object 57-9, 60-1, 172-3, 215

pronouns, indefinite 42-5, 100-1
pronouns, indirect object 56, 59-60, 60-1, 172-3
pronouns, object – 'redundant' use of 61, 203
pronouns, object – word order of 58-60, 203
pronouns, personal 14, 56-62
pronouns, possessive 48, 52-3
pronouns, relative 66-9, 101, 219
pronouns, subject 56-7, 62, 86, 119, 209
purpose 95, 99, 160, 224

qualified statements 17
que (conjunction) 88, 185
que (relative pronoun) 66, 219
quedar, quedarse 59, 84, 202
querer 58, 101, 117, 124, 126, 135, 149, 154, 175, 198
questions 44, 95, 107, 154, 174, 186, 219-20, 236, 245

relative clauses 66-7, 153, 163-4, 218-9, 221
reported speech – see 'indirect speech'
requesting, verbs of 153, 157, 187-8
resultar 202

saber 16, 77, 115, 117, 124, 135, 146, 149, 191
se as reflexive pronoun 51, 138-9, 171-2
se as indirect object pronoun 61, 173
se as passive substitute 139
seguir + gerund 134, 235
según 57, 86
ser 15, 18, 19, 52, 57, 70, 80, 84, 96, 115, 119, 124, 146, 149, 169, 201-2, 209-13
ser, article with 18, 19
si 89, 178-81
soler 198
spelling 33, 107, 122, 239-46
sports teams, article with 16
sports teams, gender of 5
sports teams, singular / plural 9
statements 17, 153, 184-6, 224, 236
subjunctive 88, 89, 114, 117, 123, 126, 135, 136, 143-50, 153-64, 168-72, 178-81, 186-7, 198, 221-4, 239
supposition 117, 125, 127, 194, 197, 233
syntax 81, 136, 155, 218-24

tan 31-2
tanto 29, 32, 37, 41, 42, 45, 90
tener 13, 18, 101, 115, 117, 120, 124, 126, 146, 149, 169
tener que 58, 193, 195-7
tercer(o) 27, 33, 104
thinking, verbs of 34, 154
time of day 15, 75, 110, 210
time phrases 98, 100, 113, 118, 232-6
todo 37, 38-9, 42, 45

u – see '*o, ó*'

verbs, continuous forms 131-3, 212, 232, 234
verbs, indicative forms 89, 90, 113-27, 143-4, 145-6, 147-8, 153-64, 168-9, 174, 178-81, 192-8, 221-2, 239
verbs, irregular 114-5, 119, 121, 123-4, 126, 127, 131-2, 146, 148-9, 169, 170, 172
verbs, radical-changing 115, 123, 131, 145-6, 148
verbs, reflexive 119, 138-9, 169, 171, 204
verbs taking *a* + infinitive 77
verbs taking *con* + infinitive 79
verbs taking *de* + infinitive 81
verbs taking *en* + infinitive 84
verse 203
vos 56, 113, 114, 145, 147, 170
vosotros 50-2, 56, 58, 59, 62, 113, 114, 122, 137, 146, 168, 170-2, 174, 245

wanting, verbs of 101, 122, 136, 154, 198
word order 29-30, 58-61, 101, 193, 194, 196, 203, 218-21

y 88
ya, ya no 236